BEYOND SURVIVAL

BEYOND SURVIVAL

Managing Academic Libraries in Transition

Elizabeth J. Wood, Rush Miller and Amy Knapp

LIBRARIES

UNLIMITED

A Member of the Greenwood Publishing Group

Westport, Connecticut • London

Library of Congress Cataloging-in-Publication Data

Wood, Elizabeth J., 1945–
    Beyond survival : managing academic libraries in transition /
    Elizabeth J. Wood, Rush Miller and Amy Knapp.
        p. cm.
    Includes bibliographical references and index.
    ISBN 1–59158–337–3 (alk. paper)
    1. Academic libraries—United States—Administration.   2. Organizational change—United
States—Case studies.   I. Miller, Rush.   II. Knapp, Amy, 1962-   III. Title.
    Z675.U5W766   2007
    025.1'977—dc22   2006027895

British Library Cataloguing in Publication Data is available.

Library of Congress Catalog Card Number: 2006027895
ISBN: 1–59158–337–3

First published in 2007

Libraries Unlimited, 88 Post Road West, Westport, CT 06881
A Member of the Greenwood Publishing Group, Inc.
www.lu.com

Printed in the United States of America

The paper used in this book complies with the
Permanent Paper Standard issued by the National
Information Standards Organization (Z39.48–1984).

10 9 8 7 6 5 4 3 2

University Library System, University of Pittsburgh illustrations and the ULS Marketing/Commu-
nications Strategy/Plan (Appendix) are used with permission from the University Library System,
University of Pittsburgh.

To those whose energy, inspiration, and collegiality help make our work lives satisfying and to those who have added joy to our personal lives.

Elizabeth J. Wood
Rush G. Miller
Amy Knapp

Contents

Foreword

Libraries face a daunting challenge as they engage the new electronic information environment. All must answer the question of how to extend past successes as essential components of scholarship, research, teaching, and learning into an unpredictable future.

Promoting past success or defending status quo is a recipe for disaster. Our community needs fresh ideas and practical experience to help us engage this changing landscape in a proactive and positive fashion—advancing our traditional values while transforming operations and services.

Beyond Survival: Managing Academic Libraries in Transition addresses this call for fresh ideas and practical experience. It explores how a wide array of contemporary management theories, concepts, models, and processes apply to today's libraries. Very importantly, these ideas are tested in and adjusted to the uniqueness of familiar library situations. This text describes how several leading libraries have acted to work with these fresh ideas to build new organizations ready and able to thrive in the emerging environment.

In today's rapidly changing information landscape, libraries face opportunity and challenge. The only constant in this landscape is uncertainty: We can only speculate about where libraries will be at the end of the next decade. More than in any preceding era, we know that libraries must change, but we do not know how to make this transition. Somehow these organizations must understand the changes taking place in their users' behavior, the format and nature of information, new information technology, and networked access services in order to transform to organizations that can thrive in dramatically different conditions.

This book is the result of practical experience with contemporary management approaches in several of the North America's leading academic research libraries. It is about real people, real organizations, and real experiences. There is a strong emphasis on describing what works and what does not transfer to library organizations. Good advice is given on myths and misconceptions about contemporary management practices as a way of sharing lessons learned from the libraries engaged in transition.

All who seek to be a part of the new information environment will find the ideas and experiences described here to be enormously valuable in thinking about their own futures.

Duane E. Webster
Association of Research Libraries Executive Director

Acknowledgments

Those who in some way helped bring this book into being are too numerous to list individually. However, four University of Pittsburgh University Library System (ULS) staff members deserve special mention for the information and assistance they contributed to the chapters about the ULS: Paul Kohberger, head of Technical Services; Jonathon Miller, head of Public Services; Fern Brody, associate university librarian; and William Gentz, personnel librarian.

Introduction

Although many academic libraries currently enjoy an unprecedented degree of productivity and stakeholder acceptance, there is no denying that others are struggling to redefine their role and to maintain their perceived value in a changing campus environment. What is more, if change accelerates or even if it merely continues at its *current* rate, it may be dangerous for libraries to become complacent. As Campbell (2006) warns, "Considering the extra-ordinary pace with which knowledge is moving to the web, it is equally difficult to imagine what an academic library will do and be in another decade" (30). Each successive OCLC report to members is more alarming in the specifics of how much the library's place in users' hearts and minds has eroded, relative to the Internet.

The OhioLINK library network reflects this perception in its theme for 2006—"Remaining Successful Through Transformation and Disruption in a Changed World" (OhioLINK 2006b, under "This Year's Theme")—and in observations that (1) "member libraries' services need to be more thoroughly and regularly grounded in an understanding of what our users are trying to accomplish and how they seek to accomplish it" (OhioLINK 2006b, under "Summarizing the Vision") and (2) "OhioLINK and [its member] libraries must make significant and fundamental changes for the long-term benefits rather than short-term oriented incremental changes that will put us slowly out of step with the rapidly changing environment" (OhioLINK 2006a, 5). In the May 29, 2006, OhioLINK Regional Briefing at Bowling Green State University, Tom Sanville made an aside to the effect that "there can be no link to the past definition of success."

A Council of Higher Education Management Associations (CHEMA) report (2006) points to a variety of challenges that are likely to significantly alter the future of higher education and also the context in which academic libraries exist. The author comments, "Some view these forces as dark clouds on the horizon that threaten higher education. Others view them as agents of change that will enable higher education to invent itself in positive ways" (1). He advocates that administrative units (like academic libraries) join in a dialog about how best to support their respective campuses. And he concludes with 6 critical questions for such units to contemplate:

1) How can we alter the underlying economics of our institutions and functions to be able to contain costs while serving the increasing expectations of our constituents?
2) Do we understand how the changing demographics of the country will impact the composition of our students, and have we done all we can to make our campuses welcoming to increased diversity?
3) Have we developed an understanding of the new competition we will face and the new markets in which our institution and functions may complete?
4) In a time of constrained resources, have we done enough to demonstrate how our functions can be supportive of the broader mission and strategies of our institions?
5) Are we prepared to recruit and retain the workforce of the future?
6) Are we developing the next generation of leaders of our functions and institutions? (17–18)

Beyond Survival offers ideas about how academic libraries can not only survive in the short term but actually thrive and maintain their viability in an uncertain future within the university by judiciously adopting organizational development tools and concepts. Real-world examples from the literature and from the experience of the University of Pittsburgh's University Library System are included to anchor the theoretical to daily realities of the academic library situation.

I

Why Not Just Keep On Keeping On?

Predictions from seers in the academic library profession who started sounding the alarm about the need for radical organizational change toward the end of the twentieth century—Carla Stoffle perhaps best known among them—have been confirmed to a shocking degree. The preface of *Rethinking Reference* starts out with these words: "If you have been working in a library in the 1990's, you have by now accepted—whether enthusiastically, reluctantly, or fearfully—the notion that libraries must undergo fundamental changes if they are to survive in the coming century" (Lipow 1993, ix). Schwartz (1997) notes the unprecedented rate of change in libraries in the 1990s and warns that both the extreme of unbridled but unsophisticated enthusiasm for change and that of "avoidance of instability while waiting for some other organization to come up with a 'blue print' or 'road map' for the whole profession" can lead to "organizational decay" (vii). Two other library authors predict that "the 1990's will be a decade in which not only these management approaches [adopted for business] are used in education but we will see our institutions undergoing major restructuring and ourselves approaching provision of library services in ways that are a result of a 'revenue' diet, technological advances, and changing personal philosophies of our constituents" (Von Dran and Cargill 1993, 1).

CHANGE ALL AROUND US

The world around us has irrevocably changed. Added to the familiar challenges of spiraling inflation, the information explosion, and competition with other campus units for annual budget increases are several unanticipated and paradigm-fracturing developments. "What we are about is not a temporary reduction in funding or a temporary shift in the way we do business. ... The key work of the library, and the focus of library activity, will have to change if libraries are to be an essential part of higher education in the future" (Stoffle 1995, 1).

Universities under Siege

Colleges and universities were plagued for years by a decrease in the 18- to 24-year-old age group traditionally thought of as candidates for undergraduate admission. A 1991 *Chronicle* article by Collison cites a decrease in the number of high school graduates as a cause of concern for private colleges. In the early twenty-first century, however, higher education has had to cope with the opposite problem. After years of stopgap cost-saving measures such as postponing building maintenance, freezing salaries, and holding noncritical positions vacant, many colleges and universities now face the problem of insufficient human and other resources to handle increasing enrollments. "Rising demand created by growing numbers of high school graduates is further stressing the educational system" (Pulley et al. 2003, A1). Not long ago, two dispirited academics wrote, "Good higher education is expensive.... The future appears bleak for higher education to adequately answer the educational needs of eligible students" (Sigband and Biles 2004, 38).

Along with the lack of resources to provide a high-quality education on many campuses, all but the most prestigious institutions are assaulted by competitive threats from many quarters—commercial entrants into the education market, steady pressure from two-year schools that can adapt faster to the changing interests and needs of students, and distance education opportunities (expensive to develop and support and also manifesting the unintended consequence of weakening the connection between a university's brick and mortar facilities and structure and the intellectual content it can deliver). A recent *Chronicle* article comments on such pressures: "While cuts in state aid and philanthropy have put the squeeze on community colleges, state universities, and traditional private institutions, many for-profit education companies are flourishing." The article goes on to qualify this statement by explaining, "For the most part ... the growth has not come at the expense of traditional colleges. But as the for-profits continue to expand their presence and their curriculums [sic]—with the addition of degree programs, like teacher education, that have long been the mainstay of traditional colleges—that dynamic could change" (Pulley et al. 2003, A12).

If taxpayer support is any gauge of how society in the United States views the value of a college education, an education is increasingly regarded as one more privilege of wealth, rather than a general good that should be within reach for all members of society. As early as 1993 Jane Bryant Quinn pointed out taxpayers' lack of concern for college students with this comment: "The G.I.'s got it. The Boomers got it. But access to low-cost college degrees is slowly being peeled away from the luckless postboomer generation" (51). And this opinion shift comes in tandem with the necessity for state and federal funding sources to weigh the interests of higher education against the K–12 educational system, an aging interstate highway system in desperate need of renovation and expansion, a decline of epic proportions in stability of the social security system, and other equally if not more compelling budget priorities. The *Chronicle* predicted at the end of 2003, "In 2004, colleges and universities will experience financial pressures that could reduce a hardened corporate CEO to tears," citing falling revenues along with increasing costs for virtually everything, including "new construction, employee health care, computer security, legal services, and debt service on borrowed money" (Pulley et al. 2003, A1).

And unfortunately, higher education has compounded its problems by pricing itself nearly out of the market with successive tuition increases. As a result, the price differential between public and private institutions is narrower, and one unintended consequence for poorly funded public institutions is stiffer competition from peers in the private sector that can afford to discount tuition and/or give more generous financial aid packages. One article notes, "As higher education lurches into the 21st century, the lines of distinction between the private and public sector are becoming more and more blurred.... Today ... both ... are competing on net price (sticker price plus financial aid) especially for nonresident students" (Kurz and Scannell 2005, 23). Another adverse reaction is the tendency of state legislatures to set stringent limits on tuition hikes (Pulley et al. 2003, A1).

No Longer the Heart of the University

Academic libraries are in trouble too. They have been edged out of the top spot as the "go-to" place for virtually all aspiring researchers by the delicious (if deceptive) convenience and immediacy of the Web. Worse yet, some funding entities now view academic libraries more as bottomless pits than as what economists call a "self-evident good." In fact—although alumni and older members of the campus community typically are nostalgic about hours spent prowling the stacks or meeting friends in the elegant rooms of yesterday's library—some faculty, administrators, and students now consider the academic library a costly and largely irrelevant relic. One of the most dramatic expressions of how libraries have lost position relative to Internet and Web search engines is in an OCLC report (De Rosa et al. 2005): Among college students across all regions surveyed, libraries ranked abysmally low compared with search engines. Answering survey question number 1345 about what sources of information were *perfect* for their lifestyles, 64 percent of college student respondents chose search engines, 30 percent indicated that the online library fit best, a paltry 24 percent chose the library proper (a ranking that tied with the online bookstore), and only 21 percent responded that bookstores were their top lifestyle choice. It must be noted that the description of this survey's methodology pegs the number of college student respondents at a mere 396 souls, representing Australia, Singapore, India, Canada, and the United Kingdom, as well as the United States.

At times the very technology that has improved library service in a myriad of ways almost seems to have carried within it the seeds of destruction of the library's unchallenged sovereignty as the preferred campus information provider. Initially portrayed as a way to cut costs, boost efficiency, and enhance access, technology undeniably has proved a catalyst for quantum changes in library operations. As such it has become invaluable to staff and users alike. But it did *not* bring about a net reduction in total library costs. In fact, the digital environment is astoundingly expensive in terms of both operational and personnel budgets.

Hardware, software, electronic materials, and even the networks (hardwired and wireless) require expensive upgrades that come at a breakneck pace. Information technology professionals, who work in libraries but support only the systems and not the core work of finding information and connecting users with it, are vital to what librarians do. But they command high salaries, and they can be difficult to retain. All of these technology costs have meant ever stiffer competition for the library's share of college and university resources and at the same time have increased scrutiny of academic library aims and operations.

There's no going back, and who would want to? In developed countries and increasingly in developing ones as well, the entire fabric of human lives and activities is becoming more and more dependent on computers to function—items and processes ranging from scholarly research to university registration and records to now-commonplace applications like retail inventories, e-commerce, automobile combustion systems, geographic guidance systems, subcutaneous dog and cat identification tags, and even running shoes enabled by a microprocessor to adjust support for various types of surface conditions. But the cost of technology—not as familiar to library managers as decades of rising labor rates, materials and equipment cost increases, and other kinds of budgetary pressures—has to be one of the largest *unanticipated* contributors to the economic predicament forcing change in academic libraries. "Factors creating the need for a budget paradigm shift for libraries predate the general economic crisis of the 1990's and make the library situation even more critical. For academic libraries, the budget crisis began in the 1980's, driven by the price increases in scientific/technical journals and the dramatic changes in information technologies requiring more capital investment and increased operational expenditures" (Stoffle 1995, 5).

Slow, Steady Decline

Apocalyptic warnings aside, for the most part, the environment has devolved more at the creeping rate of geologic change than with the breakneck speed of a tsunami. Since the dawn of the twenty-first century, academic libraries have experienced an inexorable decline in purchasing power, in some cases diminished influence on campus, and (perhaps most troubling) erosion of their fabled status as sole provider or even preferred purveyor of information. Indeed, it seems that their stakeholders—library users and holders of the purse strings alike—are insatiable. Despite the ongoing university administration mandate for libraries to do more with less, users know that they deserve the latest and greatest; and they are unabashedly asking for it.

Such a slow, steady rate of decline is unfortunate in that—lacking a devastating crash to wipe out all traces of past glories—some administrators haven't yet strayed from the vain hope that libraries are in a *temporary* economic downturn. Deaf to the warnings of Stoffle and other farsighted colleagues that academic libraries are now and forevermore will be operating under an entirely different and constantly changing set of circumstances, such diehards behave as if prosperity is sure to return and as if "business as usual" will again be the norm, providing they can just keep the doors open for a little longer. No need really to make more than judicious budget cuts and incremental service changes. "We tinker with the organization, even eliminating a unit here or there. We struggle to maintain the old and to provide the new, doing neither very well. Many of us are on the road of slow decline, rather than the road to improvement" (Stoffle 1995, 6).

Clifford Lynch (2003) is less alarmist but still adamant that radical change is needed: "Rather than considering how to redesign or recreate or enhance libraries as digital libraries, we might usefully focus our attention on the human and social purposes and needs that libraries and allied cultural institutions have been intended to address." He advocates a spirit of adventure in so doing: "[Librarians] must be careful not to overly emphasize the parts of this knowledge ecosystem that are familiar, that we are comfortable with intellectually, socially, and economically, to the exclusion of the new, the unfamiliar, the disturbing, the confusing" (78).

An *ARL Bimonthly Report* article warns that merely holding the line in terms of managing materials budgets will not satisfy either current or future needs of the academic library and its users for long. "'Muddling through' is what we do most of the time. It is a reasonable strategy for bridging the gap between present resources and future expectations—providing expectations are in a reliably upward direction" (Landesman 2004, 1).

During sustained economic downturns, however, the author counsels a bolder strategy than just conducting massive annual cancellation projects. "The short term result [of muddling through] is unsatisfactory and—since it consumes resources leaving little to invest in longer-term solutions—ensures a poor outcome for the long run as well" (Landsman 2004, 1). Instead, Landesman urges considering the materials budget as an "investment fund" of sorts. She asserts, "To ensure that mediocrity does not become an ever more apt description of our collections … libraries must move transitioning and transformative options to the top of the priority list. These options look expensive only if judged against the marginal increase in our materials budgets" (1). She points out that when such annual increases are considered "in the context of the total costs of research collections, they loom less large" (1). And she goes on to give practical advice about how to be a good steward of materials budget dollars without sacrificing the library's long-term interests.

Happily, many academic library administrators have heeded such calls for change, embracing the new economic realities and directing resources toward emerging user needs such as expanding access and convenience via the more-portable electronic formats. The fortunate ones like University Library System at the University of Pittsburgh have even provided such expanded access to users without making inroads into monograph or serials budgets. In addition, well-supported libraries and library consortia (e.g., ARL and OhioLINK) have taken advantage of feedback from LibQUAL+™: They have demonstrated their user-centered philosophy by making changes where they perceive important gaps between what users feel is ideal in terms of library service and what they perceive that they are actually getting. As a result of such responses to their stakeholders, some academic libraries are enjoying an unprecedented degree of influence on campus; and their credibility as a part of the teaching and learning community is at an all-time high.

In contrast, some smaller, modestly funded, and less well-managed academic libraries are still floundering. Lacking (1) the budget flexibility to acquire a broad range of electronic databases, (2) the political capital to stave off budget cuts, and (3) the credibility to convince teaching faculty that absent sufficient resources, these libraries are not able to both maintain legacy services and also pursue innovations at full tilt. Such libraries end up, as Stoffle (1995) says, not doing a sterling job at either good stewardship or innovating (6). Where this is the case, both their current position and their future viability are at risk.

The fact that the decline in the position of some academic libraries has been gradual can be regarded as a boon. However, the situation undeniably remains serious. Academic libraries that have not already done so must soon take stock of what is needed for the future. Unless they emulate pioneering peers such as the University of Pittsburgh, the University of Arizona, and other forward-looking institutions that have instituted radical change, they surely will perish—not in one or two waves with the force of a megaton bomb but in a much less dramatic series of events that ultimately will tip the precarious balance of their existence.

Although academic libraries will not disappear overnight, if they refuse to change and to continuously monitor their respective environments, they will condemn themselves to marginalization. Even libraries that can never aspire to ARL status would prefer to remain a vital part of their respective universities, rather than a poorly funded artifact of past glories.

The good news is that all is not lost. Academic libraries have mustered enough survival skills to stay in business. They still have time, and they already have many of the resources needed to effect the kind of change that will make a difference now, at the same time that it positions their organizations for a bright future.

Clearly it is time for radical change. "As academic librarians, we need to look outward, study the trends, and prepare for the future rather than being blind-sided by it" (Stoffle et al. 2000, 901).

Library professionals with vision, determination, and courage have a chance to turn things around. The important thing is to set their sights on *more than survival*—to dedicate resources to what will matter in the future, even though from the present vantage point they can only imperfectly visualize that future. If they will summon the strength and discipline to focus every available resource on their best opportunities, both the present and the future hold limitless possibilities.

READINESS FOR CHANGE

Many events and developments in the 1990s and 2000s have set the stage for academic libraries to embrace change and capitalize on its advantages. Chief among them are the following: a shift in higher education's attitude toward customers; new time- and money-saving technologies; understanding of the need for accountability accompanied by the availability of tools for planning and documenting performance; new pedagogical models; and the pervasiveness of workable organizational development (OD) models and techniques.

Customer Service/User-Centeredness and New Pedagogies

Along with challenges to the primacy of traditional four-year institutions noted at the beginning of this chapter—a sharp decline in the demographic group that for decades populated the undergraduate contingent; the raising of consciousness regarding the academy's duty to reflect the nation's growing diversity within the faculty, the student body, and the curriculum (along with the educational benefits of doing so); and the advent of strenuous competition from two-year institutions, online programs, and employer-sponsored training—has come greater understanding of how higher education should treat customers. Arrogance and autocratic practices countenanced in the not-so-distant past are rapidly giving way to user-centeredness with regard to student housing, teaching, and other aspects of the college experience. Much of the impetus for change in libraries and librarians' roles comes from the educational community's reactions to sociological, economic, and other changes in the larger society:

- Changes in living and learning spaces
- Changes in curriculum and teaching methods
- Changes in the communication infrastructure

Changes in Living and Learning Spaces

Cognizant that many undergrads place a great deal of weight on such nonacademic aspects of campus life as residence halls, student unions, and recreational/sports facilities when choosing where to matriculate, many colleges and universities have dedicated considerable sums of money to upgrading such facilities. Students who bring to campus a trailer or a van full of creature comforts—instead of the two or three suitcases of belongings their parents toted—are being catered to with more attractive and more comfortable housing. More dorms are air-conditioned. Residence hall facilities are less crowded and more apt to include private sleeping space attached to common rooms for studying, eating, socializing, and doing laundry.

In like fashion, in response to undergraduate concerns revealed by gaps in LibQUAL+™ ratings, forward-looking libraries are striving to spruce up their interiors with cafés and trendy furniture and to improve service affects related to a welcoming library presence.

Changes in Academics

The academic side of the university enterprise has begun to mirror the student-centeredness exhibited by student life professionals in several ways.

One Size Fits Nobody. More than one self-proclaimed wit has observed that clothing and other accoutrements of daily life purporting to "fit all" in reality hardly ever fit anybody. Personalization is a trend in today's college or university, probably a consequence of how impersonal many aspects of one's daily existence have become, along with evidence that acknowledging individual differences in students as much as possible enhances their learning. Thus, wherever possible, large theater-style classes are supplemented by small group sessions in which individuals are encouraged by a discussion leader to ask questions, test personal values and opinions, and interact with fellow students. Residential college units within a large institution—communities of cohorts with a common academic focus (e.g., music, the humanities in general) who live and learn together instead of in isolation—are another effective tool for fighting the crushing anonymity of large campuses.

In line with this way of thinking, libraries commonly offer one-to-one personal research consultations, in part because they are more adaptable to open-ended pursuit of research than are librarian-directed brief instructional moments at the reference desk. In such extended personal consultations, which are less subject to the pressure felt at a reference desk to attend promptly to a line of supplicants, the librarian can let students take charge of their quest for research. Instead of the library professional being determined to direct this and every other reference interview through a linear progression—from general information in encyclopedias and dictionaries to exploration of increasingly esoteric sources—exploration of the topic can start with a tangential aspect and backtrack through specific and general treatments of the topic at a pace comfortable to the researcher before ultimately arriving at the desired balanced treatment.

Additional examples of personalization in the academic library world are the research databases that let users customize the search interface and save searches and the library portals that can be adapted to take researchers straight to favorite resources. Controversial because of the fear that URLs will change and that users will miss valuable new resources, the latter nevertheless are an interesting and promising development.

Active Learning. Pedagogical methods are changing radically also. The "sage on the stage" lecture-based method of delivering education—wherein students essentially were vessels to be poured full of wisdom that could later be spilled out on command—has largely given way to active learning models and techniques, methods in which students are full partners in their own education, rather than passive objects of the educational process.

Critical Thinking. In a similar vein, teaching critical thinking skills—equipping students to question ideas they encounter, rather than uncritically accepting what even an "expert" presents to them—is widely regarded in today's teaching/learning community as being infinitely more worthwhile than merely inculcating a specific body of knowledge.

Not to be outdone by their counterparts among teaching faculty, library practitioners now stress action learning and critical thinking both in for-credit library instruction/information literacy skills classes and, where possible, within the constraints of one-shot sessions.

Changes in the Communication Infrastructure

The effects of the Web and the Internet on the social and economic fabric of modern life—rivaling revolutionary changes caused by the introduction of the printing press, mechanical harvesters, weaving machines, the automobile, and even space travel—have been described and analyzed ad nauseam. An example of just one such new technology with a devastating effect on campus revenue streams is the cell phone. Prior to its advent, residence hall denizens were a captive market for whatever local and long distance charges the university cared to impose. Now that very few students can be spotted at large without a cell phone instrument glued to their ears, the reduction in university revenues is significant.

Academic Libraries and Information Literacy. While not only the content but also access costs and training demands associated with new forms of communication and publishing have caused considerable economic stress on academic libraries, in other ways such developments have been a boon to the profession. This is especially true with regard to libraries gaining greater legitimacy as important players in carrying out the university's teaching mission. The burgeoning universe of information now at everyone's fingertips requires a high degree of sophistication at every step of the research process—from the basics of defining and limiting a topic, to finding the text, to evaluating resources and choosing the most appropriate ones for a given topic, to finally citing sources completely and accurately. Awareness on the part of faculty and university administration of this incontrovertible truth has fueled the Information Literacy movement on campuses as well as a concomitant enthusiasm for the library's role in that endeavor.

Academic Libraries and Distance Education. Distance education, another breakthrough application of communication technology that is growing in popularity and prevalence at virtually all institutions of higher learning, is an excellent example of a trend within the university that has fostered corresponding changes in academic library operations. The mandate to provide high-quality library resources and services to students whose main connection with campus is the keyboard rather than the classroom has made remote accessibility not a luxury but a necessity for academic libraries. Funding for technical innovations such as chat reference, electronic reserves, portals, and database proxies, in addition to such relatively low-tech services as toll-free phone numbers, can be justified by citing the compelling needs of distance students as well as the convenience of locally based students and those residing on campus.

Accountability and Planning Tools

As higher education has been beset by waves of change from demographics to budget woes to changes in consumer expectations, accountability has become more than mere rhetoric. So too have academic libraries reconciled themselves to accountability, sometimes finding themselves in the vanguard with respect to implementing strategic planning or organizational development or other philosophies and tools in advance of their general use. Two such tools have enormously changed the way academic librarians do business in the past few decades: strategic planning and student learning outcomes assessment.

Strategic Planning

Not surprisingly, adoption of strategic planning at most universities and colleges has made it advantageous for libraries to utilize this invaluable tool for (1) aligning resources with the most promising opportunities and (2) communicating to upper administration and staff alike what resources are needed and what broad courses of action are paramount to achieving both short-term success and long-term viability. Although many librarians initially recoiled at the brusque tone of admonitions from early strategic planning advocates to "drop your dogs and pick up you stars," most now have bought into the idea of building on strengths in order to maximize favorable operating and performance outcomes in times of scarce resources.

Student Learning Outcomes Assessment

Another extremely useful evaluation and planning tool is assessment of student learning outcomes. The idea that college graduates should exhibit certain skills and competencies not demonstrable solely by their transcripts and grade point averages has been manifestly clear to employers for some time. Now mandated by an ever-increasing number of accrediting agencies in recent years (Gratch-Lindauer 2002), student learning outcomes assessment is an essential component of evaluating and improving library instruction. When targeted outcomes are not fully achieved, adjustments in instruction—tweaking the syllabus, the media used, the exercises and other learning objects, the physical setting, or any other aspect of the instructional "package"—can substantially improve student learning.

What's more, where assessment of student learning outcomes is applied holistically to include out-of-classroom student learning, additional aspects of academic library performance (the efficacy of portals, tutorials, online forms, and the like) could be examined through this perspective and improved. Measures of benefit to library users such as LibQUAL+™'s self-reported data about service quality are useful. However, *quantitative* data gathered via learning outcomes assessment may in some instances constitute even more persuasive evidence of academic library excellence.

Technologies that Paved the Way

Budget woes admittedly furnished the original impetus for many of the sweeping changes in academic libraries. "The upside of downsizing, if there is one, is that in a budget crisis we can often gain support for hard choices and for radical changes that could not be made in good budget times, even if they are sound and necessary changes" (Stoffle 1995, 11). Still, it is fairly obvious that appropriate use of new technologies made possible previously unimagined changes in academic library operations and organizational structures even before the economic downturn of the 1990s. For example, the newest contingent of library and information science graduates doubtless has little more awareness of how OCLC revolutionized cataloging processes than it has of the fact that handwriting was at one time a critical component of the library school curriculum (D. Marcum 2005, 6). Indeed, even grizzled boomers among library colleagues must strain to recall an era in which catalogers all over the country spent hours painstakingly describing every aspect of the selfsame new monograph that was being added to countless collections in peer institutions. But both standard cataloging purchased in the form of Library of Congress card sets and copy cataloging done via OCLC were implemented long before the lean years.

Outsourcing of Non-Core Functions

Arguably the most controversial innovation in academic libraries made possible by technology is outsourcing. Both the 1998 book *Outsourcing Library Operations in Academic Libraries: An Overview of Issues and Outcomes* and a 1997 article written by a University of Arizona Library team leader point out that outsourcing has been around for a while, albeit not under that name. At first, the use of outsourcing was limited to functions largely peripheral to core work in libraries—security, maintenance of photocopiers, in-house binding, courier services, and janitorial work (Benaud 1998; Renaud 1997). Renaud (1997) justifiably complains that early literature about this phenomenon "fails to place outsourcing in a strategic, rather than a short term context" (86) and that this early body of work about outsourcing also leaves questions about how and where to employ this powerful tool unanswered.

Strategic Use of Outsourcing

Gradually, however, library administrators, managers, and staff members began to see the strategic possibilities of outsourcing and to consider more academic library functions as viable candidates for it—work ranging from approval plans in the collection development area, preservation, and retrospective conversion (creating electronic records to replace paper-based ones) to document delivery and systems work (Benaud 1998).

Outsourcing and Re-Engineering

The most widely known organizational change to come from outsourcing is the spate of re-engineering efforts in libraries, most notably in technical services departments and units. By 1996 Ohio academic librarians Hirshon and Winters had written a how-to manual for outsourcing serials and monograph acquisitions and cataloging including advice about dealing with the attendant fallout in terms of staff reactions. The following year, the American Library Association published *Outsourcing Library Technical Services: Practices in Academic, Public, and Special Libraries.*

Restructuring

The same year (1997), the Association of College and Research Libraries published a collection of essays and case studies titled *Restructuring Academic Libraries: Organizational Development in the Wake of Technological Change,* much broader in its scope than any of the works focused specifically on outsourcing. According to the preface, five kinds of "boundary spanning" restructuring outcomes emerged from individual contributions to this work: (1) partnerships between libraries and campus information technology units; (2) revamping of consortia in light of new technologies; (3) softening of boundaries between public and technical services work; (4) changes in research and curricular programs; and (5) a fresh look at the joint mission of universities and academic libraries to serve the public (Schwartz 1997).

Public Services Restructuring

The case studies in Schwartz's (1997) groundbreaking book treat changes in public services that were instituted largely because emerging technologies made them possible. One of the most compelling is the account of how Harvard College Library restructured its reference services to achieve greater standardization and coordination despite one of the most decentralized administrative models existing in an academic library system. The transition from what the author calls an "organized anarchy," which was comparable to the German feudal states, to concrete improvements in coordinated service is remarkable. Positive outcomes included staff increases in public service units, improved retrieval of materials from remote storage, implementation of a document delivery system, construction of an electronic classroom, and establishment of several coordinator-level positions (Kent 1997, 180–81).

Such comparatively recent technological innovations as chat reference, self-checkout systems, and digitizing also offer great promise for enhancing current services, redeploying staff, and aligning resources better with current and future user needs and preferences. Chat reference lends itself to either local operation or outsourcing—with some libraries and consortia staffing their own chat schedule, other libraries contracting with a commercial vendor to handle after-hours queries, and still others outsourcing *all* interactive electronic reference service. The last option frees the staff of smaller and less-generously funded libraries to pursue core work such as planning, liaison with faculty and students, and teaching.

THE ROLE OF ORGANIZATIONAL DEVELOPMENT IN ACADEMIC LIBRARIES

After decades of parroting the phrase "people are our most valuable resource," managers in both the for-profit and non-profit worlds have finally realized that staff members are a resource well worth systematically cultivating, one that is taken for granted only at the organization's peril. As early as 1985, an editorial decried the fact that support staff were often left out of the development equation. Despite the growing popularity of OD activities in what the writer characterizes as the "austere and uncertain eighties," this opinion piece notes that "development programs largely ignore the library's support staff." In a burst of egalitarianism that presages current thinking, the writer goes on to assert, "These [support staff] employees are among the library's primary assets" as measured against any number of criteria and are critical to realizing the library's mission (Leonard 1985, 34).

Nearly a decade later, another author credits the thinking of Tom Peters in the following introductory statement to an article about organizational change and leadership: "Managers of organizations in both the public and private sectors, recognizing that they need to face head on the challenges of managing in these uncertain environments, are increasingly looking for ways to change organization structures and processes so that organizations can survive, even thrive" (Faerman 1993, 55). And the 1997 ACRL monograph mentioned earlier in this chapter took OD to a higher level by including campus-wide and consortial restructuring efforts in its scope as well as narrower types of restructuring.

In a landmark 2004 *Library Trends* issue devoted to OD, the editors describe OD's growing importance: "One of the growing trends in libraries, especially academic research libraries, is an increase in the number of institutions that are using OD philosophy, process, and tools on a regular basis" (K. Russell and Stephens 2004, 1). In the introduction to this special issue, the following three basic definitions from established OD authors are presented:

- A self-correcting system of people
- Collaborative management of organizational processes
- Diagnosing and solving organization problems

The essence of Pfeiffer and Jones's definition (1971) is a self-renewing, self-correcting system of people:

Organizational development is an educational process by which human resources are continuously identified, allocated, and expanded in ways that make these resources more available to the organization, and therefore, improve the organization's problem-solving capabilities.... The most general objective of organizational development—OD—is to develop self-renewing, self-correcting systems of people who learn to organize themselves in a variety of ways according to the nature of their tasks, and who continue to expand the choices available to the organization as it copes with the changing demands of a changing environment. OD stands for a new way of looking at the human side of organizational life. (153)

After reviewing some eight other definitions from Beckhard in 1969 to Burke in 1994, French and Bell (1999) offer a definition focused on long-term collaborative management of visioning, empowerment, learning, and problem solving:

Organization development is a long-term effort, led and supported by top management, to improve an organization's visioning, empowerment, learning and problem-solving processes, through an ongoing, collaborative management of organizational culture—with special emphasis on the culture of intact work teams and other team configurations—using the consultant-facilitator role and the theory and technology of applied behavioral science, including action research. (25–26)

Carnevale's definition (2003) goes one step farther by affirming that after collaborative diagnosis of organization problems, the staff should take ownership of problems and be empowered to find solutions.

OD is seen as an effort to deal with or initiate change in organization cultures ... [involving] collaboration between a change agent and members of an organizational system ... to expedite the diagnosis of organizational problems and to encourage strategies that equip organizational members to learn how to cope with their own difficulties. OD is underscored by a belief that organizational members own their own problems and are responsible for finding solutions to them. (1)

In the second *Library Trends* article, the University of Arizona's team leader for financial and human services concludes—based on an admittedly small sample of persons (12 individuals responsible in whole or in part for OD in academic libraries)—that academic libraries enjoy a wide degree of latitude in implementing OD. "The approaches to implementing OD vary. In some organizations, it has been a complete library-wide undertaking, while in others the changes started in one or two units, sometimes with an overarching plan and sometimes with no intent to shift the organization.... There is not a linear progression of OD from one step to another and it is a continuous process of change" (Holloway 2004, 5).

The most widespread and best-known aspects of OD applications to academic libraries include these:

- Holistic/systems thinking: a pillar not only of the learning organization school of thought but also a basic tenet of any creditable management theory
- Process improvement: used to rethink priorities and core work and redistribute staff members to (1) the most vital functions and (2) work that matches their training, skills, and abilities
- The demise of the hierarchy and emergence of flatter organizations
- Teams and team-like structures edging out standing committees and rigid departmental boundaries

As with any philosophy and its tools, if used improperly, OD can be an expensive experiment in terms of both money wasted and degradation instead of improvement in employee morale. An early *Harvard Business Review* article takes issue with the common practice of instituting a flurry of OD practices and activities divorced from goals for concrete short-term improvements in the hope of some unspecified future successes. Schaffer and Thomson (1992) dismiss OD activities implemented in isolation from any notion of attaining specific goals—delivering product to consumers faster, cutting breakage, or accelerating the rate of introduction of new products—as having no more effect on improving financial or operational results "than a ceremonial rain dance has on the weather" (80). This position is several compass points away from the long-term approach advocated by at least one librarian: "Let's give up the goal of getting information to people and let's assume the goal of creating a learning organization for people who care that other people have information they need and want" (Phipps 1993, 37).

In addition to reservations about OD implementation divorced from business-related short-term goals, Schaffer and Thomson (1992) oppose introducing OD training much in advance of when it can be integrated into operations. They admonish managers to eschew the inefficiency and frustration of "studying and preparing and gearing up and delaying" (87) and advise them to "avoid the cul-de-sac of fixing up and reforming the organization in preparation for future progress" (89). Instead of such unfocused zeal and wasted effort, they urge "a subtle but profound shift in mind-set: management begins by identifying the performance improvements that are most urgently needed and then … sets about at once to achieve some measurable progress in a short time" (87) so that staff will experience success and can apply what has been learned in successive projects and situations.

A more recent OD work leans toward taking the long view, cautioning that mere understanding of fundamentals has not been enough for successful implementation of teams because strict adherence to the discipline of team behaviors and conditions and repeated application of such principles are required for success. "Understanding the value and potential of teams has proved to be much easier than applying the discipline required in achieving team performance" (Katzenbach and Smith 2001, xi). An academic library leader involved in early total quality management (TQM) efforts echoes this thought: "Carrying this out [implementing TQM throughout the organization], we learned quickly, was more difficult than making the decision to do so…. Flipping departments and department heads and, on their landing, calling them 'home teams' and 'team leaders' did not achieve magically the necessary systemic change in organization values and processes" (Lubans 1996, 31). Libraries would do well to consider such advice against rushing into implementing elements of OD with enthusiasm untempered by understanding and planning.

NO PASSING FAD

The popularity of specific OD theories, processes, and tools waxes and wanes as organizations gain experience with them and adapt them to suit local conditions or replace them with more sophisticated applications. Various management and educational philosophies and tools—strategic planning, marketing, and assessment of student learning outcomes—metamorphose as they become an intrinsic part of an organization's modus operandi and not a novelty. But none of these bodies of knowledge is a fad that can be safely derided and consigned to the rubbish heap of failed strategies. These are the keys to survival and success in an ever-changing world. To abandon the effort to grow, change, and realign academic libraries with changes in their industry would be to sentence themselves to the same fate as those entities still stubbornly devoted to "making a better buggy whip" at the turn of the nineteenth century. They did not all go out of business the same day, year, or decade. But nobody even knows their names anymore.

The task of academic libraries that aspire to do more than survive, then, is to effect not incremental but fundamental and transformative change. Reorganizing on a small scale—as is frequently done to fix problems in one or two units or to move troublesome permanent staff members to a position where they cannot do much damage and are not likely to raise the director's blood pressure as often—merely postpones the inevitable reckoning. Transformative change sets an organization on the road to remaining a vital player in whatever scene lies just beyond the horizon.

2

Theoretical Underpinnings of Change

MARKETING

Academic libraries developed some awareness of marketing and its application to their operations in the middle 1980s when library schools began offering courses in it. Darlene E. Weingand at the University of Wisconsin–Madison Library School was one of its foremost proponents at the time. Marketing was the theme of the thirteenth (1984) Library Orientation Exchange (LOEX) Conference, where Elizabeth Wood was the keynote speaker. And various aspects of marketing began appearing in articles and books for the library audience, including the LOEX conference proceedings, titled *Marketing Instructional Services: Applying Private Sector Techniques to Plan and Promote Bibliographic Instruction*, as well as a book by Weingand and one by Wood. Despite the growing popularity of marketing theory in some academic library circles, however, many librarians (like most higher education practitioners) continued to regard the word *customer* and the concept of competing for users as anathema. Few operating principles/philosophies at colleges and universities had been challenged, and academic libraries had been assured of their place as "heart of the university" for scores of years.

Precursors to Marketing

There is a continuum representing stages of enlightenment from a production-focused orientation, to a focus on selling, and ultimately to full awareness that marketing must start with the customer's needs. The production orientation is based on achieving quality to the exclusion of any other attributes desired by the customer—the idea that "If you build it, they will come." This idea has been thoroughly discredited by the failure of products from the Edsel automobile to the "new" Coke. Although selling is a legitimate and important part of the marketing process, two giants among marketing theorists pointed out some time ago that "properly seen, selling follows rather than precedes the organization's drive to create products to satisfy its customers" (Kotler and Levy 1969, 15). How have academic libraries progressed along this continuum?

The Product Orientation

Although in past decades academic libraries did frequently struggle with better and worse budget cycles, at least no person or entity was stepping up to offer better or faster or cheaper information and research assistance to their users than what they could provide. As a result, library practitioners felt free to define quality in their own work and—without exception—were convinced that their efforts could start and end with producing high-quality operations. So what if aspects of research and other library use were inconvenient, time-consuming, and frustrating?

Card catalogs—with their arcane controlled subject terms, esoteric filing rules, and so on—were complex enough to represent a barrier to undergraduates and occasionally even to faculty and inexperienced reference librarians. "If it takes a professional to file it, then it takes a professional to find it," librarians would intone smugly to one another. Each index too had its own set of quirks and conventions into which users had to be initiated. Material would get processed and onto the shelves in the fullness of time unless a user was sophisticated enough to ask for rush treatment. Users were supposed to be grateful for the privilege of tracking down the location of periodical titles, finding a working photocopier, and placing Interlibrary loan requests for material outside the scope of the collection that took weeks if not months to fill.

A Library-Centric View. At the time, such negative aspects of using academic libraries were a given and were of little consequence to its practitioners. They knew in their hearts that *libraries* were not the problem—unsophisticated *users* were! Librarians knew that highly motivated users could be taught to adapt to difficulties inherent in time-honored library processes and procedures. After all, where else would users turn for resources? And to whom would they complain about the inevitable delays and inconveniences?

A Corner on the Market. Academic librarians were doing the best they could with the resources they had. Collections were as large and as comprehensive as they could be made within budgetary constraints. Too bad if paper copies of serials were AWOL or popular articles had been razored out. That's the price you pay for open stacks! What a shame if a particular monograph could be had only by request from a distant library with receipt anticipated some six to eight weeks later under optimal conditions. One must plan ahead! Cataloging was exquisite in its detail, if tortuously slow. Librarians know best! And public services librarians were eager to unveil the intricacies of any library system to properly respectful users. Job security!

At that time, academic libraries had a captive audience and a corner on the market to a greater extent even than public and special libraries—each of which had something of a reputation for being responsive to what users wanted and needed. So there was little incentive to make changes. This orientation toward customers, known as "the production orientation," is based on the belief that people will always want a product of good quality and the faulty assumption that someone other than the consumer can define what constitutes quality. The hackneyed phrase "Make a better mousetrap ..." comes to mind. It no longer holds credence in for-profit or non-profit organizations.

The Selling Orientation

Amiable people with the best of intentions, librarians gradually became aware that some improvements in academic libraries were both possible and desirable.

Changing Hearts and Minds. Staff could be taught to appear approachable, speak pleasantly, and intercede when faculty or students encountered barriers in using the library. Student users could be taught to plan ahead when their topic was outside the scope of the collection, to steep themselves in knowledge of thesauri, accession numbers, and other components of complicated databases like *Psychological Abstracts* or *ERIC,* and to visit the reserve room for supplementary course materials selected by instructors. Faculty members could be "educated" about the need to give sufficient lead time for acquisition of reserve materials not owned by the library and for pulling desired items owned by the library. University administration could be educated about the cost of converting from manual to automated circulation processes and the desirability of offering librarian-mediated computer search services via vendors such as DIALOG and BRS.

OCLC's report to members, titled *Perceptions of Libraries and Information Resources,* comments as follows: "Trying to educate consumers whose habits and lifestyles are changing and have changed seldom works. It hasn't changed for companies and it probably won't work for libraries" (De Rosa et al. 2005, 6–8).

Spreading the Word. But for a long time in the history of libraries, the emphasis still was on (1) spreading the word about the academic library's virtues through promotion and publicity rather than asking users what they value and (2) teaching users to cope with difficulties and barriers, rather than eliminating them. This stage of awareness is typical of a *selling orientation,* another precursor to true marketing that relies on persuasion if not outright manipulation and stops short of finding out what customers value.

When *they themselves* are the unfortunate object of the selling orientation, librarians realize that it is not satisfactory. Years ago a frustrated librarian observed wryly at an ALA exhibit hall, "Vendors don't give us what we need. They want to sell us what they have a *lot of,* whether we need it or not." It is curious then that even after "customer service" became an increasingly important buzzword, some of our professional colleagues failed to grasp the fact that you can't come up with something *you* feel is "good for" people and cram it down their throats just by spending a lot of time telling them why you believe they *should* want it.

But We Know What They Need, Don't We? For this reason, the concept of user-centeredness, a refinement of customer service that decrees beginning the process of planning and implementing library services with the customer's view of what matters—rather than working from the library's perspective of what is important, cost-effective, and ultimately beneficial to individuals and to the university system—is almost the final step in implementing a true marketing approach. The catch is that—absent clear and regular input from customers about what they value and how they behave in seeking and using information, along with insightful analysis of information collected about user preferences and behavior—it is *not possible* to be user centered. Some academic librarians still wrestle with assimilating this concept into their professional ethos and practices. Any profession (e.g., doctors, lawyers, fire fighters) must guard against the mind-set that because of their superior knowledge of products and services, they should be able to prescribe what folks will like and how they should behave. Galbraith (2005) comments, "One of the primary barriers to converting to a customer-centric organization is the belief that a company is already customer-centric when it is not" (14).

It remains true, however, that no outside person can determine for an individual what aspects of library service benefits him or her—any more than it is possible to decide for another person what foods taste good. Any librarian can tick off examples of customer preferences that differ from what professionals feels the user ought to want.

It appears that one subset of people who use information value convenience over authoritative sources of information—hence the all-too-common preference for Internet sources over library-vetted content. If conclusions from OCLC's *Perceptions* document can be believed, these library users actually consider the Internet to be on a par with libraries as an authoritative source of information (De Rosa et al. 2005, 6–7).

Another small subset of the population of potential users may still value face time (seeing and striking up an acquaintance with potentially suitable mates who are studying for a lucrative professional specialty like law or medicine) over mere information retrievable from onsite library sources.

By the same token, savvy student researchers may understand that they stand a better chance of finding sources that will earn them top grades by asking help from a librarian than by floundering around by themselves or consulting a classmate. But a few still exercise their right to choose in a baffling way. They are the chat reference users whose Internet service provider (ISP) address reveals that—although they are at computer terminals in the same room with the reference desk staff—they have chosen to "talk" via the keyboard instead of asking their question out loud in person at the desk. For them the psychic cost of interacting with a staff member evidently is too great a price to pay.

Marketing Orientation

User-defined is the term most faithful to the fundamental marketing concept of a social exchange where each party to the exchange surrenders something of value. Library users—much like other consumers—will expend their time, effort, money, and energy only in return for something that is valuable to them. They will risk embarrassment, inconvenience, fines, physical discomfort, and other costs only when what they stand to gain from the library is something that they really want.

Some of the clearest articulations of this marketing orientation again come from Stoffle and her University of Arizona Libraries colleagues:

The radical restructuring of our libraries must focus on adopting a user (customer) focus, committing to quality service, with quality defined by the user. (Stoffle 1995, 6)

As we focus on the needs of our customers, rather than the ownership of collections, or the needs of staff, our key work activities, our organizational structure, our services, and even our physical environment will change for the better. (Stoffle 1995, 6)

Librarians now have to put into the process [of team-based quality improvement] an effort to build a relationship with the customer, become involved with the customer … a shift from a relationship with management to a relationship with the customer. (Stoffle et al. 1998, 5)

We cannot evaluate quality as if a library was an end in itself. We must address and measure the value of the library by the standards and outcomes that are important to our customers and campus stakeholders. (Stoffle, Allen, et al. 2003, 367)

To become the information source of first choice, and to compete successfully in the future, our services must anticipate customers needs, must be individually *customizable* [emphasis added], must be of consistent quality, be available twenty-four hours a day and seven days a week, must be delivered in timely fashion (whether in electronic or print format) directly to the desktop if desired, and must be sustainable (i.e. cost-effective and scalable). (Stoffle, Allen, et al. 2003, 377)

The 2004 University of Arizona annual report (2005b) notes under the section listing threats to its competitive position that "companies like Google, XanEdu, Ebrary, and textbook publishers are designing, pricing, and marketing products and services directly to faculty and students" (35).

The Marketing Mix

The importance of the marketing mix—product, price, promotion, and place (the four fundamental building blocks of marketing, also known as "the four Ps")—is "evergreen" or timeless for academic libraries. Each part of this mix represents one element of the offering that defines and comprises a specific product. And each should be tailored as much as possible to the intended target customer for that product.

Product Features

These include tangible aspects of library "products" such as plentiful, comfortable, and attractive furniture in library study areas and also intangible things important to library users—trust in staff's knowledge and skills, for example, and the likelihood of getting a gracious response to the self-deprecating phrase "This is a stupid question but …"

Brand Image

All market sectors dealing mainly in commodities—coal, sugar, soap, and similar offerings whose essential product characteristics are not easily differentiated or distinguished one from another—have difficulty attracting the customer's attention and retaining the customer's loyalty. To compete more effectively in such environments, marketers put a premium on building and maintaining a strong brand image, one that somehow sets them apart and above competitors. This brand image could be based on a combination of style, price, commitment to service, trustworthiness, an attractive or charismatic spokesperson (even a cool, beer-drinking frog), or on a host of other elements of the marketing mix, each of which will be selected for its appeal to the most important customers.

OCLC's recent report to members (De Rosa et al. 2005) contends that—with respect to both trust and quality of information—customers view libraries and Internet search engines as equals. That's the good news. The bad news is that "in a tie, the data suggests, the nod would go to search engines" (section 6, 7). Based on this conclusion, the report sees the main hope of libraries as rejuvenating the library brand so that customers begin to associate libraries with *more than* books and see them as a vital part of their present and future lifestyles, rather than a fondly remembered aspect of their past. "The library brand is dominant in one category—books. It would be delightful to assume that when respondents say 'books', what they really mean to say is that books, in essence, stand for those intangible qualities of information familiarity, information trust, and information quality. The data did not reveal it" (section 6, 7). The authors go on to say, "The library has not been successful in leveraging its brand to incorporate growing investments in electronic resources and library web-based services" (section 6, 8). Their recommendation for doing so is fairly broad: "Rejuvenating the brand depends on reconstructing the experience of using the library" (section 6, 8). They predict that since users "will continue to self-serve from a growing information smorgasbord…. The challenge for libraries is to clearly define and differentiate their relevant place in that infosphere—their services and collections, both physical and virtual" (section 6, 8).

Price

Aspects of price include not only actual financial costs such as fines and the price of printing or photocopying but also nonfinancial costs such as delay or frustration or opportunity lost when one choice precludes pursing other alternatives. For example, if libraries select books without monitoring use and attempting to predict emerging areas of interest, they waste resources and impose on their users an opportunity loss.

The OCLC report referred to earlier in this chapter lists frequently cited negatives that can be classified as a nonmonetary cost to users in three general categories: (1) inadequate products and offerings being the most frequently mentioned at 35 percent; (2) facilities and environment coming in second at 26 percent of the negative comments; and (3) customer/user service being a close third at 23percent (De Rosa et al. 2005, 3–19). The first category encompasses unavailable or outdated materials, unavailable or outdated computers, and insufficient variety in the collection. The second category focuses most on noise (too much or too little), crowding, parking, and the inconvenience of needing to use some resources on-site. The third category includes limited hours of operation, unforgiving and inflexible return policies, and other policy issues (3–19). If an academic library intended to use surveys of this type for decision making, it would be important to bear in mind that this particular one was international in scope and that it included public libraries as well as academic ones. In addition, the number of students included among respondents was quite low.

Promotion

Promotional methods encompass four basic tools used to get the consumer's attention: (1) personal selling, (2) advertising, (3) free publicity (e.g., public service announcements, press releases), and (4) promotions such as. product demonstrations, giveaways (e.g., key chains, badge holders), and contests (e.g., bake-offs, scavenger hunts, naming contests). The effectiveness of methods two and three in reaching a particular audience can vary considerably, depending on what communication medium is used.

Selection of Promotional Method and Media Type. Within the promotional method known as advertising—distinct from other promotional methods because the sponsor pays for delivery of the message—one or more specific types of media (e.g., television versus a print source) will be chosen. Within the overall promotional category of publicity (distinguished from advertising because it is *not* paid for beyond the cost of materials and production), some print-based options familiar to libraries are posters, flyers, brochures, and table tents. Other media options for publicity include television, radio, blogs, or other electronic formats. The third promotional method, public relations, can also be broken out by media type used—for example, public service announcements on television or radio, feature articles in the campus newspaper, e-mail messages, postings on blogs, or podcasts. Often seen as a means of damage control after a controversy has emerged or a disaster has happened, public relations can also be employed to build a store of goodwill for an academic library or other organization to draw on when times get tough. Examples might include participation in a campus-wide United Way campaign or a hospitality tent at the homecoming tailgate party. Events such as a reception for international students and a series of workshops for graduate students can serve the dual purpose of instruction/orientation and building good public relations with other entities and individuals at the university.

For each specific target group of the academic library at a given university (e.g., student athletes, transfer students, honor students, new faculty, university administrators, graduate faculty in a particular academic discipline), there may be one optimal communication medium, such as e-mail, and a preferable subtype of that medium, such as a Listserv dedicated to that group, rather than mass e-mail distribution. Conversely, it may be advisable to use a variety of promotional methods and several different media (e.g., e-mail or Listserv communications, ads in the campus paper, posters, endorsements from classroom teachers that the library is a valuable resource for a given course or assignment, contests, bathroom stall newsletters, and the like) to get a particular message in front of a specific target group such as undergraduates.

Message Content. The content of promotional messages is yet another detail that can be tailored to appeal to a specific group. Again, sometimes it will be advisable to stress the same message to all groups (e.g., the fact that saving paper by limiting printing not only saves money but also conserves natural resources). At other times, it may be preferable to use a variety of messages to promote the same product to different groups. For example, messages publicizing the range of available research databases to undergrads might emphasize these benefits: the convenience of remote access, saving time and pocket change by retrieving full text online rather than photocopying, and using scholarly resources that professors prefer. In contrast, messages to faculty colleagues might stress learning outcomes such as a database feature that formats citations for students or an interface that is as intuitive as the Internet yet is restricted to scholarly content. And yet another message geared toward university administration might focus on the benefits of consortial pricing of databases and/or might suggest that having databases with substantial amounts of full text plays a role in supporting student success and student retention.

Effective Messages. The distinguishing features of an effective message are two: (1) emphasis on benefits to the user and (2) customization of every aspect of the message. As mentioned in the section about content, effective messages will be tailored to get the attention of individuals in a target group or groups—*all of whom* tend to tune out anything not both attractive and relevant to them and *each of whom* has favorite forms of communication (from instant messaging via cell phone to the evening newspaper to a personal endorsement by someone their age in a bar). The content of an effective message will connect with specific values or benefits likely to move these individuals through a continuum from awareness of the offering to interest in it to a decision about it and finally to the adoption (use) of it. And the medium or media chosen to carry the message should have potential to capture a significant portion of the intended audience.

A front page *Wall Street Journal* article analyzed how *not* customizing promotions has cost a company as well known as General Motors market share and how this oversight was inextricably bound to an outdated organization structure and culture. "Since the mid 1980's, GM's overall U.S. market share has fallen by about 15 percentage points" (Hawkins 2006, A10).

What did GM do wrong? Well, in Miami, "a vibrant market where GM has bombed for the past 15 years" (Hawkins 2006, A1), the company ran ads featuring a Cadillac driving across snow. This was a big waste of money. And they started bilingual advertising in Miami years later than competitors, a move that a company employee says "clearly adversely affected us in Miami and every other top 50 market" (A10). They ran one ad targeted at the Cuban- Hispanic market featuring a Mexican woman with the car racing around the Alamo, a Texas landmark (Mexicans being only about 4 percent of Miami's Hispanic population). Another ad that failed with Hispanic consumers was based on the slogan "Break through," which has no direct translation in Spanish. And GM management refused to listen to a Miami dealer who suggested building a Cadillac sport utility vehicle to compete with the very popular Land Rover and Ford Lincoln (which were selling extremely well in Miami), changing their minds only after the Cadillac was edged out of the top-selling luxury brand spot by the Ford Lincoln. In addition to Miami, this marketing failure affected other key cities outside the Midwest, where GM would like to be more competitive (Hawkins 2006).

Why did these mistakes happen? For a long time the GM organization structure was top heavy and uninterested in what underlings thought. "At various times there have been as many as six layers of management between top executives in Detroit and those in the field" (Hawkins 2006, A10). And even now "GM's general manager for the Southeast has 38 teams reporting to him, overseeing relations with the region's 1,400 dealers" (A10). A manager at GM is quoted as follows: "Unfortunately we all work in little silos" (A10). A dealer characterizes management's former attitude thus: "We're running this company, we know what to do, and we don't want your input" (A10). Even though GM understands the Hispanic market better now, having hired a director of diversity, marketing, and sales for South Florida, things haven't totally changed for the better. The author comments that at GM, "Marketing ideas often get lost as they bounce between departments" (A10).

With respect to academic libraries, benefits featured in an effective message would be associated with a particular library resource or service. Examples might include instruction sessions geared to the game schedule of varsity athletes, a full text research database for economics students, or—in the case of a prospective library donor—the opportunity to get his or her name on a room or a collection. These benefits can be conveyed by word choice, graphics, humor, popular icons of our culture such as babies and dogs, and other sensory input (e.g., music, smell) depending on the capabilities of the medium chosen. Think of the most effective commercial or billboard or bumper sticker you've seen lately. Libraries effective at marketing get their message out in similar ways.

Scheduling Promotional Activities. Another important detail to plan is scheduling for each promotional activity. Frequency could be once a year (library booth at freshman orientation or informational packets distributed at the annual new faculty reception) versus several times a year (publicizing extended hours for exams or shorter hours around term breaks and holidays). There can be a long series of coordinated publicity events spread out over several months leading up to a big change such as conversion to a new integrated online library system vendor. Or a shorter campaign can be conducted over the course of a few weeks to announce a new service such as electronic reserves or on-campus document delivery.

Other Promotion Issues. For a campaign intended to bring more students into the library, placing posters and giveaways in the union, dorms, and athletic facilities will generally be more effective than confining their placement to the library itself. Web announcements should not be on the library web site only but also—whenever possible—linked from the online version of the student newspaper, the university portal, and other sites higher on the Web architecture than the library page. Incentives of any kind should be geared toward whatever a specific group finds enticing enough to sacrifice the time and make the physical effort to enter the building. Raffle prizes could be cash or bookstore certificates or iPods or lunch with the dean of the graduate college or the college president, depending on what audience the library is attempting to reach. Librarians, even those who deal with 18- to 24-year-olds daily, would be wise to get input from the target population on this point. We obviously don't need any enticement. We like libraries or we wouldn't spend so much of our time here.

Place

This element of the marketing mix is more accurately represented by the term *distribution.* It includes physical locations such as the *library as place* category familiar to LibQUAL+™ users, as well as the capability of remote access to content (e.g., library catalog and databases) and/or to library services (e.g., online request forms and chat reference) via Internet and Web connections. It also encompasses factors such as the nature of the staff delivering the product or service to the end user — what are their qualifications and what training have they received?

In reaching out to today's harried, distracted, and often sleep-deprived academic library user—typically torn between the demands of work, school, and the desire to preserve a modicum of personal fulfillment—a marketing mix tailored to that person's interests and needs can make a difference. It can help libraries break through the daily and hourly bombardment of stimuli to get the attention of people in their target markets. The appropriate mix of the four Ps will set the library's offering apart from the general roar of various stimuli that all of us must tune out in order to preserve some semblance of sanity and productivity in our lives.

The University of Pittsburgh's ULS has placed a high priority on getting the marketing piece of library administration right. Their comprehensive marketing plan was developed by a professional marketing firm in Pittsburgh with lots of input from the library staff. (The logo designed for ULS is shown in Figure 2.1. Images of one of their promotions for ZOOM! [their federated search capability], the *HelpHub* logo, and the postcard used to publicize their digital publishing program are shown in chapter 7. The Marketing Communications Strategy/ Plan for 2005 is included as an appendix.)

Figure 2.1
ULS logo

At the University of Pittsburgh's ULS, all new services are developed from focus groups of students to meet needs they identify in those sessions. Promotions for students are geared to young audiences. Other promotions are tailored to the interests and needs of faculty. For newsletters, as well as other promotions, they employ professional writers and marketers, and not librarians, in order to make all efforts more readable and relevant to the target audiences. Their web site is designed by professionals in collaboration with the ULS web services librarian. And the ULS is about to start a new design process employing students to assist in evaluating needs and then hiring a professional team for design work based solidly on decisions and analysis of user input from library professionals.

STRATEGIC PLANNING

The Basics

The essence of strategic planning is allocating resources to opportunities judged most likely to move the organization toward its ideal future position instead of doling out resources across the board or cutting support proportionally—without regard to how closely a particular function is aligned with the organization's mission and ideal future position. Bryson (2004) states that "if an organization has time to do only one thing when it comes to strategic planning, that one thing ought to be a stakeholder analysis.... If an organization does not know who its stakeholders are, what criteria they use to judge the organization, and how they are performing against those criteria, there is little likelihood that the organization (or community) will know what it should do to satisfy those stakeholders" (107). Incidentally, the University of Arizona Libraries have incorporated information about stakeholder relations—meaning "how the UA library is positioning itself with the campus community and its library peers" (University of Arizona Libraries 2003b, 34) into the current situation analysis section of their strategic plans.

Bryson's (2004) participation planning matrix is instructive for academic library planners who frequently need to juggle competing stakeholder interests and concerns. "Creating ideas that are worth implementing and also implementable depends on clearly understanding stakeholders and their interests, both separately and in relation to each other, so that ... issues have a chance of being addressed effectively in practice" (340). The participation planning matrix outlines different degrees of stakeholders' involvement in the planning process: inform, consult, involve ("We will work with you to ensure your concerns are considered and reflected in the alternatives considered and provide feedback on how your input influenced the decision."), collaborate ("We will incorporate your advice and recommendations to the maximum extent possible."), or empower ("We will implement what you decide.") (341). These are arrayed in columns above rows representing the following strategic management functions or activities:

- Organizing participation
- Creating ideas for strategic action (including issue identification and strategy formulation)

- Building a winning coalition around proposal development, review, and adoption
- Implementing, monitoring, and evaluating strategic options. (341)

Bryson's (2004) explanation of how to articulate strategic issues comes with the caveat that strategic issues ideally should be dealt with *before* they have reached crisis proportions. The essential elements of the description of a strategic issue are these: "1) phrases the issue as a question the organization can do something about and that has more than one answer, 2) discusses the confluence of factors (mission, mandates, and internal and external environmental aspects, or SWOC's [strengths, weaknesses, opportunities, and challenges]) that make the issue strategic, and 3) articulates the consequences of not addressing the issue" (159).

Ideally, closing the loop by evaluating the success of strategic plan aspirations vis-à-vis stakeholder expectations and making adjustments where results have not been satisfactory is an integral part of the strategic planning process. The planning cycle is completed when lessons learned are carried over to the next set of plans. As explained in chapter 8's discussion of portfolio analysis, adjustments can include new strategies for growth or maintenance of a unit with good prospects or—where enough about the environmental scan has changed—downsizing or eliminating the unit in question in a subsequent round of planning.

Another key to intelligent and effective use of strategic planning is to revisit strategic directions and actions frequently. Entities that make strategic planning an annual ritual—after which completed plans are shelved until the next year—profit very little from this time-consuming exercise. "A fraction of this data [from business units] is used to decide budgets, but most ends up in forgotten files. And when big decisions loom," individual departments seldom are consulted (Hymowitz 2006, B1). A survey of large companies done by Makaron Associates contrasts companies "still wedded to traditional planning" (B1) that make only two and a half "major decisions" (B1)—*major* meaning those decisions with "potential to boost profits by at least 10%" (B1)—with more effective companies. Those of the 156 companies surveyed who "spotlight a few priorities and regularly hold strategy discussions—instead of reviewing scores of business unit plans all at once" (B1) make more than six such big decisions annually. One company meets weekly to talk about strategic issues with the 30 top managers and on alternate weeks includes an additional 60 managers from the lower ranks to get a broader perspective. Other companies meet monthly or at different intervals.

Although all strategic management processes are organized around common principles (a mission, vision, values, and strategic planning along with a commitment to results-oriented budgeting, performance management, and strategic measurement and evaluation [Bryson 2004, 271]), there are a number of different systems for coordinating efforts in addition to the portfolio management approach. Other approaches to realigning the strategic plan with a constantly changing environment that are outlined by Bryson include the "Integrated Units of Management Approach" (271–74), the "Strategic Issues Management Approach" (276–77), the "Contract Approach" (278–79), the "Collaboration Approach" (279), and the "Goal or Benchmark Approach" (281). Each approach has its pros and cons. Fortunately, in practice elements of several of the six approaches can be and often are used together. Bryson also gives a wealth of general guidelines for revising strategies and plans, specific tips about how to maintain existing strategies, guidance about how to change or replace superseded strategies, and advice about how to terminate strategies that no longer reflect the organization's best interests.

Warning that no organization should hide behind excuses in order to avoid strategic planning, Bryson does list several conditions under which strategic planning should not be implemented:

- The roof has fallen in.
- The organization or community lacks the necessary skills, resources, or commitment of key decision makers to produce a good plan.
- Costs outweigh benefits.
- The organization or community prefers to rely on the vision, intuition, and skills of extremely gifted leaders.
- Incremental adjustments or muddling through in the absence of a guiding vision, set of strategies, or plan are the only processes that will work.
- Implementation of strategic plans is extremely unlikely. (332)

Hoshin Planning

Hoshin planning, which first ascended to popularity in the mid-1990s, was adopted by the University of Arizona because of its claim "to help an organization achieve breakthrough services and products for customers" (Holloway 2004, 11). Like all strategic planning models, hoshin planning advocates limiting the distribution of resources to key opportunities. Its guiding principles center on identifying a few areas of operation critical to advancing the organization's mission and future aspirations and concentrating the bulk of human and other resources in those areas.

What Is Unique about Hoshin Planning?

Several characteristics set this model apart from other versions of strategic planning: (1) its focus on factors that maximize positive impacts of resource use known as "high leverage points" (Bechtel 1995, 19); (2) identification of drivers (key elements of the external environment that influence the chance of success or failure); and (3) alignment of every resource in support of the organization's highest aspirations. Although in theory all strategic planning focuses on gaps between potential and actual position, this method raises the bar by focusing effort on high leverage points or areas of opportunity that stretch the whole organization and pay off in the kind of dramatic improvements that enable an organization to leapfrog ahead of its peers in a given industry. Also known as "breakthroughs," these improvement opportunities are characterized by high importance to the customer, performance gaps of significant size, urgency, and high relevance to achievement of long-term objectives (64). As such, they are critical to the organization's success and must be made top priority for annual year goals.

The Hoshin Process in Brief

The process of pursuing the critical few breakthrough opportunities involves first identifying the "drivers" (Bechtel 1995, 66) or causal factors among a group of interrelated elements of a problem or barriers to success. Then resources can be focused on the root cause(s) blocking success in order to craft a comprehensive, long-term solution to each one (Bechtel 1995). Addressing the symptoms of an organizational problem without getting at root causes may yield a few short-term successes, but this course of action will not move the organization ahead toward its preferred future.

Then targets to measure progress are developed. Examples of hoshin performance targets could include bringing more new products to market in a given planning cycle or reducing product defects to a certain percentage of what is produced or decreasing response times for handling customer complaints. Purely financial targets (e.g., increase annual sales by 20 percent) give no information about what operational problems are contributing to shortfalls or what broad aspects of operations might be tweaked in order to meet expectations and close the gaps. Hoshin planning targets, in contrast, tell employees "precisely what are the performance gaps in the business systems that must be closed in order to assure [an advantageous] strategic position down the road" (Bechtel 1995, 22). Then all resources of the organization, from individual goals for performance of tasks and activities to overarching organizational goals, must be aligned with important changes in the external environment.

Since organizational goals stem from customer needs, such vertical and horizontal alignment of resources with the organization's highest aspirations improves the chances of a breakthrough achievement. Failure to continuously align the organization with its environment—if necessary abandoning tried-and-true "behaviors, beliefs, and skill sets which led to past success"—is likely to render an organization "inadequate to meet today's and tomorrow's challenges" (Bechtel 1995, 35) and to prevent the organization from moving ahead toward its vision.

BALANCED SCORECARD

The balanced scorecard—a refinement of strategic planning theory conceived by Robert Kaplan, a Harvard Business School professor, and David Norton, a management consultant—originated as a way for profit-making organizations to focus on nonquantitative aspects of operations—those intangible factors such as customer loyalty that can be vital to maintaining a competitive edge but are not reflected directly in such bottom-line measures as profits, return on investment, and similar benchmarks. A very significant benefit claimed for this theory is that it keeps businesses from "suboptimization" or achieving good results in one aspect of the business to the detriment of another important area. It keeps the focus on both financial measures, which reflect actions already taken, and operational measures actions that will be needed to ensure future prosperity (Kaplan and Norton 1992, 174).

Nair (2004) summarizes the central tenets of the balanced scorecard as follows: The "balanced scorecard is focused on uncovering the main non-financial drivers of the business, along with the economics of the business" (5). Sensible of the need for data as comprehensive as possible when evaluating an organization's performance, Nair advocates integrating qualitative measures with the time-honored quantitative ones in evaluating progress toward goals and plotting future courses of action. He notes that planning alone may not be enough to ensure success. "Corporations both big and small can fail for several reasons. But the most significant cause of failure is not a lack of strategy, but the incapacity to execute on a balanced strategy" (3).

Indeed, to *manage* performance and not merely measure it, collecting data that ultimately will prove useful in designing and implementing subsequent business strategies is vital: data with power to forecast the future (looking ahead to what will be relevant in the future rather than simply being lagging indicators that measure past performance); comprehensive, big picture data or data reflecting key performance factors for the whole enterprise and not merely "data from silos of business units measuring their unique targets" (Nair 2004, 4); data including nonfinancial as well as financial elements; data relevant to key forces that drive the enterprise and the industry; and data that serve to describe and document phenomena that cause desired end results.

In a *Library Trends* article about incorporating OD concepts into academic libraries, Holloway (2004) of the University of Arizona Libraries comments on the balanced scorecard model's utility as a strategic management system, an organizational performance measurement system, and/or a communication tool.

Four Critical Balanced Scorecard Perspectives

The four key perspectives that guide an enterprise in turning strategy into action are (1) financial, (2) customer, (3) internal, and (4) learning and growth. Within each of the four basic perspectives Nair poses talking points based on Kaplan and Norton's theory, inviting readers to add any additional perspectives relevant to their particular organization. Following is Nair's list, with some perspectives relevant to academic libraries added.

Financial Perspective

- *For businesses:* What are the financial targets? What kind of profit and revenue should you achieve in order to accomplish nonfinancial aspirations?
- *For non-profits:* What budget considerations (i.e., the extent, limitations, and priorities among resource allocations) guides you?
- *For both:* What drives these revenue, expense, and other targets?
- *Specifically for academic libraries:* What is the expectation of your developing outside funding sources to support a portion of library operations?

Customer Perspective

- Who are the potential customers and what subsets of the larger group do you aspire to reach?
- How do you delight them? What do these current and future customers value/find desirable?
- Who would miss your organization if it disappeared? Where would customers turn if you were not around?
- What individuals or organizations now compete for these same customers?

- What partners might be enlisted to help you in achieving some of your goals?
- What are your goals for providing access to goods and services?

Internal Perspective

- What processes must you do better than competitors in order to win customers?
- What internal activities must be conducted in order to maintain organizational characteristics and behaviors that will support your organization's mission and goals?
- *Specifically for academic libraries:* What academic or other administrative priorities influence how you will document the library's productivity and relevance to the university?

Learning and Growth Perspective

- What training and development must be done in order to deliver results that have been identified within the first three perspectives as critical to success?
- In particular, how do you train people to excel at whatever sets your organization apart from competitors?
- What organizational culture and climate nourish learning and growth? (Nair 2004, 20–24)

Bryson (2004), an authority on planning for non-profits, illustrates a chapter dealing with change cycles for strategic planning with an example of what a balanced scorecard looks like for city government in Charlotte, North Carolina. The four balanced scorecard perspectives are located under a set of strategic principles called Smart Growth Principles—meaning development that takes into account the economy, ecology, and social concerns of the community—with which they are aligned. This organization has articulated the four perspectives as "Serve the Customer," "Run the Business," "Manage Resources," and "Develop Employees."

Most of this example translates well to academic libraries. Of course, our goals under "Serve the Customer" would be different because our strategic principles would be different. Instead of reducing crime, we might derive from information literacy principles a goal about fostering user independence or making users aware of copyright and fair use considerations.

But the city's goals for running the business need no translation to apply to libraries. Developing collaborative solutions, enhancing customer service, and improving technological efficiencies are central to both academic libraries and municipalities. Many of the city's goals within the "Manage Resources" perspective fit libraries as well: deliver competitive services (with the Web and the Internet being some of our strongest competitors); invest in infrastructure (computer upgrades, software applications like bibliographic utilities, wireless capabilities, etc.); and expand revenue sources (in their case the tax base and other revenues; in our case external fund raising and development efforts). The city aims to maintain an AAA bond rating; library collections and services must support the parent institution's reaccreditation studies. And finally, developing employees by (1) achieving a positive climate, (2) recruiting and retaining a skilled and diverse workforce, and (3) promoting learning and growth is every bit as important to academic libraries as it is to any other for-profit or nonprofit entity.

Gumbus and Lyons (2004), who have written extensively about applications of the balanced scorecard (which they abbreviate as BSC) within the healthcare industry, note the importance of promoting this performance management system to employees as well as to its customers. They underscore the benefits of BSC in this way: "As Unilever knows first hand, the BSC provides a common language for all levels of an organization, aligns various disciplines and stakeholders around common strategic goals, and offers a uniform approach to managing the company's daily and long-term operations" (44). Their detailed description of methods used to achieve employee understanding and buy-in for BSC is concluded with these words: "Critical to the successful implementation of the BSC, however, is a well-crafted internal communication and marketing plan. Such a plan will not only help shape the message, but it will encourage the BSC's active adoption by all stakeholders" (46).

University of Virginia's Experience with the Balanced Scorecard

One academic library that has made extensive use of the balanced scorecard for assessing operational performance is the University of Virginia. A PowerPoint presentation titled "Assessment and Flexibility: Implementing the Balanced Scorecard, Reassigning Staff" given at the Fourth University of Arizona *Living the Future* conference in 2002 outlines the statistics the University of Virginia considers important enough to use in planning, along with their process for "job sculpting," or matching the employees' personal interests to the job so that they are happy as well as productive in carrying out job responsibilities.

Components of University of Virginia's Balanced Scorecard

The University of Virginia approached implementation of the balanced scorecard by articulating a core value to ground each of the four perspectives and articulating strategic objectives to guide operationalizing each core value. The core value capturing the user perspective was "We respond to the needs of our customers" (Oltmanns and Self 2002, 15) and its execution was guided by the following strategic elements:

- Quality service
- Education
- High-quality collections
- Access to collections (16)

The core value attached to the internal perspective is continuous improvement. The strategic dimensions are (1) timely delivery of information resources to the user, which could as easily have been attached to the user perspective but is repeated here probably for emphasis; (2) innovative, effective, and efficient use of library financial, human, and other resources; (3) incorporating assessment into the organization's operations and functions; and (4) implementing continuous review and improvement of "high-impact" processes (Oltmanns and Self 2002, 17).

Wise use of resources is the core value attached to the financial perspective. Strategic elements include (1) increasing the resource base by soliciting a higher level of private donations, external support, and also institutional support; and (2) keeping the ratio of cost to value high for services and resources provided to customers (Oltmanns and Self 2002, 17–18).

The learning/future perspective is based on developing and empowering staff and developing appropriate library systems. Strategic elements include (1) human resource aspirations (foster learning, recruit, develop, and retain qualified and productive staff); (2) facilities that maximize staff and user productivity and provision of quality services; and (3) "cutting edge technology infrastructure" (Oltmanns and Self 2002, 19–20).

The following seven items comprised categories of data collected by the University of Virginia at the time of the presentation: (1) various customer perceptions gathered via survey ratings, (2) timeliness of service, (3) cost of service, (4) volume (presumably measures of activity such as the number of items cataloged per year or the number of public service transactions), (5) funding success, (6) comparisons with peers, and (7) internal improvements. At the time of the conference presentation, a total of 26 measures ("metrics") representing the four balanced scorecard perspectives were extracted from the aforementioned data categories. Targets for each measure explicitly articulated criteria for full success, partial success, and failure so that improvements could be made in subsequent cycles (Oltmanns and Self 2002, 22–23).

Analysis of Successes and Failures

The follow-up conducted at the University of Virginia after the metrics were analyzed is worth noting. All areas were examined for the degree of success and analyzed for better ways of addressing targets. For successful efforts, the follow-up process involved noting who should be commended for the success and then asking two key questions: "Is the target appropriate for next year?" and "Is the metric still important?" (Oltmanns and Self 2002, 25).

In answer to the first question, a change such as drastic staffing cuts hypothetically could result in lower goals in a staff-intensive area for the subsequent year. The second question might be answered in the negative where it has been revealed that a given metric no longer is the most effective way to document progress toward a target. The number or percentage of staff members attending professional conferences as a means of professional development might constitute an example of the need to change a metric related to the Future Perspective (individual and organizational learning and growth). After the goal of motivating a critical mass of staff to attend professional conferences has been achieved, the metric might be discontinued altogether. Or it could be augmented to count more active types of involvement such as committee assignments or presentations made, along with continuing to count attendance.

For unmet targets, the University of Virginia examined (1) how realistic the target was in the first place, (2) whether unanticipated extenuating circumstances affected the degree of success, and (3) whether a means might be found for achieving the target in future (e.g., better funding, more staff, process improvement) (Oltmanns and Self 2002, 27).

Annual Revision of the Scorecard

The final step in using the balanced scorecard method at the University of Virginia is examining its structure annually. Again, any superseded metrics are identified and dropped or altered. In addition, any new ones needed to reflect emerging goals and priorities are written into the following year's structure. And any practical problems associated with the metrics are addressed (Oltmanns and Self 2002, 28).

Application of the Balanced Scorecard to Organizational Change

The University of Virginia has used results of the balanced scorecard planning and evaluation system principally in two types of personnel decisions: (1) requests for new positions and (2) staff requests for reassignment. Following analysis of the library's successes and failures at achieving critical goals, the results of the metrics were used in decisions about redeploying staff.

Where critical needs in the University of Virginia Library or in specific departments had been revealed (e.g., the need to integrate digital services), and where these needs could be matched to staff interests, new positions were proposed. Requests for new positions would pass muster after the following conditions were met: The job shift had been defined as permanent or temporary; a time frame for reassessment had been articulated for any temporary arrangements; and the salary implications of a reassignment had been worked out (i.e., money was available to match an increase in responsibility with a commensurate raise in pay or where an individual's salary range was fixed at a high level, responsibilities commensurate with that pay level had been identified) (Oltmanns 2004, 169).

Employee requests for reassignment were vetted by asking the following questions: (1) What would be the impact of the reassignment on library priorities? (2) How would the move affect morale? (3) Was anyone besides the applicant in question interested in the new position? and (4) Who would do the work left behind, assuming that the responsibilities abandoned were still an organizational priority? (Oltmanns 2004, 169).

Benefits Accruing to the University of Virginia Library

The authors concluded the presentation by explaining that the University of Virginia Library benefited by (1) increases in productivity, loyalty, morale, and motivation; (2) retention of valuable staff; and (3) increased understanding of and appreciation for work done in the Library (Oltmanns and Self 2002, 48).

Oltmanns and Self (2002) urge going beyond the status quo to tailor jobs to staff interest and thus to exploit staff's potential to grow and become even more productive. Settling for merely satisfactory performance can be viewed as squandering an important organizational asset, since staff members frequently can achieve more if they are better motivated and better led. As two *Harvard Business Review* authors point out, "Many managers … allow talented people to stay in jobs they're doing well but aren't fundamentally interested in" (Butler and Waldroop 1999, 152). Moreover, this *HBR* article endorsed by Oltmanns and Self identifies the practice of capitalizing on the ability of staff to grow and excel as the key to retention of the best staff. "In these days of talent wars, the best way to keep your stars is to know them better than they know themselves—and then to use that knowledge to customize the careers of their dreams" (Butler and Waldroop 1999, 144). These thoughts reinforce the general wisdom that a manager's time—a precious and limited resource—should be spent on enhancing the performance of the best staff. It should not be wasted on a task that has little potential for producing results—namely, attempting to motivate, control, or punish the worst or even the marginal worker.

ORGANIZATIONAL DEVELOPMENT CONCEPTS

In a turbulent age whose hallmarks include (1) an economy in which it seems that the jobs of everyone except the economists are being off-shored and (2) a social structure in which the generation gap has shortened from 20 or 30 years to 1 or 2 years (or is that minutes?), virtually every modern entity recognizes the need for continuous change. Academic libraries that have reorganized have brought a variety of OD concepts to bear on the process. Many institutions have embraced the learning organization principles to a limited extent. Others have become enthusiastic proponents of all elements of learning organization theory and practice. A special issue of *Library Trends* points out that "libraries of all types have adopted various organizational development practices, both in a proactive way to create healthy organizations and as a means of correcting organizational dysfunction" (K. Russell and Stephens 2004, 1–2).

The Learning Organization

The change model known as the learning organization, popularized by Peter Senge, encompasses a number of extremely useful tenets and tools for moving an organization from the common human characteristic of being change-phobic to embracing change, even becoming change-centric.

Senge in Context

In Carnevale's 2003 book about public sector change, Senge's work is placed in the context of "an eclectic set of ideas to improve organizational performance," that were "enthusiastically embraced" (15) as American competitiveness started its rapid downward slide. Grouping Senge's philosophy about improving organizational learning capacity together with other popular OD ideas and trends—what constitutes excellence, what can be borrowed from Japanese management techniques, total quality management, the need to change organizational culture, and the need for public organizations to think and behave more like their counterparts in the private sector—Carnevale enumerates eight common principles shared by these OD movements:

- *Customer or client satisfaction* is the primary goal of the organization.
- There is a strong commitment to *human capital development*.
- *Continuous improvement* (usually associated with various forms of work teams) supplants former orientations toward assigning blame and the correction or punishment of individuals.

- *Employee involvement and participation* are encouraged at all levels of the organization.
- *Empowerment,* or "the notion that those closest to the customer and client should have effective voice and discretion in dealing with organizational problems down the line" (Carnevale 2003, 16), is essential
- Developing *shared vision* is imperative.
- The public sector is expected to think and behave in *entrepreneurial fashion*—learning to raise capital, improve services, and compete more effectively.
- *Organizational culture* is thought to be the fundamental means of changing an organization as "[OD] looks to the underlying psychology of people and their reactions to the practices of organizations as crucial in their loyalty, identification, and commitment to the organization and its mission." (16)

The Five Disciplines

The disciplines or learning principles on which Senge's "life long program of study and practice" (1994, 6) is based have been adopted by our profession to such a degree that few academic librarians would question their wisdom, whether or not these concepts are consciously associated with formal implementation of learning organization practices. The following lists these articles of faith:

- Personal Mastery—learning to expand our personal capacity to create the results we most desire, and creating an organizational environment which encourages all its members to develop themselves toward the goals and purposes they choose.
- Mental Models—reflecting upon, continually clarifying, and improving our internal pictures of the world, and seeing how they shape our actions and decisions.
- Shared Vision—building a sense of commitment in a group, by developing shared images of the future we seek to create, and the principles and guiding practices by which we hope to get there.
- Team Learning—transforming conversational and collective thinking skills, so that groups of people can reliably develop intelligence and ability greater than the sum of individual members' talents.
- Systems Thinking—a way of thinking about, and a language for describing and understanding, the forces and interrelationships that shape the behavior of systems. This discipline helps us see how to change systems more effectively, and to act more in tune with the larger processes of the natural and economic world. (Senge 1994, 6–7)

Senge's (2001) take on leadership is interesting. He feels that traditional organization structures limit potential for developing a learning organization. "When executives lead as teachers, stewards, and designers, they fill roles that are subtler, more contextual, and more long-term than the traditional model of the power-wielding hierarchical leader suggest" (Senge 2001, 126). He says leaders must establish a learning infrastructure, since "learning is too important to be left to [chance]" (126). And he insists that leaders must change their attitudes and behaviors before any other meaningful change can occur. "What is important, first, is that executives see that they, too, must change, and that many of the skills that have made them successful in the past can actively inhibit learning … [since] they usually are not very good at inquiring into their own thinking or exposing the areas where their thinking is weak" (127).

Nebraska: A Learning Organization Pioneer

With their 1996 move toward adopting the learning organization principles as a way to become an agile, flexible, future-oriented organization, the University of Nebraska at Lincoln Libraries became pioneers in implementing Senge's philosophy. Giesecke and McNeil (2004) classify the learning that individuals, groups, and ultimately the whole organization experiences into two types: (1) maintenance learning and (2) anticipatory learning. They point out that because of its short-term focus, maintenance learning—the type of learning uncovered by process improvement as procedures are examined to find more efficient ways of doing things—"often misses changes in the environment" (56).

Thus, a forward-looking organization needs to go beyond maintenance learning to anticipatory learning, where new knowledge gleaned from maintenance learning is incorporated into subsequent projects and processes, ideally both within the unit that first becomes aware of a better way to do things and also across the organization where similar processes or tasks are carried out.

Learning Organization Outcomes at Nebraska

Giesecke and McNeil (2004) contend that the learning organization model is the best way to overcome barriers embedded in human nature and human behavior and to achieve anticipatory learning. "In learning organizations individuals move from fearing mistakes to using problems and errors as information to inform decision-making, improve processes, and create success" (56). They cite as validation of progress at their library the results of a campus-wide Gallup Corporation survey: "Most staff rated the Libraries as excellent or very good on these key learning organization concepts. In fact, the Libraries rated higher than most academic departments on these measures" (66). They identify three questions from this survey as relevant to learning organization characteristics:

- How often do staff members have an opportunity to do their best everyday?
- How clear are expectations?
- How often do staff members get to do something new? (66)

The Star Model for Reorganization

Star Model Essentials

Holloway (2004) identifies this OD model as the third one used by academic libraries she examined. She defines the model as "a systems approach to reorganization with five points of the star inter-related" (11), alluding to Galbraith's 1997 work on organization design. A central tenet of Galbraith's early work on organization design is the necessity of bringing about coherence or fit between three types of variables that the organization has at its disposal: organizational strategy, organizing mode, and the integration of individuals into the organization.

Galbraith (1997) briefly describes the star organization design model. It focuses on five policy areas that influence one another and are controllable to various degrees by decision makers: (1) task diversity, difficulty, and variability; (2) dimensions of the organizational structure, including division of labor, departmentalization, distribution of power, and configuration or span of control;

(3) "people" or the human resource policies and practices, including selection, training and development, as well as transfer and promotion; (4) the reward system, comprised of job design, leadership style, basis for promotion, and compensation system; and (5) information-processing and decision systems including the nature of decision mechanisms, frequency of dissemination of information, how formal communication is, and the content, organization, and functionality of organizational databases (5). Alignment of these parts of the star means that the elements reinforce one another and thus maximize support for the company or organization's strategy.

Elaboration of Star Model Concepts

Galbraith's update to the 1977 work titled *Designing the Customer-Centric Organization* (2005) summarizes the impact of each of these five organizational choices:

Strategy, which determines [the organization's] direction

Structure, which determines the location of decision-making power

Processes, which have to do with the flow of information (they are the means of responding to information technologies)

Reward systems, which influence the motivation of people to perform and address organizational goals

People (human resource) policies, which influence and frequently define employees' mind-sets and skills. (Galbraith 2005, 15)

The main thesis of *Designing the Customer-Centric Organization* is that designing the organization around the loyal customer is vital for success and ongoing viability in the current era. "Today nobody owns the customer. The customer owns you," says Galbraith (2005), with the result that "to have a relationship [with the customer], the company needs to be able to do business the way the customer wishes" (1). The implications of doing business to please the customer are the following: "It means forming long-term relationships with the most valuable customers ... interacting with these customers across multiple points of contact and integrating the results ... into a consistent company policy for the customer ... learning ... to customize the company's offerings for different customer segments ... learning about new customer needs and expanding the company's offerings to meet them ... [and finally] using knowledge of customers to package products and services into solutions that create value for the customers" (2). In summarizing Gulati and Oldroyd's 2005 discussion of customer relationship management (CRM) success factors, chapter 8 of this book expands on Galbraith's premise that long-term relationships are critical.

A third work by Galbraith (2000) portrays the ideal organization as "organic, flexible, agile, or reconfigurable" (154)—in other words, capable of endlessly adapting to changes in the environment. He explains, "The basic premise is to apply organization design thinking to create an organization that can move easily from one design to another. These moves result in combinations and then recombinations of skills, competencies, and resources" (154). This description evokes the University of Arizona, ULS at the University of Pittsburgh, and many other academic libraries committed to continuous improvement and to building a future based on user needs. No matter what theory or process undergirds and guides the change process, such a change-centric atmosphere is the ultimate goal of forward-thinking academic library administration.

Despite the widespread if belated awareness among academic librarians that change is needed, leadership in preparing for and implementing change efforts is critical to success. Lientz and Rea (2004) observe, "Change must be managed and directed. You cannot just expose something new and expect that everyone will adopt it with wild enthusiasm" (4). They cite rejection of some major innovations, from the Roman cavalry's failure to adopt stirrups to early rejection of the facsimile machine. Another example would be the electric car, coming into its own scores of years after its invention only after critical shortages of gasoline have forced exploration of alternative automobile fuel sources.

NECESSITY: THE MOTHER OF INNOVATION

The accessibility of such tools as marketing, strategic planning, balanced scorecard accountability, and OD concepts could not have come at a more fortuitous time for academic libraries! Forces driving change had built to an intensity that was too great to ignore. The times were ripe for change, and library leaders were ready to take the plunge.

3

Embedding and Perpetuating Change in Academic Libraries

NO IDEAL TYPE OF ORGANIZATION

Clearly fundamentally changing the organization rather than tweaking parts of its structure and processes is key to getting beyond the survival mentality. But there is no one ideal type of organization. At a Harvard Business School conference called *Breaking the Code of Change,* one presenter observed that "people are extraordinarily clever at circumventing any structure to accomplish what they prefer" (Cohen 2000, 179). Top performers—those self-motivated, energetic, change-centric individuals that all managers would love to clone—will find a way to work and be productive under any organizational structure. You can't totally stymie them by an experiment in reorganization, no matter how ill conceived. By the same token, there is no organizational structure that—in and of itself—will change the attitudes, behavior, and work habits of the other end of the human resource spectrum.

Managing Change Avoiders

Hard-core deadwood—those individuals too stubborn or too damaged to appreciate where their own self-interest lies, beyond a naked yearning to control things, to escape responsibility, or to maintain a familiar environment—can rarely be transformed into productive employees. They persist in negative behaviors despite evidence that their personal and professional strategies are bringing them and the organization nothing but grief. We've all worked with them and sometimes supervised them. These are the folks who will spend 20 minutes arguing, rather than acceding to a request or suggestion to do something that would take them 5 minutes to complete. Folks who can't always be relied on even to show up, much less deliver what is expected of them. Folks who complain bitterly about being left out of the loop yet who consistently allege that they have mysteriously failed to receive messages from distribution lists that include their names. Somehow, every other person on the list got the message and read it without incident.

It is a mistake to squander the energy of a supervisor or a team or any other important organizational resource trying to change such individuals. Stoffle and her coauthors (1998) say, "The train has left the station, and we—as an organization—have to concentrate on the people on the train ... we did what we could for [those people who did not buy into organizational change] and now we just have to move on" (10).

The Hierarchy Endures

The hierarchy is still a viable model for some organizations, depending on the personality of the top leader or leaders, the organizational culture prevalent among rank and file, and the competitive situation in which the entity operates. Virtually all organization development experts—even those whose main focus is teams—acknowledge the validity and enduring value of the hierarchy as either a stand-alone organizational structure or a necessary adjunct to the team structure in a hybrid organization comprised of both models working in tandem.

In Favor of Hybrids

Sponsorship: Always a Best Practice

Despite his focus on teams, the author of *8 Lies of Teamwork* sees value in management practices associated with the traditional hierarchical organizational structure. He notes that the three things he deems necessary for sponsorship of successful teams—assigning a sponsor to each team, holding the sponsor accountable for team success or failure as measured by how well it advances the parent organization's goals, and expecting the sponsor to monitor what is going on by conducting kickoff and progress review sessions—are simply best practices that should be followed in order for oversight to be effective under *any* organizational structure. If these elements of support are denied to teams or any other subordinate unit, then the group in question will be predisposed toward failure (Wachter 2002, 121).

The Collaborative Spirit

Robbins and Finley (2000) express the following opinions about the merits of teams versus hierarchies: (1) "There are ways to get the collaborative spirit short of adopting the team structure" (120), and (2) "It is perfectly possible to have a healthy organization without teams in the narrower, structured, 'self-directed' sense. Instead of teams, you foster a teaming environment, which is just as good and lots easier to manage" (123).

Teams in Tandem with Existing Structures

An early *Harvard Business Review* article republished in an anthology gives the following endorsement of the hierarchy's ongoing worth: "We believe that teams will become the primary unit of performance in high performance organizations. But that does not mean that teams will crowd out individual opportunity or formal hierarchy and processes ... teams will enhance existing structures without replacing them" (Katzenbach and Smith 2004, 21). The article further asserts that values embodied by teams and characteristic of teamwork can be found in other organizational structures.

Taking a similar tack, librarian authors question whether teams and other sweeping organizational changes à la the University of Arizona are the only valid model for academic libraries. R. Werking states, "I am perplexed by the opinion piece 'Choosing our Futures'.... It offers neither research findings nor detailed accounts of what has transpired at the University of Arizona, but instead issues clarion calls to change" (Lee, Juergens, and Werking 1996, 232). Werking continues, "Let us look before we leap into any brave new world, by thinking first and organizing afterwards" (232). Juergens urges a slower approach than the University of Arizona took without disputing that changes manifestly do need to be made. "The changes must be as broad as the authors [Stoffle, Renaud, and Veldorf] outline; however, done over time, we can reach the same goals without so much pain" (227). Her response concludes with this thought: "Because we have such different pasts, we will choose different paths to different futures" (228).

Another management theorist quoted in *Library Trends* foresees a blend of the old and the new orders with increasing reliance on collaboration and consensus: "Although the old-fashioned 'command and control' model of leadership will continue to be important, especially in situations where clarity and speed are requirements, most organizations will find that a facilitation model of leadership works better" (Stringer 2002, 220).

Balancing Teams and the Hierarchy. Katzenbach and Smith (2001) state that "a balanced leadership approach will integrate the two [the traditional single-leader discipline and the discipline of the team structure] rather than constantly favoring one over the other" (2). They go on to warn that leaders who fail to effect such integration end up with what they dub "*compromise units* [emphasis added], small groups who fail to grasp and apply either of the two disciplines and become dysfunctional" (2) Expanding on this idea, they describe a *Y* where effective small groups in any organizational structure share five fundamental characteristics but branch off to operate under whichever management style is dictated by task requirements. "Leaders and other members of small groups must master all three branches of the *Y:* (1) the elements of effective group work; (2) the discipline of single-leader groups; and (3) the basics of real team performance" (4).

Examine the Task. Indeed, Katzenbach and Smith (2001) identify the prime indicator of the need for teaming as a task whose expected work product necessitates that group members work together and produce a "collective contribution," rather than working in parallel activities to "deliver performance through the combined sum of individual contributions" (12). The example given contrasts a task that can be pursued by several people working independently (e.g., testing variations in wording for a message in an upcoming ad campaign) with a task that requires group members to be joined at the hip, working in a "real-time collaboration" and "integrating multiple skills and perspectives" (14), for example, redesigning an entire successful product line for relaunch in a younger market segment. The litmus test for deciding which approach to adopt is whether the "value of ... merging perspectives" (14) is a required element for delivering a successful work product.

Process Improvement as a Stand-Alone Event

It follows from this line of reasoning and from observation of successful academic library efforts that process improvement does not necessarily require comprehensive reorganization. Cataloging/acquisitions, reserves, serials/govdocs processing and other technical specialties lend themselves to process improvement and often can be re-engineered without changing the overarching organizational structure. Reference and other public service processes also sometimes can be revamped without total restructuring of the organization. A historical example is the 1979 merger of a technical services and a public services unit at the University of Michigan (Holbrook et al. 1984, 29–32).

The Management Role Is Still Valid

A library school professor observes, "A key problem in using teams rather than hierarchy is that organizations do not hire, fire, and promote teams but, instead, hire, fire, and promote individuals" (Owens 1999, 572). The inference is that some elements of the hierarchy remain effective in today's organization. In a similar thought, Wachter (2002) dismisses the popular administrative fantasy that implementation of the team model will decrease the number of management positions needed in an organization. Although conceding that well-run teams do increase productivity by accomplishing results with less work, he says that, ideally, "the most-effective team based organizations will have as many supervisors and managers per capita as do traditional hierarchical organizations. The role changes and becomes more fulfilling, but does not go away" (11).

This view is validated by John Lubans (1996), at one time Deputy University Librarian at Duke University: "I do have a new leadership role. My work is evolving into four major categories of coaching, consulting, encouraging, and leading" (34). He explains the professional growth stemming from Duke's adoption of total quality management (TQM) and the concomitant change in his role in this way: "Cutting supervisory ties moved me beyond the textbook into reality, putting meaning into the belief ... that 'once relieved of their traditional responsibilities, managers can attend to more important issues for the organization's future'" (36). He characterizes Duke's venture into TQM as follows: "We pushed the hierarchy to its productivity limits, virtually taking a team-based approach within the hierarchy" (29). The context for this remark is that—although technical services was restructured and teams were empowered to make many decisions—department heads could chose to retain their hierarchical position, rather than becoming team leaders, and some did so. The lesson to be drawn here is that the hierarchy still is relevant and should not be dismissed as an anachronism.

Top Management's Role

In *8 Lies*, Wachter (2002) unequivocally affirms the validity of top management as the ultimate authority in an organization and explains how that fact

plays a role in the success of teams: "Accountability begins at the top of the organization and works its way down. Leadership must always have prime accountability for success or failure. If not, we empower leaders and managers to cause
teams to fail" (56). He explains, "Leaders instill vision, meaning, and trust. They
empower followers. Leaders also exercise power, the ability to translate inten-
tion into reality by initiating and sustaining action" (45). In a chart summarizing linkage between key elements of the strategic plan, he defines the vision as
"what we [the organization] are in the process of becoming or achieving in the
future" (21) and notes that the vision is "established by leadership" (50), which
he has defined elsewhere as the organization's appointed leadership, the executive team. This take on the leader's role is at variance with the view attributed
to Senge that leaders should see themselves as mere "stewards of the vision not
possessors of the vision" (Phipps 1993, 21).

Wachter (2002) elaborates about the changed role of other positions of authority within the traditional hierarchy of a team-based organization as follows:
"A supervisor in a team based organization coaches, teaches, builds teams, and
creates a climate for performance [developing] people capable of excelling.... A
manager must still allocate resources across several teams, form teams around
tactical and business requirements, ensure consistent business process across
team and functional boundaries, and share process improvements across the
organization" (47–48). And he distinguishes the team's role from the hierarchy's
responsibilities thus: "The team makes tactical decision, husbands resources,
defines processes, and enforces process discipline" (48).

A librarian writing about leadership echoes some of these thoughts. Observ-
ing that the importance of leadership hasn't diminished in libraries, Shoaf (2004)
opines that "a new library leader is emerging. One with different talents and a
more supportive mission" (363). These new qualities are enumerated as leading
change, articulating a vision for the library, coaching, living the service ethic,
putting staff first, and creating "a culture of leadership" (365). Each of the preceding leadership qualities departs from the old command and control style of
management and embraces a more collaborative role. Like the leadership at the
University of Arizona, the University of Pittsburgh, and many other academic
libraries, the individual discussed in this article "manages rather than imposes
change on staff. He or she leads the staff through change with a combination of
pliable adaptability, wisdom, and compassion" (364). Such an individual is good
at both articulating and communicating a vision for the library. "This means that
persuasion and an ability to impart beliefs and conviction" is necessary in order
for staff implementing this vision to "move toward it with certainty and assurance—certainty that it is the correct path and assurance that it will help achieve
the library's goals" (364).

Facilitating is another of what Shoaf (2004) sees as vital new skills. "[Coach-
ing] is about communicating and expediting ... about recognizing talent and
putting it to work where needed" (364). He urges leaders, most of whom make
decisions about operations from a vantage point far removed from the front
lines, to get back in touch with both front line staff and customers, to the extent
of making anonymous checks on service points if indicated. He also urges conducting strategic planning not in a vacuum but with a primary focus on "people

strategy" (365), since the staff makes the difference between whether plans get lip service or actually get woven into the organization's daily routines.

Finally, he joins the chorus in favor of empowering all staff members and relying on individuals throughout the organization to take responsibility in their respective domains for doing whatever it takes to achieve customer satisfaction. "A culture of leadership can help staff to develop creative thinking and risk-taking actions, but requires a commitment from the top" (365). Conceding that "most of us are not there yet" (375) in terms of being ready to abandon the command and control model of leadership, Shoaf nevertheless is optimistic about positive outcomes if and when we get there. "The new library leadership with the right stuff will propel libraries into an uncertain future with grace and aplomb" (375).

Although they are not the only game in town, teams can be enormously beneficial to an academic library or other complex organization as long as one limitation is kept in mind. No organizational structure—not even teams—can change human nature enough to make all human beings equally talented, energetic, and motivated. A librarian observes, "It is doubly ironic that a few staff [members] continue to practice their team leadership in controlling ways.... This has shown to me the intractability of the hierarchical model" (Lubans 1996, 36).

The tendency to recreate the hierarchical model in teams pointed out by Lubans may stem not from the power of the hierarchical model but simply from the inability of *any* system to circumvent human nature. Some people simply cannot step away from behaviors that are core to their identity and previous job success. No matter what structure is imposed, they will not treat others collegially in order to unleash the power of the group. These are the staff members who will always "kiss up and kick down." They will not willingly share information or power. They can't seem to learn to listen more than they speak, in order to air all points of view and take advantage of the wisdom of a group.

Most who write about teams advise that even staff members who do not initially take to the team environment often can be counseled and taught more appropriate behaviors. As mentioned in the beginning of this chapter, however, some people cannot be won over to the individual and organizational benefits of teams or taught to function effectively in a team. Their role in the organization should be insulated as much as possible from the work of teams, so that they do not sabotage team outcomes. Regrettably, some who cannot adjust and cooperate with teams probably should be handed their walking papers and a carefully worded letter of recommendation.

TO TEAM OR NOT TO TEAM?

A few academic libraries that have had bad experiences with teams may be adamantly opposed to instituting any form of them. At the other end of the continuum, there may be libraries that view teams as the answer to every problem and that grossly underestimate the amount of resources needed to implement an effective team structure. Quite likely neither position is entirely tenable in today's resource-strapped, fast-changing academic library environment.

Popular Myths about Teams

Several OD practitioners with impressive client lists are intent on debunking the following popular myths and magical beliefs about teams.

Myth #1: Teams Are a Panacea—A Good Tool for Every Environment and Situation

"Teamwork is not appropriate for every situation" (Wachter 2002, 156).

"Teams are unnecessary when tasks are simple and routine, do not require employees to coordinate their work, and do not require a variety of experiences or skills" (Polzer and Luecke 2004, 11).

"Teams are inherently inferior to individuals in terms of efficiency" (Robbins and Finley 2000, 213).

"Teams cannot solve all your organization's problems. Nothing can" (Robbins and Finley 2000, 64).

"If you don't commit to the idea of trusting people and to the free flow of information through an organization, developing teams isn't just the wrong idea, it can be catastrophic" (Robbins and Finley 2000, 221).

Myth #2: Building Teams Is a Desirable End in Itself

"All too often ... the impetus for teamwork is an executive's desire to gain cooperation and buy-in from employees or to improve morale." Teams should be given more meaningful responsibilities than to "make inconsequential decisions and solve unimportant problems" while management makes "the real decisions" (Wachter 2002, 18).

"If we want to get results from teamwork, we must make teamwork [an integral part of] the way we do business" (Wachter 2002, 37).

"Teamwork is ... a tool to implement culture, strategy, process, and financial imperatives. Efforts to build teamwork outside the context of these organizational drivers are doomed to fail" (Wachter 2002, 38).

"If you just want to make people feel good, throw a party. It is a lot cheaper than setting up teamwork outside the business" (Wachter 2002, 39).

"Organizational leaders can best foster team performance by building a strong performance ethic rather than by establishing a team-promoting environment alone" (Phipps 2004, 81).

"Team talent, efficiency, intelligence and clout are pretty useless unless the team has some clue where it is going and how it is to contribute to the organization's overall strategies for success" (Robbins and Finley 2000, 115).

"A team shouldn't even exist unless it represents the best way to help the organization achieve its goals" (Polzer and Luecke 2004, 25).

Myth #3: Operational Expertise Should Be the Primary Criterion for Selecting Team Members

"The wise manager will choose people both for their existing skills and their potential to improve existing skills and learn new ones" (Katzenbach and Smith 2004, 23).

"Team requirements fall into three fairly self-evident categories ... technical or functional expertise ... problem-solving and decision-making ... and interpersonal skills." Among interpersonal skills, these authors include the willingness to take appropriate risks (Katzenbach and Smith 2004, 11).

"Teams must be composed of members who collectively bring all the necessary skills—whether technical, problem-solving, interpersonal, or organizational—to the job" (Polzer and Luecke 2004, 34).

"Unfortunately, attention to technical skills [in selecting team members] often overshadows attention to interpersonal and organizational skills, which in the long run may be just as important" (Polzer and Luecke 2004, 35).

"Include individuals with varying abilities and attitudes, to promote role adoption and variety in response, facilitating innovation" (Bradigan and Powell 2004, 146).

Myth #4: One Strong Leader Is All You Need to Make a Team Succeed

"There are many models of team leadership, ranging from traditional iron-hand rule through various degrees of self-direction to apparent leaderlessness" (Robbins and Finley 2000, 207).

"Strong leadership is useless if the people following ... are incompetent or uninterested in the team task" (Robbins and Finley 2000, 207).

"Investing leadership in a single person is not an absolute necessity as long as there is agreement among [team] leaders on means and ends" (Polzer and Luecke 2004, 30).

Myth #5: Teams Lead the Organization

"Teams can and do share management responsibilities.... [However,] the responsibility for leadership rests firmly on the shoulders of the executive team" (Wachter 2002, 21).

"If the staff team can't or won't make a decision, the president or CEO will. As the leader, that is their job" (Wachter 2002, 80).

"I reject the views ... that the best that high-status leaders can hope to do is compose a team well and then keep their distance to avoid unduly influencing members' deliberations" (Hackman 2002, x).

Myth #6: The More Members, the Stronger the Team

"When group size becomes very large, the problems generated [by decreasing motivation, difficulty coordinating, and other inefficiencies] far out-weigh the incremental resources brought by additional members" (Hackman 2002, 117). Positing an inverse relationship between size of a team and potential productivity, Hackman holds that smaller is usually better and pegs the ideal size for a team at no more than six members (116–19).

"Teams by their very nature can't be very big." Core members, the people who will be held responsible if something goes wrong, are "100% dedicated to the team task," in contrast to others who support and interact with the team in a multitude of ways. The ideal number of team members is 10 or fewer (Wachter 2002, 215–16).

Even one person can be considered a "virtual team" when that individual possesses the breadth and depth of expertise normally associated with a functional team (Wachter 2002, 218).

"Virtually all effective teams ... have ranged between 2 and 25 people" (Katzenbach and Smith 2004, 10).

"The optimal size for a team depends on its goals and tasks. In general ... five to ten members ... when the tasks are complex and require specific skills. Larger teams (up to twenty-five people) ... if their tasks are simple and straightforward and team members agree to delegate tasks to subgroups as needed" (Polzer and Luecke 2004, 38).

Myth #7: Sports Teams Are the Model for Implementation of Work Teams

"True, [professional] sports teams are groups of people with selected areas of expertise, who share a common goal (winning). But they are led the old-fashioned way, by a supervisor/coach who is above them in the hierarchy." In addition, they neither encourage individual members to make their own decisions, nor create a safe environment for learning through mistakes, nor reward ordinary players anywhere nearly as well as the superstars (Robbins and Finley 2000, 201–202).

"Every sports analogy [comparing athletics teams to work teams] ... leaves out a fundamental part of the equation. Players compete for positions on [sports] teams and only the very best make it" (Wachter 2002, 67).

Myth #8: Teams Do the Work of the Organization

"Teams think, [individual] team members do work" (Wachter 2002, 30).

"The truth is that team members actually do all the work! ... If we allow the organization to believe that teams actually do work, we create an environment where individuals can shirk responsibility and accountability by hiding behind the team" (Wachter 2002, 110).

"Every member of a successful team does equivalent amounts of real work" (Katzenbach and Smith 2004, 13).

Myth #9: Teams Are More Productive than Individuals

"The truth is that teams are inherently inferior to individuals, in terms of efficiency," in cases where an individual has enough information and other resources to complete a task. This is true because one person operating autonomously will not encounter the interpersonal frictions, delays, and misunderstanding that are part and parcel of operating within the team environment (Robbins and Finley 2000, 213).

"Most of the activities addressed within organizations are best handled through normal work processes or by people acting alone [instead of by teams]" (Polzer and Luecke 2004, 7).

Myth #10: Consensus Is the Only Acceptable Decision-Making Mode for Teams

"Unfortunately teams and team based organizations never actually use consensus, it takes too long" (Wachter 2002, 122).

"The petty sorcerer would grind action to a halt by insisting on complete consensus" (Wachter 2002, 122).

"What often appears to be consensus is simply the outcome of some people voting in favor just to end a deadlock and move on," or assenting "with the understanding that their colleagues will support them on another matter" (Polzer and Luecke 2004, 51).

"[Consensus] takes a lot of time and psychological energy, and a high level of member skill.... There can be no emergency in progress. Bring your pajamas" (Robbins and Finley 2000, 44).

Myth #11: Relationships Are Paramount and Maintaining Harmony Is Job One for Teams

"Many people have the misconception that teamwork is about maintaining good relationships. Consequently, teams will often sacrifice results in order to maintain harmonious relationships" (Wachter 2002, 27).

"When 'getting along' becomes the hallmark of teamwork ... fear of offending someone causes open and honest communications to stop" and "teamwork fails to produce results" (Wachter 2002, 87).

"When teamwork is about results ... relationships take care of themselves" (Wachter 2002, 123).

"The nearly universal human desire to have harmonious interactions with others, to be approved rather than rejected by our team mates, and generally to keep anxieties as low as possible ... sometimes leads us to do thoughtless things that perhaps we should not do, and to go further than we ought to go in pleasing our fellow team member or our clients" (Hackman 2002, 109).

"Conflict is common place and expected. Since it cannot be—and shouldn't be—eliminated, the team must learn to manage and make the most of conflict" (Polzer and Luecke 2004, 86).

"Group emotional intelligence ... is not about harmony, lack of tension, and all members liking each other" (Druskat and Wolff, 2004, 48).

"Critical thinking and rigorous debate invariably lead to conflict. The good news is that conflict brings issues into focus, allowing leaders to make more-informed choices" (Garvin and Roberto 2004, 104).

"Cognitive or substantive conflict relates to the work at hand ... disagreements over ideas and assumptions and differing views on the best ways to proceed.... Not only is such conflict healthy, it's crucial to effective inquiry" (Garvin and Roberto 2004, 104). In contrast, affective or interpersonal conflict is destructive, and given its devastating impacts on both the team and the parent organization as "personal friction, rivalries, and clashing personalities," this type of conflict can lead the decision process off on tangents. In addition, it almost always will "diminish people's willingness to cooperate during implementation" (104–105).

Myth #12: All Right-Thinking People Enjoy Working Closely with Others

"Most of us enter a potential team situation cautiously because ingrained individualism and experience discourage us from putting our fates in the hands of others or accepting responsibility for others" (Katzenbach and Smith 2004, 14).

"People—average Americans, anyway—need their space to feel calm and safe" (Robbins and Finley 2000, 209).

"In designing a team [physical] environment, do not expect people to crave constant contact with one another.... There must be no communication snags anywhere. But people need their privacy too" (Robbins and Finley 2000, 210).

Myth #13: Individuals Are Completely Subsumed by the Team

When organizations do not honor individual contributions as well as team results, "dedicated individuals choose not to support teamwork" and other team members tend to "abdicate responsibility and avoid accountability" (Wachter 2002, 24).

"There is a synergy between achieving team goals and achieving individual goals" and when this fact is not reflected in the reward system "most competent team members opt out, leaving teamwork in the hands of those poor souls who neither desire nor aspire to achieve" (Wachter 2002, 70).

"Effective teamwork means a continual balancing act between meeting team needs and individual needs ... the things that each of us wants, things that have nothing to do with teams or jobs" (Robbins and Finley 2000, 22).

"In teaming physics, the team is decidedly the weaker force. The stronger force remains the collection of personal wishes and wants that team members bring to the team" (Robbins and Finley 2000, 21).

"People will only agree to team if it meets their own needs first" (Robbins and Finley 2000, 23).

"Just as each member must contribute to the team's work, each should receive clear benefits" (Polzer and Luecke 2004, 21).

Myth #14: The Team Has Primary Responsibility for Its Own Success

"Any significant change requires active champions if it is to succeed" (Wachter 2002, 138).

"Unfortunately, teamwork ... does not sell itself" but requires a champion to overcome organizational barriers and pockets of resistance (Wachter 2002, 141).

Support people for a team include "team sponsor—a manager the team can run to when it needs protection or direction" and "facilitators—outside people who help keep the team on track" (Robbins and Finley 2000, 216).

"Whether a team is formed by a manager or by a group of staff members, a team must have a sponsor" (Polzer and Luecke 2004, 27).

"The sponsor should champion the team's goals at the highest level, reminding the leadership of how the team's success will contribute to the organization's success" (Polzer and Luecke 2004, 28).

Myth #15: Teamwork Means More Meetings

Teamwork actually can reduce the number of meetings needed to accomplish a task or project. "Teamwork makes meetings more effective. One of the hidden powers of teamwork is the ability to focus meetings on accomplishing results rather than activities" (Wachter 2002, 28–29).

Myth #16: Team-Building Exercises Carry Over to the Workplace

"Everyone is ecstatic, certain that the lessons of teamwork [from undergoing physical and mental exercises together] will naturally translate to something wonderful once they get back to the office…. But teams are not failing because people have fears and phobias, or are unable in a broad generic way to 'trust'…. Their trust issues are specific to [work] roles and procedures—not to one another's willingness to catch them when they fall" (Robbins and Finley 2000, 198).

Myth #17: Personality Type Is the Key to Team Dynamics and Team Results

"The Myers-Briggs type inventory does not measure anything that matters to teams. Teams do not rise or fall on how people are (either real or perceived) down deep inside. They rise or fall on what they actually do, how they actually behave toward one another on the outside" (Robbins and Finley 2000, 205).

"All teams care about is what you *do* [emphasis added] in real terms, as seen through the eyes of your teammates. What you are inside is your own business" (Robbins and Finley 2000, 205).

A Guide to Implementing Teams

How Sweet It Is When Teams Work!

It is beyond the scope of this book to go into detail about how to set up and nurture an effective team. The literature on this topic is extensive and makes fascinating reading. One of the best practical resources for learning how to implement teams is *The New Why Teams Don't Work: What Goes Wrong and How to Make It Right*. Far from being against teams, *The New Why Teams Don't Work* celebrates what they can accomplish under the right circumstances. "*Team intelligence is intelligence about working together* [emphasis added]. A team that is smart about itself knows where its strengths and weaknesses are. Team members know what each of them wants and needs. They know about one another's peculiarities, and how to get the best from one another. And they know when to stop bugging one another" (Robbins and Finley 2000, ix–x).

What Teams Need

Although "productivity by attrition" (Robbins and Finley 2000, 9), meaning financial gains made by downsizing and either eliminating or combining jobs, has been achieved by countless private and public entities, the type of improvement that does *more than* buy time and temporarily stave off disaster is still out of reach for many organizations that have implemented teams. For those who implemented change haphazardly, "communication, quality, and true productivity gains—all the promises teams make and managers get so excited about—remain elusive" (9).

Problems arise when teams are not properly set up and supported. "When they fail, it is often because the organization employing them has turned to teams in order to trim middle management , without giving the new teams the attention, tools, vision, rewards, or simple clarity that they need to succeed" (12). Like several other authorities on teams, these particular authors write not to condemn the team structure but to make explicit what is needed for its success—to expose root causes of failure and to offer strategies for stamping out the betrayal, lying, and stupidity (read human nature) that all too often cause teams to fail (x).

Between them Robbins and Finley have an extensive grasp of management theory and practice. Their instinct for what makes people tick is awesome. They describe human behavior and motivations clearly and instructively. And their language is colorful and interesting, without jargon or verbosity. For example, descriptions of common problems in team interaction are put into context by this chapter introduction: "We [advocates of teams] tend to picture the perfect team" whose members "fall somewhere between angels and the characters sketched in apparel ads, " whereas "real teams … are made up of living, breathing, imperfect people" (62). An abundance of strategies for understanding and coping with difficult people follows this colorful comment.

Robbins and Finley conclude with a stirring tribute to "the glory of working together and getting things right" (259). They compare the best team dynamics to the way families function. "Like families, all teams are flawed" (258); and like families, when the crunch comes, teams show a fierce loyalty toward the very members whom—in private—they may criticize and in some ways cordially dislike. "In the best teams you see a circle—of sympathy, support, and a limited kind of love … when team members sincerely want the best for one another" (258).

QUESTIONS TO ASK BEFORE DECIDING ON TEAMS

In weighing the advantages and disadvantages of moving from a heavily hierarchical organization to one powered by teams, the following questions/issues should be carefully pondered.

Readiness for Change

Among the permanent staff, is there a critical majority of people open to change? Senge (2001) speaks of "internal networkers" among the rank and file whose "authority comes from the strength of their convictions and the clarity of their ideals." He goes on to say, "This, we find time and time again, is the only legitimate authority when deep changes are required, regardless of one's position." He cautions that finding them in the organization is critical to successful change, since "much time and energy can be wasted working with the wrong people, especially in the early stages of a change process" (128). A case study about a self-managed reference team at The Ohio State University's Health Sciences Library stresses the importance of Harrington-Macklin's advice to seek volunteers in order to secure the right level of commitment and to forestall any other individual's resenting being excluded (Bradigan and Powell 2004, 147).

However, some individuals and groups within the organization are apt to be less open to change. It goes without saying that tenured and union-affiliated library staff members are anything but putty in the hands of library management. Even classified staff members who are not unionized may have de facto tenure because of civil service laws and regulations. If they are resistant to change, they cannot always be won over. Performance reward systems not withstanding, not all employees can be motivated to improve or to move on.

Those long-time employees who enjoy some protected status may be both comfortable with a much lower performance than the majority of people could tolerate and also be bulletproof with respect to either rewards or punishments/disincentives. They cannot be seduced and they are beyond shame. Robbins and

Finley ascribe such entrenched status quo behavior to an attitude of entitlement. People who for years have not been held to account may as a result have become comfortable with mediocre or substandard performance—for themselves and for the organization. Such problem employees trade on the popular notion "that people have an inherent right to fair treatment, a living wage, and decent conditions," and have adopted the attitude that they need do nothing to earn such treatment from the organization (Robbins and Finley 2000, 84–85). If such unhealthy and unrealistic attitudes predominate among staff, there is much work to be done before teams stand a chance of succeeding.

Desire for Autonomy

What proportion of the permanent staff has the "worker bee" mentality? Some of your most productive employees may be better followers than leaders. Not all good employees desire increased autonomy and responsibility. In fact, some may be terrified by the thought of having empowerment thrust upon them and being held accountable for forces and factors they feel they can neither influence nor control. University of Arizona writers quote a staff member as having said, "Don't ask me to think. Just tell me what to do" (Diaz and Pintozzi 1999, 34).

Before leaping to implement teams, it is critical to separate the sheep from the goats, as it were. Only individuals receptive to having more autonomy and responsibility can be counted on to wholeheartedly support their teammates and to participate fully in new processes based on a team structure. When changing to a nonhierarchical organizational structure is being planned, any productive staff member disinclined to accept autonomy and increased responsibility must be carefully considered. Such a person may be a better candidate for a resource person who supplies functional expertise as needed than for core membership on a team.

Potential to Develop Team Skills

How many employees have strengths that with appropriate coaching and training can be parlayed into good team skills? Not everyone is capable of developing the ideal communication, negotiation, prioritization, and dialog skills. Some have a tin ear for the nuances of team-like interactions, despite their best intentions and extensive training and practice. Others may not be capable of learning quantitative tools, concepts, and techniques and consequently attempt to limit use of quantitative approaches. They cannot be allowed to sabotage efforts to supplement qualitative information with quantitative data. Again, depending on what other skills such staff members have or can acquire, it may be that neither group should be assigned as core members of any team.

Leadership

What leadership qualities and positive organizational dynamics does your organization have and what desirable qualities does it lack? If the existing hierarchy already has the qualities you are looking for, it may be advisable to institute temporary project teams that will be disbanded after their work is done, rather than undertaking the cataclysmic upheaval of full-scale change to the team-based organization.

Do current leaders have both the vision and the ability to inspire trust in subordinates in sufficient quantities for fulfilling the organizational mission? Does one or more of your current leaders have the skills and personal charisma to promote cooperation across functional lines, to reward innovation, and to foster acceptance of change by creating a safe environment for experimentation? If yes, the hierarchy may still be a viable structure for your organization and drastic changes may not be needed. If important things are lacking in the current organization, however, then by all means fix the problem! But the old saw still applies: If it *ain't* broke, don't fix it.

Out of the Frying Pan, Into the Fire?

What would be your object in flattening the organization? If it is to increase participation and access to top management for employees at the lower echelons of the hierarchy, the team structure *may* achieve this aim, but improvement is not guaranteed. What does the organization stand to lose and to gain by going to a team structure? How widespread are the problems with participation and communication?

Many supervisors and managers may already be doing an excellent job of encouraging participation and fostering a robust flow of ideas back and forth between their units, other parts of the library, and top management. If this is the case, a flat organization can exacerbate communication problems and feelings of disenfranchisement for the rank and file instead of making things better.

In a flatter organization, mangers have fewer staff members to whom they can delegate anything and assuredly will have less time to spend exchanging ideas with staff under their span of control. So if staff members cannot send input upward through a supervisor and if only team leaders and *aggressive* team members have the ear of top management, then the voices of many good employees will be heard less often than before. This circumstance would be unfortunate for both staff and the organization.

A flatter organization does not decrease the need for increased attention to communicating. On the contrary, it ups the ante. Typically in the flatter organization, responsibility for communication no longer is centralized in the administrative offices. Teams and other groups who are immersed in their own goals and processes may not be conscious of the need to keep colleagues, other teams, or the administration apprised of their needs, their aspirations and plans, or their progress. The result can be increased organizational tension and, not infrequently, missteps in formulating and implementing strategy or even mission drift stemming from lack of coordination and the absence of a top-level unifying force.

Are Sufficient Resources Available?

Are there sufficient financial and nonfinancial resources for bringing your staff up to speed in organizational skills and management techniques, for ongoing training, and for an appropriate level of review of team processes and actions? Team members do not magically become egalitarian, tolerant, and supportive of the organization's future rather than their own self-interest. All of them need training in interpersonal and management skills to maximize their contributions to the team.

For example, team members need to know how to question and explore their own perceptions as well as those of fellow team members. If a team lacks this skill, it is possible for a team member whose personal agenda conflicts with the organization's best interests and/or the team's goals to cloak self-interest in team rhetoric. When this happens, team colleagues can be fooled/manipulated into uncritical acceptance of a personal agenda that conflicts with team priorities. There is no point in setting teams up for a fall by ignoring the importance of training.

What about Performance Problems?

What strategies will be used within the new organization for dealing with employee performance problems? A clear and specific charge for each team, empowerment within well-defined boundaries, appropriate oversight of the team process, appropriate team training in confronting and intervening in nonproductive or disruptive behavior, and a reward system focused on results consistent with team goals—all of these things help keep team members on track. But teams often are better at dealing with motivating a diamond in the rough than at dealing with the hard cases among staff. Where there are significant individual performance problems, supervisors with hierarchical authority often are better equipped to set expectations, monitor progress or the lack of it, and document unacceptable performance than a team or team leader is. This is especially true when team membership and team leadership turns over frequently.

Steep Learning Curve

It takes training and experience to understand and deal with the complex environment within which an academic library exists. If such training is not supplied and if the prevailing notion of teaming centers on the misconception that all viewpoints should factor equally into the shared vision of the organization's future and current aspirations, then resources can be squandered as team members with little or no experience in budgeting, planning, marketing, and campus politics build air castles instead of buckling down to critical tasks. Their reach may well exceed their grasp.

Conversely team members inexperienced in such arenas may insist on staying in the comfort zone of familiar things and not reaching high enough. The result is reinventing the wheel instead of pursuing ambitious changes and true innovations that would advance progress toward achieving organizational aims.

A Moving Target

To sum up, teams are a moving target and not a permanent entity. Members come and go. Leaders come and go. Team focus must change periodically in order to remain in alignment with the priorities of the parent organization. Management's relationship with teams can get better or worse. It is a Sisyphean task to build and maintain teams, an endeavor that should not be undertaken without the resources to succeed.

HOLD YOUR NOSE AND DIVE? OR DIP IN ONE TOE?

A lot has been written about how fast large-scale organizational change should be implemented. Gen X and Gen Y are said to be inured to change and often to thrive on it. No doubt the same will be true of Gen Z when it has been identified and studied. For that matter, even staff nostalgic for the free-wheeling 1960s and 1970s—when the pace of academic library change was slow enough to accommodate frequent coffee breaks and many philosophical discussions about minutiae whose substance few people recall and when nobody questioned the wisdom of librarians, much less the value of libraries—recognize that "the times, they are a changin'." But *how* to foster effective change is one of the most profound mysteries of the academic library profession.

How Slow Can You Go?

In the mid-1980s, Rogers, Hayden, and Ferketish (1985) identified the key to successful change efforts within an abbreviated time frame as a combination of information and employee readiness to embark on change. "An organization requires less time to implement a value-driven change when it readily provides information and employs a workforce that has the capabilities and willingness to undertake the change effort." In contrast, they observed that "change in less-equipped organizations takes longer" (114). Phipps's (1993) interpretation of Senge supports the latter opinion about motivating people to change. "Our complex organizational systems will find their own rate of growth. Driving people to be ever faster in their change processes ... will fail to move them any faster than they are capable of moving," whereas "giving them support to follow their own vision, to use their own abilities for systems thinking, to share at their own levels, will allow them to achieve whatever is the maximum rate of change" (27). Change "by fiat" (28), which she defines as "demanding, cheerleading, intervening with recognition or rewards for speed" (27), ultimately delays the rate of lasting change.

Support for Comprehensive Change

Robbins and Finley (2000) categorically advise against "the dribble method" (176) of implementing change, warning that successive waves of incremental change can exhaust and demoralize staff. They say that typically a slow timetable for implementation fails to diffuse resistance to change and actually "heightens the sense of mistrust of management that many employees already have" (176). In their experience, "Companies that dole out changes in small doses over longer periods of time, hoping to minimize negative impact, are surprised at the sudden dip in morale after about the second or third dose" (175), and "organizations that have had the best success with change make major steps in short time frames, with the end product carefully described up front" so that "team members tolerate the short-term pain for the longer-term payoff" (176).

The Case for Waves of Change

Authors of a book about managing information technology (IT) change titled *Breakthrough IT Change Management,* in contrast, espouse implementing discrete

waves of change interspersed with periods of regrouping "measuring the results, gathering lessons learned, preventing reversion, and preparing for the
next wave" (Lientz and Rea 2004, 12). If waves of change in different areas are
staggered, then there is time for marketing change to staff, monitoring their reactions and involvement, and measuring progress toward goals for the changes.
They feel that managers who grasp "how to organize the changes in a particular wave of change so that they are inter-related with each other, yield positive
results, and are consistent with longer term change" (31) will avoid the disadvantages of the two most popular models for change: the exhaustion and disillu-
sion of continuous change and the shock and overwhelming disruption of "big
bang" change, where all needed changes are made at once (31).

Small Steps toward Change

Schaffer and Thomson (1992) assert that organizational change can be implemented via either a large-scale effort involving the entire organization or with
"a few modest pilot projects" (88). No less an authority on academic library
change than the University of Arizona Libraries crew echoes this sentiment in
their reference to Tennant's concept of "zooming" or the process of making small
changes constantly. "By establishing an organizational culture of 'zooming' ...
the organization itself can begin to respond quickly to change on an incremental, evolutionary basis. Such an organization will tend to go where it should
much sooner than one which resists change" (Stoffle, Allen, et al. 2003, 370).

Fitting New Strategies to an Existing Organizational Structure

Kaplan and Norton (2006), the inventors of and the authorities on the balanced scorecard system of organizational performance management, caution
against getting caught up in what they call "restructuring churn" (102). Too
many cycles of organizational restructuring initiated without thoughtful and
thorough consideration of what corresponding changes in organizational performance are desired are virtually guaranteed to be frustrating, expensive, and
ultimately ineffective in terms of advancing the organization toward a better
future. Kaplan and Norton begin an article with this provocative statement:
"Strategic dreams often turn into nightmares if companies start engaging in
expensive and distracting restructurings" (100). They go on to explain how and
why prolonged cycles of drastic restructuring can create problems as bad as
those they were intended to solve, if not worse. "It takes time for employees to
adapt to new structures, and a great deal of tacit knowledge—precisely the kind
that's become most valuable—gets lost in the process, as disaffected employees leave. On top of that, companies get saddled with the vestiges of previous
organizational decisions, such as obsolete local and regional headquarters and
legacy IT infrastructures" (102).

Conceding that escalating competitive pressures and a constantly changing
economic environment are powerful motivators for considering restructuring,
Kaplan and Norton (2006) nevertheless advise against looking to repeated
reorganizations to solve organizational performance problems. The world
has changed since the nineteenth and twentieth centuries, they remind the
reader. Now competitive advantage "is derived less from the management

of physical and financial assets and more from how well companies align such intangible assets as knowledge workers, R & D, and IT to the demands of their customers" (102*)*. Of course the guiding philosophy they advocate for balancing financial concerns with intangibles is the balanced scorecard performance management system successfully used by a fair number of non-profit organizations, including some academic libraries, as well as by some of the leading companies.

These high priests of OD advise giving up the quest for perfection. "Companies do not need to find the perfect structure for their strategy ... a far more effective approach is to choose an organizational structure that works without major conflicts and then design a customized strategic system to align that structure with the strategy" (Kaplan and Norton 2006, 102). Key elements of this "customized strategic system" will be familiar to librarians cognizant with good management and OD principles. They include procedures and practices for planning, for allocating budgets that support organizational priorities, for performance management, for monitoring and reporting on progress, for revising strategies where results are out of bounds, and for effective communication and the conduct of productive meetings (103). For details about how the balanced scorecard framework works to identify strategies that will support the organizational structure, Kaplan and Norton refer readers to their book, *The Strategy-Focused Organization* (2001).

MORE QUESTIONS TO EXPLORE

Lientz and Rea (2004), authors mentioned in a preceding section of this chapter, pose list after list of extremely helpful questions for change makers to ask in the planning, implementation, and review stages of any organizational change.

That's Not Just Ancient History

For example, they point out that it always is good to ask what happened in previous change efforts. They contend that by finding out what departments and individuals resisted and/or threw a monkey wrench into previous change efforts, planners can discover the informal political structure at different supervisory levels and use this information to make subsequent change efforts more successful. For this reason, they counsel exploring and responding to staff misgivings at all stages of the change process, rather than rushing to cut off questions and disagreements. In this way concerns can be addressed and softened by stressing the individual and organizational benefits of the proposed changes as well as by adapting the proposed change process to accommodate potential problems that surface. The alternative is strengthening incipient resistance to change and driving it underground, where it will be virtually impossible to counter (Lientz and Rea 2004, 46).

These sentiments are subscribed to by librarian authors as well. Engaging dissenters and addressing their concerns is important in effecting lasting change. "No significant change will occur without some degree of skepticism or deep sincere disagreement about vision. In some environments, conflict arising from the work of organization development—substantial change—is akin to competing for the soul of the library" (Stephens and Russell 2004, 248).

The Planning Process

An extremely valuable feature of *Breakthrough IT Change Management* (Lientz and Rea 2004) is the explanation of how winning change goals, objectives and strategies are selected and winnowed down to strategic essentials.

Common Goals

First, Lientz and Rea enumerate and explain the most common goals for organizational change, most of which will be familiar to academic library administrators: (1) reducing the cost of work; (2) reducing the number of employees needed to do the work; (3) empowering employees so that routine tasks and decisions can be executed by front-line staff; (4) streamlining and simplifying work so that employees with more training and experience can be redirected to more productive (and often higher level tasks); (5) increasing employee productivity; (6) increasing quality and/or reducing error rates; (7) reducing cycle times for processes; (8) increasing sales (or in the case of non-profits, increasing penetration of current and potential user groups); (9) increasing cooperation among employees within departments; (10) reducing disharmony between departments and increasing collaboration and cooperation across departmental lines; (11) updating or changing the value structure of the organization; and (12) streamlining and realigning the organization to pursue a new or greatly revised mission (Lientz and Rea 2004, 58).

Weighing Alternatives

Next they pose questions applicable to the process of evaluating possible change objectives and selecting the best of the objectives generated:

- Is the degree of risk inherent in a given objective one that management can support?
- Is the projected time span for making the change realistic?
- Can interim changes be accomplished as part of the overall change objective?
- Is there adequate staffing for the work needed to attain the change objective?
- Are there sponsors for change and are there experienced managers in place who can address the objective?
- What are the risks to the business (in the case of non-profits, the core functions) if the objective is selected for implementation?
- What are the risks if the objective is *not* selected? (Lientz and Rea 2004, 60)

Testing the Options

Next they advise generating a list of potential change strategies to address the objectives and considering how each proposed change strategies will affect the organization: the degree to which each individual strategy supports a given change objective; the potential impact of the proposed strategy on key organizational processes; the degree of alignment of fit of a proposed organizational change strategy with existing business strategies (e.g., expand into new markets, develop a portfolio of new services); the availability and adequacy of managerial personnel, other staff, and additional resources to support the proposed change strategy; the change strategy's fit with the culture of the organization and with departments most involved in the changes; and significant risks associated with the scope and timing of the change. It is also important to consider whether the entire organization must change or whether only a few departments will be significantly involved (i.e., will re-engineering technical processes in one or two units bring about sufficient improvements?). And will the change be sudden and major or continuous and gradual or discrete waves of change consistent with long-term goals? (Lientz and Rea 2004, 62–63).

Keeping Score: How Effective Was the Planning?

Finally, Lientz and Rea (2004) offer scorecards to assess the effectiveness of the planning effort for both goals and strategies, noting that "because of the need for consensus and support, how you undertake actions in change management is often as important as the end result" (64). They go on to point out that "this is particularly true in these early planning stages. During implementation of change, the focus shifts toward getting results" (64).

Key factors to evaluate in initial planning stages include the following: (1) Extent of participation in the planning process by managers, (2) extent of rank and file employee involvement, (3) number of managers involved in the work processes to be changed and the operational areas affected, (4) extent that front line employees have contributed to development of objectives and strategies, (5) amount of time the entire group has spent reviewing and agreeing on change objectives, (6) extent of resistance to change in general, and (7) extent of resistance to specific change strategies. Generally, the greater the involvement and contribution toward planning, the better the chance of success (63).

At first glance, Lientz and Rea's (2004) precepts about how to interpret rankings for two of the factors listed in this scorecard seem counterintuitive. They warn that too much enthusiasm from managers at the start of the change effort can be counterproductive, since it can burn itself out and leave the process without support for the long haul. "Implementing change is [like running] a marathon. Enthusiasm is great, but it must be measured and sustained by results" (14). Just as surprising is their assertion that resistance is not entirely negative. Often resistance can to some extent be used to the change maker's advantage. While hearing questions, fears, and objections to the idea of change or toward specific change strategies may be disheartening to change makers at first, Lientz and Rea urge exploring the reasons behind such concerns and reservations rather than sweeping negative comments under the rug. The dialogue with resistant employees, usually the ultimate experts regarding details about the work for which they are responsible, often yields valuable information that strengthens the strategy and improves the odds that its implementation will succeed (189–90).

Assessing Outcomes

Scorecards for evaluating change feature four different perspectives: (1) employee performance during implementation of long-term change (participation rates, degree/depth of engagement in various aspects of the change, and extent of support for/commitment to the change); (2) management performance during implementation; (3) performance of the change process during implementation; and (4) assessment of the change process in its entirety, by focusing on performance of the change management team and the success of the change management process throughout the change effort (Lientz and Rea 2004, 211–16).

Change Implementation: Management Scorecard

The management scorecard has a great variety of measurements, reflecting the wide scope of management responsibilities: involvement in, commitment to, participation in, and support for change; the number of issues that required management involvement to resolve and the average time it took management to deal with an issue; effort put forth to resolve resource allocation problems, chiefly personnel resources; budgeted versus actual costs; amount of time planned for the change effort versus elapsed time; and number of surprises or unanticipated issues and developments that emerged during implementation (this number should be low), along with average time needed to deal with surprises, and management's ability to mitigate the impact of any surprises (Lientz and Rea 2004, 213–15).

Change Implementation: The Process Scorecard

The process scorecard employs a group of measures dealing with both process details and assessment of big picture impacts of change. Process details focus on the work and how well IT systems support improvements in the work—availability of meaningful and workable process measures, increases in the volume of work addressed after the change, improvements in average time to handle a single transaction, number of exceptions (groups of transactions not handled by the new IT system), number of manual work-arounds still needed after implementation of the new IT systems, and number of shadow systems eliminated versus the number remaining (shadow systems being ways to gather and analyze important data not produced by the new IT systems and processes (Lientz and Rea 2004, 215–16).

Work process changes are one gauge of big picture impacts. Some benefits from this type of change are realized quickly (e.g., improving delivery times, expediting handling of customer service transactions, or increasing some aspect of product quality). Other benefits from process changes are incremental benefits and are attained over the long term *after* benefits from the waves of "quick hits" or substantial short-term improvements have been realized. For example, after a quick hit change that implements a faster dispatch system, a company subsequently may also reduce the error rate in filling orders, thus increasing satisfaction among its customers and/or suppliers. If this happens, then over the long term the company should become able to compete more effectively against rivals (Lientz and Rea 2004, 215–16).

Another big picture item is the number of issues that arise and are resolved during implementation versus the number and types of issues that remain unresolved. Still another key factor is how robust the change process proved to be: its adequacy for addressing and resolving issues and problems, its completeness (to what degree long-term as well as intermediate goals and objectives were realized), and its flexibility (how well it does handling new problems that emerge as a result of changes) (Lientz and Rea 2004, 215–16).

Advocacy of Learning Organization Concepts

Although *Breakthrough IT Change Management* (Lientz and Rea 2004) is specifically geared toward changing technologies and IT systems as well as implementing e-business strategies, most of its precepts and recommendations apply to management of any type of organizational change. Many of the concepts the authors propound and the principles they endorse are compatible with learning organizational philosophies adopted by many academic libraries. The change management scorecard is a case in point.

Key qualitative factors recommended for evaluating change management from planning through the implementation stage include the following elements: (1) Overall quality of change management team effort; (2) ability of the team and the change process to resolve problems; (3) performance on cost and schedule parameters set for the change, (4) average time to resolve issues that surfaced during the planning stage or afterward, (5) number of surprises (unanticipated problems and issues) that emerged and were addressed, (6) average time needed to address a surprise, (7) quality of teamwork, (8) extent of collaboration and cooperation among team members, (9) turnover of team members, (10) extent and quality of lessons that were learned throughout the change process, (11) how the team organized and used the lessons learned to improve and strengthen subsequent change effort, and (12) lessons learned that can and will be applied to future change efforts (Lientz and Rea 2004, 216).

GOOD HUMAN RESOURCE PRACTICES

Whatever organization model is chosen, clearly the success of the endeavor will be enhanced by following good management practices in recruitment/retention, training, performance measurement systems, and other aspects of the quality of work life within the library's control.

Recruitment and Retention

Much has been written about using human resources effectively, in particular focusing energy on recruitment and retention of the kind of staff the organizational structure and culture needs in order to achieve and sustain its highest possible productivity and strategic priorities. Addressing diversity targets is critical for every academic library in today's increasingly multicultural society. Articulating essential and preferred criteria for any open positions—qualities that will both support current priorities and leave grow room for addressing emerging issues as current priorities evolve and new concerns surface—is another important consideration. Salary and benefits must be commensurate with the responsibilities of a position and with the qualifications of finalists for the position.

Retention is fully as delicate a feat as hiring good people in the first place. Retention issues—salary, and so on—overlap somewhat with recruitment concerns. Salary compression—the phenomenon in which salaries of new hires eclipse those of seasoned and valued staff—can be the kiss of death for retention. Where this problem is rampant, typically the most valued staff will move to greener pastures while those with outdated skills, limited motivation, and other performance deficits cling like limpets. Mentoring can be key to supporting and bringing along new hires unused to academe or new to working in libraries. For all of their energy and skills, new staff members may need help in navigating the shoals of campus politics and expectations for promotion and tenure.

In addition, it is wise to think ahead to (1) building in career progression opportunities for valued senior staff and (2) succession planning for key positions in the organization. Talented and marketable folks will not stay if appropriate opportunities for advancement (either promotion within grade/rank or the chance to move up into leadership positions) are lacking in the organization. These issues should not be left to chance. The organization can take several giant steps backward when it loses a key staff member and experiences either a delay in finding a suitable successor or finds that it cannot find a candidate with equivalent skills and personal qualities and must settle for a less-capable replacement. Inexperienced individuals with growth potential often surprise both themselves and the organization eventually. But while they are developing, the organization can lose momentum at a critical juncture in its development.

Training

Training is an ongoing need for both new and longtime staff. In many academic libraries the idea of subject specialists with advanced degrees in various academic disciplines has gone onto the chopping block. Now reference and instruction librarians are exhorted to become "deep generalists," who know as much as possible about as many diverse subject areas as possible. Fulfilling this expectation is a tall order even with abundant support for training in software applications, databases, citation tools, and sundry other areas that today's librarian is expected to master. Absent time to learn, financial support, and the blessing of unimpeachable mental health, this concept could be a recipe for mediocre service if not personal disaster.

And then there are the interpersonal and team behaviors to perfect. Social misfits and malcontents can no longer be sheltered from expectations or hidden away in a library unit where their lack of social skills will do no harm. Gone forever is the heyday of academic libraries when personnel budgets were exempted from cuts or raids, nonproductive staff could be carried by their more capable colleagues, when talent could be stockpiled against future need, and when twice-daily coffee breaks were an inviolable right for the entire staff. Whether the organizational structure is hierarchical or flatter and more team-like, in today's stripped-down academic library, everyone must pull his or her own weight and then some. And virtually all functions are interdependent to the extent that an employee's repertoire of skills and behaviors for communication, negotiation, managing conflict, leadership, and the like can make or break the organization.

Measuring Performance

Measuring individual and organizational performance is as complicated as ever. But now, to a greater extent than ever in the past, academic libraries are called upon to empower, coach, and motivate personnel and to guide them to their full potential rather than merely documenting performance and administering rewards or punishments. This heightened responsibility necessitates an unparalleled sophistication about organizational development, together with formidable time management skills and unflagging energy.

TECHNOLOGICAL INFRASTRUCTURE

Identifying and utilizing appropriate technologies and partnering with vendors, consortia, and other entities to develop new ones is also critical to holding one's own in the academic library environment. The freedom of wireless connectivity, no longer a novelty in many academic libraries, is taken for granted by a majority of today's patrons. They don't ask *whether* it is available. They ask how to configure their laptops in order to use the wireless access.

Staffing patterns and building policies are affected by availability of new technologies as well. Instruction librarians are asking themselves whether they should be available on demand to students who might want to instant message them for help, sometimes even from the classroom. Reference and circulation librarians are questioning whether restricting use of cell phones is effective or realistic in an era when phones and similar devices have transmogrified into multifunction tools that facilitate voice communication; handle e-mail and instant messages; can capture, broadcast, and receive both still and motion pictures; and—for all we know—may by next year be capable of brewing a beverage superior to Starbucks' most popular menu items.

TWO EXEMPLARS OF ORGANIZATIONAL CHANGE IN ACADEMIC LIBRARIES

Because of the transformation starting in 1991 from an institution that didn't even have an online integrated library system to its current preeminence among libraries that innovate, the University of Arizona Libraries is the model for *comprehensive organization-wide continuous* change. As subsequent chapters of this book show, the University of Pittsburgh's University Library System (ULS) models comparatively smaller scale organizational change implemented in successive cycles with time in between for gains from each such event to be consolidated and for organizational learning to be incorporated into successive change efforts. Each of these remarkable academic libraries has succeeded in transforming a prestigious and venerable but also hide-bound and largely unresponsive organization into an institution in the vanguard of customer service and innovation among Association of Research Library members.

4

Lessons in Organizational Change from the University of Arizona Libraries

AN ORGANIZATIONAL DEVELOPMENT PIONEER

Starting in 1991, the University of Arizona Libraries was on the move. As staff members put it, "External forces, new leadership, and internal stagnation collided. Something new and unique was about to happen in the library" (Diaz and Pintozzi 1999, 27). Teams were implemented after much discussion of the ideal management structure for this library system. All aspects of planning and operations were fair game for discussion and change. The learning organization was adopted as the library system's guiding principle and hoshin planning was chosen as a planning and evaluation tool. Over time a revolutionary performance evaluation management system (PEMS) was developed and implemented. Arizona instituted an annual Living the Future Conference to exchange ideas and progress reports with peer libraries interested in innovation. The end result was an organization with an inverted organizational chart—one with the dean on the bottom conceptually and all staff above her in the pyramid of empowerment—and zero tolerance for planning or operating from any frame of reference that failed to keep user needs as its primary focus. The reality at Arizona and most other institutions of higher learning is that a dean cannot abrogate ultimate responsibility for signing off on actions and decisions. But the chart is a powerful symbol of shared responsibility and empowerment.

During the late 1990s, the academic library world sat up, took notice, and began emulating this innovative and energetic organization to varying degrees. The paradigm of the academic library characterized by an inflexible and all-powerful hierarchy, accompanied by a patronizing attitude toward users and their needs, a prescriptive and self-serving perspective about setting priorities, isolation from information about users, deeply rooted reverence for the status quo, and isolation from and indifference to market forces was fractured. Little in the academic library environment has been the same since. As glorious as this well-documented saga of transformation is, however, there are two important lessons to be gleaned from the University of Arizona Libraries experience with change: (1) Theirs is by no means the only way to pursue organizational revitalization; and (2) an extremely supportive environment is required to succeed at the rapid, large-scale change they undertook.

Many Paths to Transformation

First of all, despite its stunning success at organizational transformation and its reputation as the founder of the immensely popular annual Living the Future Conference, Arizona makes no attempt to prescribe what is best for other libraries that need to change in order to align themselves with the new realities of a constantly changing environment. Virtually everything written by Dean Carla Stoffle and her staff contains a disclaimer about the Arizona way not being the only viable model for academic library organizational change. For example, "this essay is not an attempt to sell the University of Arizona answer to the problem. ... There will be many solutions and many paths to take" (Stoffle, Renaud, and Veldorf 1996, 214). Indeed, one of the key assumptions made by the University of Arizona Organizational Design Project Steering Committee was that "there is no perfect organization, and this redesign will not solve all problems" (Kollen, Simons, and Tellman 1997, 211). They happened to choose (1) the discipline of the learning organization and (2) the structure of teams as guiding principles for reorganization. Both Senge's five disciplines approach and the team structure made sense in the University of Arizona Libraries' circumstances and have served Arizona exceedingly well in their innovative approach to retooling. But the University of Arizona Libraries has not claimed that theirs was the *only* way to restructure and prepare for the future. The Arizona experience manifestly does not represent a cookie cutter approach that every academic library must adopt in order to foster change.

It Takes Resources

The second lesson to be learned from Arizona is, to paraphrase the truism about real estate, "resources, resources, resources." If anything is obvious from the wealth of documentation about the University of Arizona Libraries' transformation from a hierarchical organization fueled by complacency and self-interest into a flatter, nimbler, user-centered organization committed to and surpassingly adept at effecting change, it is the fact that tremendous resources would be needed to replicate their experience.

In a book chapter celebrating many milestones along the path to becoming a learning organization, Diaz and Phipps (1998) have been disarmingly candid in disclosing the enormous amount of resources needed to get their change effort off the ground and to address ongoing challenges in maintaining the momentum of change while simultaneously keeping the library doors open and the stakeholders reasonably content. Articles by Arizona staff have also been frank about bumps and wrong turns encountered along this library's road to organizational glory.

The University of Arizona Libraries Advantage

The following factors comprised an environment uniquely rich in support for change at Arizona:

- University support
- Corporate support
- Library budget allocations earmarked for change

University Support

University support for the library's change process took a number of forms, beginning with hiring an innovative new director in Stoffle.

CORe. At the outset of the library change process, there was an unprecedented degree of university support for the effort. The entire University of Arizona was engaged at the time in a program review effort called Continuous Organizational Renewal or CORe, which served as a framework if not a mandate for change in the library. This university focus on renewal set the stage for support from the university provost to the degree that "when some new activity or program [stemming from team-based management at the library] had to be embarked on that was somewhat outside ... the established policy framework, or slightly beyond the scope of what had been done in the past, an exception could be made and we could move forward" (Stoffle et al. 1998, 5).

It is not uncommon for an academic library to find itself leading the charge on campus to employ customer service or the five disciplines or some other type of change process, struggling to convince forces outside the library as well as within its walls that its vision for change will work. But the University of Arizona Libraries had the full support of university upper administration from the beginning. Since it was the first entity on campus to get serious about teams—about six months in advance of the rest of the university's interest in total quality management—it was "seen as a leader in this area as the campus move[d] in the same direction" (Giesecke 1994, 198–99). Because there were no skeptics or powerful opponents at the university level, Dean Stoffle's ideas and leadership elicited enthusiastic support for two aspects of staff needs during the transition: (1) training and (2) health and wellness monitoring.

Human Resources Support. Initially, the university's Employee Development and Training Office consulted in developing staff training to support the change effort including the basics of team development, team dynamics, and leadership roles within the team structure (Diaz and Phipps 1998, 411). Key to this effort was development of a customer service training module expressly for the libraries that was adapted to each team's needs (416). And after restructuring of the campus Human Resources (HR) department, one of its units, the Human Resources Team (HRT), began to participate directly in the change as full members of some of the library's annual project teams. In addition, trainers from another HR unit began to work actively with library teams in conducting needs assessments (Diaz and Phipps 1998, 423).

Health and Wellness. A second major source of support for Arizona staff during the change effort was the university's Employee Wellness Department. Initially, it provided advice such as how to manage stress, and later it cosponsored a health screening program with the library.

Corporate Support

A partner in other aspects of campus renewal, the INTEL Corporation provided a full-time consultant to the University of Arizona Libraries and provided training modules in techniques for conducting effective meetings, using facilitation tools, implementation of management by planning (a strategic planning method developed in Japan), and the principles of quality management (Diaz and Phipps 1998, 409). INTEL advisors estimated that "it would take at least seven years to approximate the sense of accomplishment associated with self-directed teams" (Bender 1997, 19).

Library Budget Allocation

In best strategic planning fashion, the Libraries carved out budget allocations to support the reorganization. In 1994–95 alone, some $28,900 was dedicated to training and team support projects. These funds were used to employ outside consultants, to augment the pool of resources for salaries and professional development, and to secure a variety of nonfinancial rewards and recognitions for team accomplishments (Diaz and Phipps 1998, 418). Outside consultants played a variety of roles in transforming the University of Arizona Libraries.

Library Management Consultant. Coordination and training by Maureen Sullivan under the auspices of the Association of Research Libraries' Office of Management Services (ARL/OMS, subsequently rechristened Office of Leadership and Management Services) in developing teams from 1992 to 1994 was an important part of the Arizona experience (Diaz and Phipps 1998, 410). Sullivan introduced the fundamentals for implementing teams to the staff, demonstrated how to chart work flow, and used assessment instruments to help staff learn about their personal preferences and styles and to gauge how well the teams were operating in their initial stages of development. It is worth noting that quite a few libraries have benefited from such consultants, whose services are within the means of most academic libraries.

Diversity Consultants. Not content with local expertise in the task of fostering organizational diversity, the University of Arizona Libraries found funds in 1994–95 to hire the Equity Institute, a national group, to conduct two days of training on diversity issues. Then in 1995–96, an ARL/OMS diversity consultant made a site visit (Diaz and Phipps 1998, 422).

Quality Consultant. That same year (1995–96) an outside quality consultant worked to teach teams the fundamentals of total quality management (TQM), grounded in Deming's work (Diaz and Phipps 1998, 414).

In addition to bringing in the aforementioned types of consultants and several others, the Libraries were creative in deploying available resources in support of salaries commensurate with outstanding performance, professional development funds, and other rewards.

Salaries. In 1994–95 the library budgeted funds to increase staff salaries (Diaz and Phipps 1998, 417). The 2001–02 current situation analysis points out that the library was to offer competitive starting salaries for all librarian ranks along with the availability of "substantial" monetary awards for career progression (University of Arizona Libraries 2002, under "Human Resources: Strengths"). Similarly the 2003–04 current situation analysis mentioned that monies for market adjustments and merit had been allocated by the university for that academic year and commended the long-standing library practice of internally funding merit, promotions, and counteroffers as a viable fall-back strategy in case university monies should dry up in subsequent years (University of Arizona Libraries 2003a, 2003b).

Professional Development. In addition to dedicating some 1994–95 funds to salaries, other monies were used create a "career progression" fund to support learning opportunities ranging from training on new software to attendance at Educom, stress management seminars, and training in Senge's theory of the learning organization (Diaz and Phipps 1998, 419). And Arizona has continued to protect funds set aside for individual and organizational learning. A library annual report notes, "The Libraries have systems in place to promote staff development including travel money, twenty days of available professional leave each year, and $2,000 faculty grants for our librarians conducting research" (University of Arizona Libraries 2004, 4). In addition, the previous report notes that in spite of budget cutbacks, merit money was set aside to reward exceptional performance (University of Arizona Libraries 2003d, 1).

Nonfinancial Rewards. Nonfinancial types of recognition have been utilized as team rewards as well. In 1994–95, for example, money and time were set aside by the library for such nonsalary rewards as staff recognition meetings, dinner celebrations upon the completion of projects, and awards of small items such as calculators, cups, and T-shirts to teams (Diaz and Phipps 1998, 417).

BARRIERS TO CHANGE

Even such a well-conceived and well-supported change effort as that of Arizona Libraries encounters its share of problems and obstacles—particularly when it is a pioneering effort with no existing model among peer libraries for the type of structure envisioned after the change. Again Diaz, Phipps, and other Arizona staff have been forthcoming about the elements of their process that did not work as well as anticipated in the early years. Many of the following problems exemplify classic missteps of an organization new to the team structure:

- Overload and competing priorities
- The pace and scope of change
- Team structure and process problems
- Cost (both out-of-pocket and staff time) associated with training

Overload and Competing Priorities

By attempting such ambitious organizational change *at the same time* as serials cuts, other budget cuts, and the implementation of a new integrated library system, Arizona Libraries at times overwhelmed its staff members. The result at Arizona was some resistance to both the restructuring itself and the training about the nature of change in the first two years. "We challenged ourselves and the staff to capacity (and at times beyond capacity) to absorb and turn the training they received into learning by practice" (Diaz and Phipps 1998, 410).

Such a tendency to go overboard in setting team goals is typical of a newly minted team-based organization, according to OD professionals. "New teams are famous for declaring 30 goals or outcomes when they first come together" (Robbins and Finley 2000, 39). The resulting tension, they say, has a deleterious effect on teams. "Uncompleted tasks slowly paralyze individuals and teams—until the simple act of getting together to discuss progress looms insurmountable" (41).

Planning Took a Back Seat

Staff-driven strategic planning implemented in the third year was initially seen as peripheral to "the functions assigned to the team that directly served the customer" (Diaz and Phipps 1998, 419), work that teams considered vital. As a result, staff members generally were "unwilling and unprepared to reprioritize their work in order to focus on developing skills and capabilities for a new future" (419).

Lack of Commitment to Some Projects

Although all projects for implementing change were fully funded, there was not sufficient ongoing dialog between the coordinating Management Review Team (MRT) and the rest of the staff, including team leaders, to ensure commitment to some project goals. Hindsight suggests that more frequent communication and sharing of ideas would have improved understanding at the team level about the learning organization principles guiding the MRT's thinking, about the connection of individual projects to the restructuring effort, and in particular about the importance of team goals in laying a foundation for the new organization (Diaz and Phipps 1998, 419).

Low Attendance at Early Training

In 1994–95, staff uncertainty about how to honor both functional and team responsibilities hampered training efforts. "Competing priorities also got in the way of staff attendance at the training that was provided" (Diaz and Pintozzi 1999, 30). One of the first training events, a session designed to explore organizational values and trust, failed to produce the anticipated enumeration of shared values when not all staff attended and consensus about values could not be reached (Diaz and Phipps 1998, 409).

Unrealistic Attendance Expectations

The percentages set for staff participation in cross-cultural training in the third year of the transition were too high at a time when there were many competing proprieties, such as learning to work in teams (Diaz and Phipps 1998, 413). Again, according to the OD literature, this is a common phenomenon—initial uncertainty about how much of one's functional responsibilities can and should be put aside in order to learn and perfect teaming skills and to do the work of the team.

Timetable for Change

Learning that change would not happen quickly was one of the biggest surprises for the University of Arizona Libraries staff. This fact was revealed in a variety of ways at different stages in the change process.

Training Takes Time

Initial training sessions geared toward coping with organizational change did not enjoy much success. Because in the first year of restructuring there was too much uncertainty about the nature of the proposed changes, such sessions failed to lessen feelings of vulnerability and fear (Diaz and Phipps 1998, 409). In addition to realizing the importance of providing information about the nature of proposed changes, Arizona gradually became aware that the deep learning associated with change would take time. "Training is a starting point ... there has to be follow-through, reflection, feedback, and practice over a long period of time for real change to take root" (Diaz and Phipps 1998, 410).

Team Skills Develop over Time

Because of the upheaval of comprehensive organizational change, development of team skills was even slower than it might otherwise have been. "We were naïve about how much time it takes to learn coaching skills, new ways of running meetings, and new ways of communicating with people at a time when everyone else is involved in a change process" (Diaz and Phipps 1998, 411).

Developing Foundation Documents Is a Cyclical Process

The team charged with soliciting input to and drafting a mission, shared vision, and aspiration statements in the third year encountered two significant problems. First, since insufficient time had been allotted for the task, they failed to narrow four versions down to a single acceptable mission statement. And second, a jocular remark about the team's goals for dissemination and adoption of the mission statement backfired. Some staff members were offended and consequently had one more reason to air negative feelings about the organizational change effort (Diaz and Phipps 1998, 415).

Motivation Can Suffer from Tight Time Lines

Motivation was yet another victim of tight time lines. Team rosters turned over too fast for teams to see the fruits of their labors. "Giving ourselves a one-year time frame in which to complete our projects misguided us.... Knowing that we were only a one-year team ... contributed to our uncertainty that what we designed would be followed up on and expanded to staff who did not participate" (Diaz and Phipps 1998, 418).

Acquiring New Skills and New Behaviors Takes Time

Awareness of the need for change notwithstanding, behavior does not change overnight. Even in the third year, many team members had a surprising amount of difficulty mastering new skills and tools and staying customer-focused. They were not accustomed to prioritizing tasks, improving process efficiency and effectiveness, incorporating customer perceptions into modifying their work, or being held accountable for their work in a quantifiable way. They needed time to understand and internalize such concepts. "The conflict between [maintaining the status quo by] ... offering ... current unexamined services and [the new ethos of] preparation for the future, which involves studying processes and developing skills and capabilities, is real and difficult to address" (Diaz and Phipps 1998, 419). Still foundations were laid in the third year; and gradually these new management and customer service skills became more firmly established and integrated into the organizational culture.

Getting Staff Buy-In Takes Time

Another example of overly optimistic expectations about the speed of change negatively influenced the effectiveness of training. Initially, there was resistance among team leaders (all experienced supervisors) to training modules predicated on the idea that in preparation for teaching they themselves might profit from instruction in learning theory and particularly in how to gear training to different learning styles. Once more, awareness and buy-in were achieved not instantaneously, but over time (Diaz and Phipps 1998, 416).

Resolving Complex Problems Takes Time

In that 1994–95 year, the team charged with improving communication throughout the Libraries found itself unable to recommend changes within the specified time frame because of the complexity and variation among the Libraries staff in individual preferences, needs, and goals for communication. Given more time—despite the inherent complexity of the problem—this group *was* able to recommend a number of ways to improve communication (Diaz and Phipps 1998, 413). Within the hierarchy, a central body is responsible for communication. Within the team structure, however, the onus is on every person and group to figure out who needs information about what is being done and being planned and to see that the information is shared in a timely fashion. Developing such awareness throughout the organization takes time.

Team Structure and Process Problems

Lacking any model of how to implement teams in an academic library, of necessity the University of Arizona Libraries learned much about this undertaking by trial and error. Other libraries can benefit from insights that Arizona gained the hard way.

Size

The size of several functional teams remained a problem as of 1999, making it "difficult and time consuming [for members] to work together as a group" (Diaz and Pintozzi 1999, 20).

Common Understandings

Common understandings of the concept of empowerment remained elusive (Diaz and Pintozzi 1999, 30).

Communication and Commitment

Diaz and Phipps (1998) assert that incomplete communication about such issues as the importance of project goals and how team goals related to the larger restructuring effort engendered "a reluctance on the part of some team leaders and staff seriously to commit to the new organization concepts and disagreement on content, design, and participation goals" (419) set by the MRT. In addition to time problems noted elsewhere, the authors grant that the MRT's ownership of the project goals worked as a barrier to open communication in support of the learning community ideal of testing assumptions and developing shared visions of the future. "We [MRT members] were resistant to being criticized, especially after we had put in so many hours of hard work.... We were only lightly open to having our assumptions questioned" (419).

Skill Sets and Team Conflict

Since facility in using decision-making tools and processes was not acquired instantaneously, a certain amount of team conflict was engendered by "poor or inadequate communication, or simply because of varying styles or approaches to problem solving" (Diaz and Pintozzi 1999, 30).

Unclear Expectations

Lack of clear expectations for teams seems to have derailed the success of some learning organization projects.

Skills Inventory. Although a skills and abilities inventory was widely administered (19 of 25 teams completed it), no team seemed to have followed up on its results to provide training to its members in any formal and systematic way. Since the importance of the inventory and its intended use evidently were not fully communicated, it was seen largely as busywork, completed grudgingly, and shelved rather than used to guide individual and team learning as intended (Diaz and Phipps 1998, 416).

Customer Satisfaction Survey. Although an all-purpose customer satisfaction survey was developed in the third year of Arizona's organizational transformation, it was not used after the pilot year; and for some time staff appeared unconvinced of the necessity of continuous assessment of customer satisfaction. Just as worrisome, at the end of the first stage of reorganization, no team had yet published its customer service goals or operating principles (Diaz and Phipps 1998, 416).

Documenting Work Processes. In the same period of time, teams that were expected to create documents about work processes sufficiently detailed to facilitate cross-training and enhanced teamwork did not understand the scope of this charge. Consequently, many produced only checklists of procedures. A few documents were helpful but many were too sketchy to use in training (Diaz and Phipps 1998, 417).

Needs Assessment. In 1995–96, efforts to "engage in a deeper level of assessment of [team members' training] needs" were successful in some teams but not all. Hampered by insufficient levels of commitment from members, some teams fell short of this aspiration (Diaz and Pintozzi 1999, 30).

The Cost of Training

Clearly the individual and team learning that are bywords of the learning organization are expensive in terms of both staff time taken away from daily operations in functional areas and also out-of-pocket costs for speakers, training materials, and the like.

Creative Solutions

When much of the early training did not "take," Arizona gained the key insights that (1) "training does not equal learning," since time for practice is a necessary complement to rote learning and (2) "training at the point of need is the most effective method to ensure that learning takes place" (Diaz and Pintozzi 1999, 30). Consequently, the Libraries began to conserve dollars allocated for training by scheduling sessions closer to the time that new skills could be applied.

One way that Arizona resolved the issue of competing priorities between teamwork and functional area work was to make funds available to units to partially replace team members pulled away from their respective functional areas. "If critical work could not get done, then the team could request additional one-time funds to fill in behind the teammate assigned to a cross-functional team" (Stoffle et al. 1998, 9). An academic library colleague remembers hearing from Arizona staff an estimate that they were "overstaffing" the libraries by 30 percent to accommodate time for team training, team activities, and the other extra work stemming from the drastic reorganization effort (R. Miller, e-mail message to author February 23, 2006). This practice of supplemental staffing may be difficult to sustain without compromising other organizational priorities. It is worth noting that even when such extra personnel costs are *not* a line item in the budget, whatever work goes on in teams still represents a deficit in support for functional areas whose staff participate in teams. Thus, it should be accounted for in any cost/benefit analysis of efficacy of the team structure.

Training Is a Process—Not an Event

Without a doubt, however, the most important lesson brought home by the University of Arizona Libraries' experience is that training is an everlasting work-in-progress, rather than something that can be chalked up as a victory before moving on to other priorities. Staff turnover exacerbates the training problem, since departing staff members take with them hours and hours of training and experience funded by precious operating funds. But even when staff retention rates are good, training is not something done once and forgotten about. In *any* organization today and particularly in one committed to Senge's precepts, continuous learning is the sine qua non for keeping up with current developments as well as getting positioned for the future. Learning comes at a cost—one that many believe is *mandatory* rather than optional. That is why resources dedicated to learning must be factored into cost/benefit analysis and protected from budget fluctuations.

Three Categories of Need for Ongoing Training

University of Arizona Libraries annual reports and strategic plans for various years underscore these truths by emphasizing the ongoing need for training in three general areas: information technology skills, individual learning, and learning organization/team skills.

Information technology skills:

- "Lack of needed skills within current staff to support computer systems" (University of Arizona Libraries 2003d, 13)
- "Potential lack of capability to provide library technical support for customers due to closing of labs on campus" (University of Arizona Libraries 2003a, under "Information Technology: Threats")
- "Lack of staff knowledge and capacity/time to learn/know software and hardware (University of Arizona Libraries 2003a, under "Information Technology: Threats")
- "Multiplicity of demands on finite human resources and costs not directly projected in project statements impose extra demands on systems organizations" (University of Arizona 2003a, under "Information Technology: Threats")
- "Lack of needed skills within current staff to support our new systems" (University of Arizona Libraries 2003a, under "Information Technology: Weaknesses)

Individual learning:

- "Limited funds for training and staff development reduce opportunities for career staff to move into new work" (University of Arizona Libraries 2003d, 14).
- There are "more demands for continuing education for librarians" (University of Arizona Libraries 2005a, 5).

Learning organization and team skills:

- "A significant number of staff do not have a background or understanding of team concepts and the fundamentals of the learning organization" (University of Arizona Libraries 2003c, under "Human Resources").
- "Permanent loss of positions without a restructuring of current work flow could result in burnout, job dissatisfaction and overall decrease in productivity. Staff acceptance to changes in work structure and involvement in designing future work is necessary to meet new customer needs successfully" (University of Arizona Libraries 2003b, under "Threats: Changing Roles; New Work").
- The "growing need to learn new approaches to work and team management meet barriers in the form of increasing cost and competing time demands for training" (University of Arizona Libraries 2004, 28).
- The "growing need to learn new approaches to work and team management meets barriers in the form of increasing cost and time demands for training. This is compounded by a reduced lack [sic] of SOS staff [the Staff and Organization Systems Team] to plan and coordinate training programs and other forms of web-based tools

for performance support" (University of Arizona Libraries 2002, under "Human Resources: Weaknesses of the Library").

- "25% of staff do not have a history or in-depth experience with our team-based customer-focused, learning organization" (University of Arizona Libraries 2002, under "Human Resources: Weaknesses of the Library").
- "Staff input indicated that there was a need to beef up programming and support for training and learning" (University of Arizona Libraries 2000, under "Staff Development: Current State").
- "Work teams and team leaders have identified the need to provide more new employee orientation programs, such as facilities tours, and other modules that teach staff about working in a team-based environment" (University of Arizona Libraries 2000, under "Staff Development: Current State").
- Data from an October 1998 focus group seemed to indicate that staff had an incomplete understanding of two components of a new performance management system piloted that year—namely the team project planning process and the developmental review process (University of Arizona Libraries 1999, under "Human Resources and Staff Environment"). Among other causes for insufficient understanding of these two components, the focus groups cited "lack of adequate training" (University of Arizona Libraries 1999, under "Human Resources and Staff Environment").

TIPS FROM ARIZONA FOR OVERCOMING OBSTACLES TO ORGANIZATIONAL CHANGE

Although Arizona clearly surmounted difficulties in its reorganization and currently is recognized as a leader in academic library innovation, in hindsight Arizona staff members offer some tips for a smoother transition from a hierarchical organization to a team-based structure. Again, many echo the dictums of the OD and other management literature. They lend weight to generic advice because they are from the non-profit sector and specifically from an academic library.

- Involve staff
- Think long term
- Focus on mission-critical aspects
- Set attainable goals
- Articulate a clear charge
- Provide a supportive environment
- Develop a shared vision

Involve Staff

First of all, participation is a fundamental requirement for any meaningful and lasting organizational change. "People have to know that they have a chance to shape their future, in light of the environmental pressures to change" (Stoffle et al. 1998, 8). Given the participatory nature of the team organizational structure and the learning organization disciplines, involving staff would seem almost too obvious to mention. Yet University of Arizona Libraries authors repeatedly stress its necessity for effective organizational performance in the team-based environment. "Widening the circle of responsibility is the key to developing awareness of accountability and self-responsibility" (Diaz and Phipps 1998, 418). Such grassroots involvement is particularly critical to effective development and implementation of training and other team support processes. Both of the preceding comments resonate with Carnevale's definition (2003) of OD, which stresses that because staff own their own problems, they must be empowered to find their own solutions.

Think Long Term

Allowing sufficient time for deep understanding to develop and for attitudes and behavior to change is a central theme in writing about the Arizona experience as shown in the following quotes: "We were forewarned … that the kind of change we were embarking upon would take up to ten years" (Diaz and Phipps 1998, 411); "There has to be follow through, reflection, feedback and practice over a long period of time for real change to take place" (410); "When undergoing change, it is important to work with people where they are in their own development" (410).

Focus on Mission-Critical Aspects

In an effort to do everything required for restructuring and organizational culture change, Arizona designated 14 of 28 areas of need as critical to address in the first year. "This led us to select too many projects and to ignore the concern expressed by the Strategic Long Range Planning Team that we had lost focus on the 'critical few'" (Diaz and Phipps 1998, 418). Setting out too many projects makes it virtually impossible to complete any of them in sufficient depth to be effective or to make substantial progress toward the organization's overarching aspirations.

The University of Arizona Libraries notes that proficiency in using a planning tool known as ID Graphing would have been a great help in the early years of their restructuring (Diaz and Phipps 1998, 418). The plethora of failed or only partially completed projects in the first three years prompted Arizona to use this tool along with others in subsequent years in order to focus on its highest strategic priorities and to drastically limit the number of annual projects.

Set Attainable Goals

Setting challenging and measurable but attainable goals is a cardinal rule of planning. Tasked with the impossible, staff members typically react by developing attitudes and behaviors ranging from cynicism to burnout. Diaz and Phipps (1998) acknowledge that unrealistically high goals for participation in training during the first three years resulted in staff resistance to learning at their library (418). (These authors nevertheless assert that team leaders' learning was enhanced by the necessity of developing innovative ways of achieving the degree of penetration necessary for building a sound foundation of skills for the new organization.)

Bender (1997) too points to the necessity of prioritizing goals and limiting their number. "The challenge [of cross-functional teams appointed by the Strategic Long Range Planning Group at Arizona to develop a set of projects derived from the strategic plan for implementation each year] has been not only to come up with projects that benefit our customers, but to design a number of projects that are 'doable' given the number of other projects and objectives assigned to project team members, and the size of the budget required" (20).

Articulate a Clear Charge

"In some cases we did not communicate as clearly as we could have with the project owners about our expectations for each project" (Diaz and Phipps 1998, 418). As a result, teams were confused and some meetings dragged on longer than they needed to.

A charge should not be so specific as to dictate what elements of the organizational culture and operations must be changed or to preempt creativity in implementing solutions to problems. Either of those two conditions would undermine the autonomy and empowerment of teams. But it should communicate broadly what is expected (the scope and limits to the group's responsibilities) in quantitative terms and within a specific time frame; and it should be written down. Lack of clarity can promote undesirable duplication of effort by among teams, waste time, cause frustration, and ultimately prevent groups from connecting their efforts in a meaningful way to the larger entity they are meant to serve.

Develop a Shared Vision

Bender (1997) notes that "the central concepts and desired outcomes underlying the University of Arizona Libraries' Restructuring ... all are predicated on the existence of a shared vision" (22), something that at that point had not yet been developed. She predicts that all real and imagined barriers would be "much more taken in stride once a shared vision is designed and adopted by the library" (22).

Other librarian authors agree that, lacking such a shared purpose, teams tend to forgo innovation and revert to the old ways of working. "The tradition of simply doing one's best and continuing to do the same work in the same way is strong" (Diaz and Pintozzi 1999, 33). The converse is true when a shared vision has been developed, articulated, and distributed throughout the organization. "A common vision can ... make the difference between making tremendous strides into the future together and taking baby steps in different [opposing] directions" (35).

Provide a Supportive Environment

A supportive environment for teams has several key components, depending on which writer one consults. Polzer and Luecke (2004) cite these four: (1) leadership support in recruiting people, garnering resources, and warding off whatever organizational forces "would be inclined to torpedo the team effort," (2) a nonhierarchical structure where information is shared, boundary-spanning collaboration is the norm, and employees are empowered, (3) a reward system that balances encouragement and recognition for both individual and team achievements, and (4) experience in working in teams (21).

The University of Arizona Libraries identifies several additional things that improve an organization's chance of success in implementing teams: training, management review and guidance, communication, and other components of a supportive environment.

Training

Training is a support element endorsed by Arizona as well as virtually all others who write about teams. Teams and other working groups need both general training (e.g., analyzing data, prioritizing, making decisions) and also training and practice in using specific tools designed for such activities. Examples of the latter are the plus/delta process and team climate questionnaires used to assess team functioning (Diaz and Pintozzi 1999, 33). This kind of training permits teams to make the solid, data-driven decisions for implementation that are the hallmark of the learning organization.

Management Review and Guidance

Another vital element of a supportive environment that Arizona (in common with OD professionals) identifies for successful implementation of teams is management review and guidance. "We [the MRT] had to learn how to give constructive, thought-provoking feedback to another team without taking over their work or creating communication barriers" (Diaz and Phipps 1998, 419).

Communication

An excellent system of communication, characterized by distributed responsibility and the use of multiple channels (everything from e-mails to open houses), is yet another vital component of success in a team-based environment. "Lateral communication from team to team and from individual to individual has replaced much of the vertical communication that characterizes traditional hierarchical organizations. Responsibility [for deciding who needs to know what plans and details] … is also distributed…. It is equally important to consider the channels available and to select the appropriate method(s)" (Diaz and Pintozzi 1999, 31).

Bender (1997) too cites communication as a challenge, particularly where decision making has been shared among teams and the Library Cabinet. She identifies typically poor attendance at meetings where progress is reported as the cause of "a lack of common understanding of goals, uncertainty about what empowerment means, uncertainty about which decisions require consensus decision-making, and which to do" (21). All of these problems could have been ameliorated by better attendance and attention to what was being communicated.

Additional Components

Subsequent descriptions of Arizona's evolution to a learning organization with a team-based structure document desirable elements of support that were added over time: changes in the personnel review process, corresponding changes in the reward structure, and articulation of competencies expected of teams and their individual members.

Performance Review Process

As a first step toward reforming the performance structure and processes, between 1992 and 1997 Arizona substituted a "culture of trust and non-inquiry related to individual performance" (Phipps 1999, 117) for the old annual performance review system, which did not reflect the new team structure or the adoption of customer-focused organizational values (C. Russell 1998, 164).

In concert with McClure of Syracuse University, a performance effectiveness measurement system (PEMS) was developed in order to "measure the effectiveness of ... services and teams with the same performance-measurement philosophies and methods used to test and improve ... overall organizational effectiveness" (C. Russell 1998, 160).

Compensation Reforms

Shortly after PEMS was implemented in 1998, University of Arizona Libraries began development of a compensation system with the following components: base pay tied to individual performance, quarterly bonus pay aligned with organizational performance ratings from surveys and other customer feedback, and career progression or merit increases based on demonstration of competence and "value to future library work" (Phipps 1999, 116).

Articulation of Competencies

And, finally, the Science/Engineering Team developed a list of core and mastery-level competencies. Core competencies, which "constitute the collective knowledge unique to our profession" and which enumerate how library professionals "add value to services provided to users" (Holloway 2003, 95), make it possible to hold staff accountable for a basic level of performance and let them know what they need to do in order to succeed. These sets of abilities, which are the hallmarks of librarian effectiveness, can be grouped into job expectations in two main areas of performance: (1) professional competencies (e.g., instruction, developing collections and access to information resources, reference assistance, and marketing/liaison work) and (2) personal competencies including general interpersonal skills (e.g., effective communication) and the ability to contribute to teams and to the organization as a whole.

Core *skills* (e.g., technical abilities such as knowledge of the format and conventions of typing catalog cards or facility in using computer applications such as HTML) are expected to vary over time. For the most part, however, basic core *competencies* (e.g., knowledge/skills associated the theory and practice of a functional responsibility such as instruction or reference) remain stable (Holloway 2003, 95).

The concept of mastery-level competencies, indicative of in-depth expertise that exceeds expectations, is useful for guiding professional development aspirations and for assessing eligibility for merit pay and promotion (Holloway 2003, 95–96). Like core competencies, mastery-level competencies "are likely to shift and expand as new areas of expertise or specialization are identified" (Holloway 2003, 96).

CAUTIONARY ADVICE FOR CHANGE MAKERS

Who among academic libraries has even an approximation of Arizona's financial and other resources to dedicate to change efforts? Manifestly *not* small- to middle-sized academic libraries. And probably not even all of Arizona's 100-plus ARL peer institutions. There can be no point in aspiring to follow exactly the same path to current viability and future vitality without equivalent support! Arizona staff members cautioned in a group interview, "There is a great deal of stress and anxiety…. Reinventing an organization may sound great in the literature, but you do not get there the day you decide you need to change. It is a very long process" (Giesecke 1994, 199). A decade later, Holloway (2004) observed that "implementing a new structural organization within a university is not for the faint-hearted. It takes the courage of conviction as well as support from university administrators" (8). Happily, there is more than one route to library revitalization, just as there is more than one way to accomplish most worthwhile aims in life and work.

Rush Miller, dean of the University of Pittsburgh ULS and a long-time observer of the academic library scene, observes, "The real import of the Arizona experience is that it prompted many of us to be bolder in leading real cultural change in our libraries. I know that I took my strategic plan steering committee to [Arizona] to one of their early conferences and we gained a great deal from it. We rejected their model when we realized how high the overhead would be for us. But many of the principles such as shared vision, flatter organization structures, customer focus, etc. were very helpful to us in affirming our own directions in the change process. Dean Stoffle and [Arizona] staff [members] were real pioneers in communicating the need for drastic organizational change for us all" (R. Miller, email message to author February 23, 2006).

5

Evolution Not Revolution: First Cycle of Change at the University of Pittsburgh's University Library System

THE UNIVERSITY LIBRARY SYSTEM IN CONTEXT

By any measure of academic achievement, the University of Pittsburgh is a world-class research university, ranking among the best nationally and internationally. Founded in 1787 as the Pittsburgh Academy (the first academic institution west of the Alleghenies), the university has grown from a log cabin school supporting the educational needs of local students on the edge of the American frontier into an internationally recognized leader in higher education. Located in the heart of the cultural and educational district of the city of Pittsburgh, Pennsylvania, the University of Pittsburgh is a formidable educational and research center with an excellent reputation for quality, comprehensive undergraduate and graduate programs, as well as a research program that ranks in the top tier of American research universities.

The stature of the institution is evidenced by its rankings among universities in the United States and worldwide. A member of the elite Association of American Universities since 1974, the University of Pittsburgh ranked twelfth among all U.S. universities in National Science Foundation science and engineering funding in 2002 (NSF 2005). Worldwide, Pittsburgh was rated forty-third among all institutions of higher education in rankings published by Shanghai Jiao Tong University (2005). The university has approximately 5,000 faculty members who provide educational leadership for 34,000 students from more than 70 programs and departments, almost one-third of them graduate and professional students. More than 1,600 are international students. In 2005, the university awarded 372 doctoral degrees. The university's educational and general) budget is $1.4 billion with an additional $650 million per year in sponsored research dollars. In addition to programs on the Oakland campus, the university supports four regional campuses in western Pennsylvania and international programs in countries around the globe (University of Pittsburgh 2005).

The University of Pittsburgh's University Library System (ULS)—supporting this impressive university system—ranks twenty-third in overall size among 110 academic members of the Association of Research Libraries (ARL) and is among the upper echelon in the delivery and implementation of information technologies as well as collaboration in collection sharing and access. For example, in 1996 the ULS implemented digital library services for users around the globe with its China Gateway Service. This service delivers material from Chinese, Taiwanese, and Korean libraries at no cost to scholars worldwide.

In 2004, Pittsburgh's ULS book collection numbered 4.7 million volumes. From 1994 to 2004, the collection grew by more than one million books, and the serials titles rose from 23,380 to 44,924. Its total budget in 2004 was $25.6 million annually, with an acquisitions budget of more than $13 million. This last figure represents an $8 million increase over 10 years (ARL 2005). Given the current organizational vitality and standing among peers enjoyed by the University of Pittsburgh and by its ULS, it is difficult to credit that a mere decade ago the library system was at a crossroads. As is true of many large organizations, although change within the ULS was necessary for survival, it also was difficult and slow in implementation. The library deserved its strong reputation, but it had become somewhat complacent. Its transformation from a traditionally structured conservative library into a more innovative, agile, and forward-looking organization is a unique and inspiring tale.

A LEGACY OF PROBLEMS BECOMES CRITICAL

Circa 1994, the situation within the ULS was approaching a crisis. The ULS ranked well above two-thirds of the academic members of the Association of Research Libraries in the size of its holdings and the strength of its materials and operations budgets. Many of its distinguished collections were of national and international importance. A complex aggregation of scholarly resources, the ULS had 16 different physical locations on the Pittsburgh campus. Despite its reputation as one of the nation's top research library systems, however, a multitude of serious problems within the ULS had eroded support on campus from students, faculty/staff, and university administrators. Also, the directorship had become a revolving door. A two-year national search for a director failed; and when the search was reopened, it still took two more years to secure a director (1990–94).

Although staff and librarians managed to maintain service commitments, the lack of permanent leadership within the ULS—together with the general lack of support on campus—took its toll. For example, in the mid-1980s, the archives—out of workspace and unable to secure appropriate storage space—was ordered by the library director to cease acquiring new material. This prohibition, still in place in 1994, resulted in the loss of countless valuable materials that were donated to other area institutions.

The personnel budget for the ULS was negatively affected by the long-established practice of hiring additional catalogers as the only means of coping with backlogs and of dealing with specialized collections acquired over the years. Over time, this disproportionate emphasis on in-house cataloging, along with a general lack of fiscal support, precluded adequate development of technology-based initiatives including digital collections. Salaries for library faculty and staff had been kept artificially low in order to maximize the number of individuals employed. Consequently, employees who were underpaid, and many of whom felt unappreciated, suffered low morale. Many openly expressed negative feelings about the organization.

The organizational culture of the ULS during this period was characterized by a rigid hierarchical structure, the lack of a faculty governance system of any kind, administrative fiefdoms within departments and units in which assistant directors ruled their respective areas with impunity, and a lack of effective internal or external communication. Individual agendas were being pursued to the detriment of the organization's well-being. These and other problems limited productivity and innovation and worked in opposition to rational deployment of fiscal support and human resources, as discussed subsequently in this chapter. Unchecked, such problems would have had serious ramifications for the continued operations of the libraries.

Organizational Problems

Like many ARL libraries at the time, ULS at Pittsburgh had a long history of resistance to change and was held back by an archaic hierarchical management structure typical of large research libraries for much of the past century. A Blackwell case study titled "Balancing the Books" describes the ULS organizational culture at that time in these words: "[The ULS] was a capital-and-people-intensive operation weighed down by insulated departmental silos, long-entrenched library practices, complacency, poor customer service, and a host of inefficiencies" (Bates n.d., 1). Previous attempts to extricate the ULS from its decline had failed to grapple with root causes of the ULS's problems.

The Hierarchy and Communication

The ULS organization was hobbled by an entrenched hierarchy and such rigid demarcations between departments that issues and problems could not be approached except at the highest echelons of the library system. The only way that front line counterparts in different silos could work directly to thrash out mutually advantageous solutions to problems would be to take the discussion to lunch and subsequently feed the issues and alternative approaches to their respective bosses (the assistant directors for Central Technical Services, (TS) Public Services/Administration, and Collection Management) in hopes that rapprochement would eventually be effected at the top levels. This was a cruelly slow and cumbersome process in a time when the environment outside the ULS was changing so rapidly.

Mixed Attitudes about Change and Operational Priorities

Over time some library personnel had developed mechanisms for dealing with changes in their responsibilities and daily routines. Not atypically for an academic library with the ULS's size, national prestige, and long history (more than 200 years of operation), however, the technical service staff for the most part had been operating day to day in much the same manner for a number of years. Prior to the re-engineering project, many Tech Services staff literally had been in the same position, at the same desk, doing essentially the same tasks for decades.

Focused on quality, the cataloging staff enjoyed a strong reputation among other cataloging professionals; and they had at one time been pioneers. For example, Pittsburgh was the first library outside of Ohio to join OCLC, and Pitt was an early site for the OCLC Gateway network. Given its long-standing reputation for excellence in such partnerships as the OCLC Enhance program, NACO (Name Authority Cooperative) Program, and CONCER (Cooperative ONline SERials) Program, quality was the Cataloging Department's raison d'etre.

How could a reputation for excellence have turned into an organizational deficit? Although it is difficult to argue that quality is not important, what was lacking was any sense that a balance could be reached between quality and the volume of materials processed in a reasonable amount of time. Although the quality of the ULS's cataloging was exemplary, the time required to produce such quality was not acceptable in terms of user needs. In short, staff there worked to rule, rather than to provide service to either external or internal publics. Although processes were largely automated, they remained excruciatingly slow and unnecessarily convoluted.

Not unique or surprising in a cataloging unit at the time, the prevailing philosophy was that everything must be done in-house; and allocating responsibility for tasks was extremely conservative. Everyone must be the consummate expert in his or her area of responsibility. Instead of cross-training staff or, indeed, questioning *any* long-standing practices, layer after layer of staff was added until the departmental personnel budget became bloated.

The practice was to customize all cataloging records from sources like OCLC or the Library of Congress in-house. Any title for which a quality record was not available would be warehoused until it finally had been cataloged by an institution whose work ULS staff trusted. Indeed, unless an acceptable record could be found in OCLC, the book was shelved and then not searched again until six months had elapsed. Only after two years could the book be designated for original cataloging. The result was monumental cataloging backlogs (tens of thousands of volumes of older materials were stockpiled, awaiting cataloging in 1994) and significant barriers to patrons needing access to either unique, current English language imprints or foreign language books, many rare and valuable to scholars on campus.

Over a long period of time, the department's entrenched orientation toward technical quality as an end in itself reflected neither concern for nor awareness of the greater good of the ULS. It is easy to see how people in the TS unit, lacking contact with end users, became disconnected from both the patrons whom they served and their colleagues in other units. For experts devoted to high-quality cataloging, technical correctness was sacrosanct. From their point of view, customer needs were best served by perfect cataloging records, regardless of considerations of timeliness of access or budgeting. There was no question of browsing the shelves for new materials. If a determined patron was able to discover that a needed current title had been received and was in-house (a fact not reflected by the OPAC at that time), it was possible to retrieve said work. However, the process could not be characterized as user-friendly.

Since TS was not organized for patron access to new or backlogged materials, the burden of identification and retrieval of in-process materials fell to the Public Services librarians and staff. All too often, these folks had to take personal responsibility for retrieving high-demand in-process materials for exasperated patrons, sometimes covertly. This created an unnecessarily adversarial relationship between personnel from the two units.

Thus, insupportable delays and the lack of opportunity for the vast majority of users to even know that many current materials existed within the collection (at that time some 3.8 million volumes) constituted a pernicious if covert threat to the ULS's fundamental mission—supporting university priorities for serving its primary users. Not surprisingly, rumblings of dissatisfaction among some academic departments and schools about this and other deficits in library service had significantly eroded support on campus for the ULS, its staff, and its administrators.

Unexamined Work Processes

As typically happened in the early years of library automation (the 1960s through the 1990s), up to this point the University of Pittsburgh libraries system had merely "paved the cow path" when new technologies were implemented instead of rethinking the value added by multiple and repetitive processing steps. So the ULS had not been able to reap the full rewards in efficiency and effectiveness from the new technologies. In TS, this problem was particularly evident. Quality assurances built into the system required that even the most basic cataloging tasks had to pass through far more levels of review than were necessary. Unit heads reviewed and revised virtually every step of the labor-intensive process of identifying, ordering, receiving, cataloging, and physically processing each item added to the collection. These steps added little or no value for the end user.

The serials exchange programs set up with other countries are an example of antiquated processes in TS that badly needed revisiting. These operations had for decades been treated as sacrosanct, despite the growing commercial availability of many publications included in the agreements and the probability of significant cost savings had the method of acquisition for the majority of such material been converted to contracts with serials vendors. Failing to take advantage of the emergence of cheaper and more efficient avenues for acquiring such material demonstrated how entrenched in routine the department had become.

Performance Problems

Compounding the problem of inefficient and ineffective processes was some staff members' negativity toward change. This aversion to change inhibited productivity, severely limited the volume of through-put, and made discussion of ways to improve processes slow and difficult to implement. Also, as in any large organization, there were a few staff members in the ULS who had basic performance deficits: unsatisfactory attendance and unwillingness to support library-wide priorities. Some staff members simply would not accept input from outside the department or unit. Many in TS had grown accustomed to setting their own policy and procedures for what work would be top priority in their department. They felt strongly that they should determine how the work should be accomplished without oversight from the ULS administration or other units. Something of a siege mentality existed in the unit. Again, the focus was not where it should have been—on serving the immediate research needs of primary clientele.

Changes in the External Environment

The list of factors threatening the ULS's reputation on campus and its continued viability was extensive. Also, this was taking place at a time when virtually the entire higher education community—under the combined assaults of a weakening political and financial base, a dip in the traditional student demographic base, and radically changed consumer expectations—had perforce begun to open its mind to the concept of customer service. Business leaders on boards of trustees had begun to question the lack of sound business practices in higher education. Companies they led were forced to rightsize operations to remain competitive in an emerging global economy. Quite understandably, they urged academic administrators to follow suit in demonstrating fiscal restraint and doing more with less.

At the same time, funding bodies reflected taxpayer concerns about ever-increasing costs for tuition and taxes, which at that time comprised a majority of the funding for universities. The good times of incremental increases to base funding year after year were coming to an end, probably forever. The need for greater accountability for resources and programs led to greater scrutiny of most university operations, academic libraries among them.

How could the ULS be considered a good steward of financial resources and a progressive library without recognizing the validity of an orientation toward customer needs? How could the ULS hope to maintain sufficient fiscal resources to meet the challenges of a changing environment while wasting huge sums of money on inefficient operations?

And how could the provost and other university administrators ignore low staff morale in the libraries, campus-wide discontent with the library system's inadequacies, unresponsiveness, and other problems when evaluating the ULS's performance, its leaders, and its contributions to the University of Pittsburgh's mission? Clearly, in the view of its constituents, the status quo was not working to produce an effective library system. If not remedied soon, this situation would have invited a mandate for change from university administration in order to avert disaster.

A Budgetary Black Hole

Among the morass of emerging problems, the aspect of ULS operations most out of control was personnel management. The TS Department had become a budgetary black hole. One of the least defensible long-standing practices in TS had been to hire new staff members each time a collection was added. When cataloging of new material required fluency in Hebrew or Polish, for example, additional staff members were added without a thorough review of the workflow, entertaining the possibility of outsourcing, or consideration of staffing needs of units outside TS. As a result, while the TS staff grew significantly over time, staff numbers in other units remained constant. New public services could not be considered when so much of ULS operations were oriented toward perfect cataloging in-house. Nor could new technology be implemented or electronic resources be mounted as long as TS remained the elephant in the corner of the room.

Not surprisingly, by 1996—with more than 60 permanent staff plus in-house contract catalogers for special projects such as the Polish National Alliance and the Kosciusko Collection—the personnel budget for TS had bloated to a staggering $2,034,363 (including fringe benefits and student employees) with no end in sight (Kohberger n.d.b, under "Background"). Such automatic increments to staffing and the concomitant failure to reexamine priorities and reorder allocation of resources choked off any chance for the ULS to realign resources with its best opportunities. In 1994, the ULS had only five or six research databases, was handicapped by a poor technology infrastructure, had never tried strategic planning, and had a budget unaligned with overall library priorities. Approaching the new millennium, there was no way for the library system to pursue innovations such as digitizing local resources or capturing the full benefits of the Internet and Web for library users.

ANTICIPATION OF THE NEED FOR CHANGE WITHIN ULS

In 1994, Dr. Rush Miller, formerly dean of Libraries and Learning Resources at Bowling Green State University in Ohio, became director of the ULS. He had been recruited to clean up the mess in the ULS. But he had been warned by colleagues that the library system at Pitt was a career-threatening "rat's nest" with a reputation for "chewing up directors." After considerable hesitation, Miller decided that—though risks admittedly *were* high—assurances of support from the university's new administration made taking on the challenges within ULS an attractive personal and professional opportunity. This in fact proved to be the case.

New Leadership, Old Problems

Clearly, Miller inherited a host of insidious problems that he was determined to tackle. Unsatisfied with the library system's lack of orientation toward the future and the inadequacy of its resources to pursue any significant innovations, he decided with the help of library managers and staff who had potential to be change agents to put the ULS's house in order and to free up sufficient resources to transform the libraries into an efficient, effective, forward-looking, and user-centered organization.

Twenty-First Century Expectations

Miller understood the big picture much better than some of his contemporaries in academic library leadership and had built his reputation on the successful management of organizational change management. He believed that in the twenty-first century more would be required of academic libraries than carrying on business as usual. Libraries in the coming era would be fully involved in redefining the very concept of what a library should be in an age dominated by technologies that changed at a rapid pace. Libraries as organizations could not continue to operate in traditional ways. Many time-honored traditions and assumptions would need to be questioned and examined in light of emerging technologies and changing user expectations and needs. Although *values* would not necessarily be different for libraries and librarians in the future, how those values were interpreted and implemented would be different in ways that might not be fully evident in the mid-1990s. But any library wedded to the status quo and reluctant to take a hard look at where changes were required would soon find itself relegated to a poorly funded and marginalized artifact of past relevance instead of a vital partner and preferably a leader in the campus learning community.

Internalization of the Vision

Miller's staff internalized his vision, as is evident from these excerpts from the foreword to an early draft of the Tech Services Reorganization Plan: (1) "Technical Services must, in conjunction with the rest of the ULS, rethink its mission and goals and develop a plan to achieve them as economically as possible if the ULS is to have resources to combat materials inflation and to support new library services"; and (2) "When our strategic plan is in place it will guide us in managing the 'continual change' that is necessary for us to initiate new services and to improve existing services for our users over the next three to five years" (Kohberger et al. 1996b, 1).

Shifts in Patron Expectations

Beginning in the 1990s, faculty on every campus in the United States began to expect ubiquitous access to information. Expectations that libraries would provide additional electronic resources were rising despite lobbying for increases in university funding for academic programs (e.g., upgrading campus access to the Internet and the World Wide Web, setting up expensive labs for up-and-coming new scientists, making more faculty merit money available, upgrading classroom computing and projection equipment). Would the money stretch far enough to achieve both goals?

In addition, students were yielding daily to the blandishments of commercial vendors of inferior resources collections and the wilderness of the Internet. They were already beginning to value immediate access to information, assistance with any and all technologies, facilities for collaboration with their peers, and a host of other things unknown to preceding generations in preference to traditional collections of books that they could see and touch and were supposed to venerate. The public was beginning to wonder, "Were academic libraries still relevant to student learning?"

Preparing for Change Initiatives within the ULS

As described in subsequent paragraphs, having secured the provost's support for large-scale organizational change and having negotiated favorable terms (the ULS would get to *keep in its budget* all personnel savings from reorganization), in 1995 the ULS initiated both a strategic planning process and the re-engineering of TS. The fact that ULS leadership anticipated the need to implement changes before the university administration required them to do so meant that in this course of action—as in later ones—the ULS was a model of proactive leadership within the academic library community. The story of how the ULS managed these dramatic changes follows.

The Case for Damage Control

Most librarians are aware of strategic planning basics. They realize that it "starts with a vision of an ideal future and focuses on present conditions and actions needed to prepare and position the library for that future" (Wood 1988, 100). And even neophytes have an inkling that a sound strategic plan—one grounded in the careful analysis needed to articulate library strengths and to identify the most important opportunities to bankroll with available resources—takes time to write.

What some in our field may *not* understand, however, is that early in the strategic planning process, implementing a given isolated course of action *in advance* of having a full-fledged strategic plan in place may be advisable and can be imperative. Staff wedded to the way things always have been may in fact attempt to use the pretext of waiting for the completed strategic plan to stall any change in the status quo, even necessary damage control. Stranger yet, on occasion a well-meaning but timid library administrator will be tempted to go into a holding pattern, suspending all action until the plan has been completed and communicated to stakeholders in the library's future.

The wise library manager, however, does not yield to specious arguments urging a state of complete paralysis in anticipation of writing and implementing a strategic plan. A delay of as little as six months to one year in attending to a bona fide financial crisis or in remedying an equipment failure that seriously compromises daily operations, for example, would be unconscionable even for those fully committed to the benefits of strategic planning.

An analogy can be made to a medical emergency. Obviously, an arterial hemorrhage must be stemmed before attending to any underlying condition requiring long-term treatment. An ambitious plan to build muscle strength or introduce a healthier diet simply is not relevant to the patient until he or she has been stabilized enough to live through the next 15 minutes. Such was the case with the ULS TS Department. Accordingly, the management group in partnership with the staff of ULS performed organizational surgery to re-engineer the TS structure and processes. They wielded a scalpel, with great delicacy and consummate skill. And the patient did not die on the table, despite the delay of a few more months in articulating and implementing a finished strategic plan for the entire library. In fact, savings from this timely organizational reform would give the ULS a head start in identifying sufficient resources for pursuing new initiatives called for in the strategic plan.

University of Pittsburgh's Vision for Change

Miller saw that radical change would be needed to pull the University of Pittsburgh's library system out of its downward slump and keep it from being sidelined in the future. The vision guiding such change was this:

- ULS must become a learning organization where problem solving and creativity would be fostered at all levels of the organization.
- The current hierarchy of departmental silos must be replaced with a flatter and more fluid structure capable of embracing change, capitalizing on new opportunities, and taking calculated risks where substantial potential rewards were in the offing.
- Quality must be redefined to encompass customer service considerations as well as technical correctness in such things as catalog records.

So the ULS rejected the quick fix approach of across-the-board budget cutting to free up funds for innovations and embarked on a bold three-pronged strategy to position it for success in the near term and also for securing a robust and viable future: (1) the crisis in personnel costs would be addressed in a re-engineering effort focused on reconsidering and streamlining technical processes rife with bottlenecks and inefficiencies; (2) the organization would work toward developing a culture of continuous change and an organizational structure flexible enough to permit continuous realignment of the library system with its rapidly changing environment; and (3) at the same time, a year-long strategic planning process would be initiated in order to uncover the system's foremost strengths and target its best opportunities.

Toward the end of the twentieth century, a librarian author pointed out that at the time few academic libraries were willing or able to pull support from tradition operations in order to fund innovations: "Given the political strength of staff and customers wedded to legacy services, the campus library may be tempted to ... continue to support legacy services at past levels while funding emerging services with marginal funds" (Renaud 1997, 89). The ULS at the University of Pittsburgh was not satisfied with this kind of weak compromise.

Instead of staying with the herd, the ULS ventured into uncharted territory, exemplifying what Renaud's article advocated: "The campus library needs to make tough choices based on a clear understanding of its portfolio of collections and services that shift resources to high value, future-oriented work" (1997, 89). Fortunately, the ULS did not need to pull support from what the customers cared about (periodical subscriptions and research databases). But initially some staff members resisted discontinuing the legacy practice of focusing strictly on technical quality in cataloging at the expense of library users' need for access to current imprints and their desire for a greater number of research databases.

RE-ENGINEERING TECHNICAL SERVICES

The planning phase of the re-engineering spanned the period from September 1995 to September 1996.

First Steps

In late fall 1995, an interim coordinator of TS was appointed and the assistant director for TS was reassigned to head the Archives Service Center after taking a one-year development leave. To buy time for developing a plan outlining staffing needs for the soon-to-be re-engineered TS Department, hiring for vacancies in TS was frozen. Remaining staff were temporarily reassigned to cover key responsibilities in vacancies left by attrition (Kohberger n.d.b, under "Phase One"). Next, the library director appointed the TS Working Group, a team of three unit heads from the Serials/Acquisitions and Cataloging departments—each selected for his or her potential to be a change agent. These team members would lead the re-engineering process and work with a library consultant (Jennifer Younger, then at Ohio State University) to ensure that the re-engineering process would be coordinated with the ongoing strategic planning process and would not be in conflict with its vision or values.

The first step of the re-engineering process was conducting meetings in each of the eight subordinate units within TS—Original Cataloging, Copy Cataloging, Card and Book, Order Services, Receipt and Search Services, Serials Acquisitions, Periodical Check-in, and Government Documents—to discuss the merits and drawbacks of the current organizational structure and to brainstorm possible improvements. From the outset, improving communication within and between the units was seen as an essential component for the eventual success of the process.

Then supervisors were charged with conducting a self-study to prepare for process improvement in which they would do the following: (1) identify key tasks or functions performed; and (2) state who did the tasks, describe how efficient the current workflow was, and analyze what value was added to the ULS's operational success by each step of the process. Costs for current ULS Technical Services operations were estimated, benchmarks of practices at peer institutions were established, site visits to technical services departments at peer institutions were made, and vendor services for various portions of the technical processing—from selection and ordering of material to receipt, payment, cataloging, labeling, and placement of the shelves—were fully explored (Kohberger n.d.b, under "Phase One").

The Library Consultant's Role

In August 1996, the consultant's report to the ULS was received, reviewed, and analyzed by supervisors in TS. In her first paragraph, Younger grounded her recommendations firmly in the new ULS vision noted earlier in this chapter: "The following memo contains my recommendations for maintaining a high level of service to the University of Pittsburgh Libraries and library users while reducing costs and streamlining processes" (Younger 1996, 1).

The Context for Re-Engineering

Placing the re-engineering effort of the University of Pittsburgh's Library System in context, Younger noted that "like others struggling with the press of daily activities [the ULS] has not reviewed as critically as could be done the underlying assumptions, habits, or overall use of resources" (1996, 1). She went on to highlight three major types of opportunities peers of the ULS were exploring: (1) "Purchasing more services from vendors where such services are available and cost [effective]"; (2) "rethinking local services and policies to ensure that the value being added is still needed and not simply a continuation of what has always been done"; and (3) "work[ing] to create shorter work flows with fewer steps and fewer redundancies between work units" (1).

Acknowledging the difficulty of undertaking this big a change in the status quo, Younger (1996) gave the TS staff the following vote of confidence: "The strength to do so [examine long-standing beliefs and practices] … [lies] in the willingness of librarians and staff to ask the hard questions, to examine new ways of doing work and to put their knowledge to work in making effective changes" (1).

Recommendation: Eliminate Redundancies/Repetitive Steps Where No Value Is Added

In a narrative time line of the TS, Paul Kohberger, the head of the department, summarizes the consultant's main recommendations:

Briefly, J. Younger's report advised T.S. to eliminate redundancies from processes. For example, how many units do English language cataloging and at what level of expertise?

Also she advised us to consolidate various approval plans with one vendor and investigate value added services.

Another area she highlighted was to examine cataloging policies and procedures and to streamline them whenever possible, emphasizing record acceptance rather than modification. (Kohberger n.d.b, under "Phase One")

Recommendation: Consider Outsourcing or Adopting a Team-Like Structure

Not surprisingly, the most significant recommendation for addressing runaway personnel costs was this: "Purchase bibliographic records for books requiring original cataloging from a vendor" (Younger 1996, 3). Younger gave two extremely cogent arguments for doing so at the University of Pittsburgh, foreshadowing elements of the re-engineering plan ultimately endorsed by TS Working Group members:

"This [outsourcing of original cataloging] is particularly efficient in situations where the volume of materials in particular languages, subjects or formats is small, making resident expertise in these areas relatively expensive. It is also a useful method when there are other demands on the time and expertise of the catalogers, such as for general problem solving, training, reference, or cyclical need for assistance in cataloging unusually large numbers of books and/or serials. Alternatively, for original cataloging, develop a team approach between librarians and staff such that the librarians focus on the most complex of issues in cataloging and problem solving while the staff handle the more straight forward cataloging of individual titles. (Younger 1996, 3–4)

Ultimately, the ULS would decide to outsource the acquisition, cataloging, and processing of mainstream English-language material as well as cataloging of the backlogs of foreign language materials. Team approaches to original cataloging, the handling of journals, and the general concept of outsourcing evolved from consideration of Younger's recommendations together with advice and observations found in the professional literature.

Other Issues, Including Learning Organization Concepts

Younger's 1996 report continued, spotlighting issues such as treatment of domestic and foreign newspapers, the cost-effectiveness of serials exchange programs, and the workflows in government documents. Last, but still very important, she advised three conceptual shifts that would bring the ULS closer to its ideal of becoming a learning organization:

- *Accountability:* She urged establishing goals, measurable criteria, and specific targets for assessing quality in TS operations. (She gave the example of agreeing on an acceptable percentage of errors in bibliographic records.)
- *Systems thinking:* She counseled incorporating into the development of TS policies and procedures "a broad understanding of public service unit goals and requirements" (5) in order to ensure that TS is effective in doing the right things and is operating in a cost-effective manner. She also advised thinking library-wide in terms of where specific responsibilities and tasks such as periodical check-in should ideally be carried out — whether in the Central TS Division or in public service units housing the collections.
- *Fostering a culture of change:* Younger encouraged staff to keep the momentum of change rolling. "Use this report as a starting place for generating more ideas of what can be done differently and more cost effectively at the Hillman Library. Consult broadly among library staff and librarians for suggestions. Ask colleagues at other libraries what they have done in the last year to 'do more with less'" (3–6).

The Human Resource Considerations

When contemplating the re-engineering of TS, understandably, the ULS administration sought counsel about how to maximize positive outcomes and minimize individual and organizational disruption.

Approaches to Downsizing

Anticipating recommendations for reducing the number of staff in TS as the most likely outcome of that department's self-study, the ULS consulted the university's Human Resources (HR) unit about options for accomplishing a staff reduction. The HR department outlined the following pros and cons of the two most common strategies for downsizing: option one, layoffs versus option two, a phased approach to reassignment within the same organization.

Layoff Strategy Advantages

- Immediate removal of displaced and disaffected staff
- Short period of disruption with fewer long-term risks
- Cost-effectiveness for the long run

Layoff Strategy Disadvantages

- Adverse public opinion: Emotionally charged community memory of recent layoffs in the collapse of Pittsburgh's steel industry
- Bad fit with university culture: Perception of this strategy as suitable only for the business environment and inhumane in the academic context

Relocation Strategy Advantages

- More humane treatment of staff
- Retention of expertise in experienced staff
- Dilution of intensity of disruption

Relocation Strategy Disadvantages

- Expense of retaining staff with high salaries
- Potential for relocated staff to spread disaffection throughout the ULS
- Increase in long-term risk with longer duration of disruption

Biting the Bullet: Relocating Existing Staff

Despite the calculated risks of a phased approach to change, the ULS administration opted for the more humane option of downsizing by reassignment of existing staff. The near-catastrophic effect of the collapse of the steel industry on the economy of Pittsburgh and environs played no small part in this decision. As Lientz and Rea (2004) advise, change managers must be sensitive to three layers of culture in deciding how to implement change: the organization culture, the culture of departments/units directly involved, and the culture of the region or country in which the entity operates—particularly its "mores, ethics, and habits" (19).

Open Communication

The single factor of organizational dynamics that is most critical to the success of the change process and the thing that typically takes the longest is engaging the hearts and minds of staff whose working environment and lives are about to be altered. Determined to secure active participation in the re-engineering process, rather than grudging compliance coupled with covert resistance, the libraries conducted a series of open meetings in April and May 1996 to air any staff concerns about the re-engineering process.

The reader might recognize this strategy as an ideal approach to effective organizational change. Lientz and Rea (2004) talk about the tension and sometimes outright contradictions between what they call "quick hits" that are made in an environment of organizational crisis (such as the ULS's re-engineering of TS) and the organization's long-term goals for change. They point out that where there is urgency to address problems and when the leadership needs to shake up a complacent staff, information can be helpful in resolving such contradictions and conflicts between short- and long-term change efforts. And they give the following guidelines for addressing such problems and concerns:

- Point out that the change is necessary because of the problem and its impact
- Delineate how *not* making the change will make things even worse
- Explain how things will improve with the long-term changes (Lientz and Rea 2004, 189)

The HR Consultant's Role

The ULS also enlisted Jean Ferketish—then director of the University of Pittsburgh HR department's Organization Development Office and an organizational consultant with national and international standing—as an in-house consultant to support the change process. When undertaking any large re-engineering project, it is important to involve neutral outside experts to provide guidance and support as the process evolves. In retrospect, involving objective outside consultants from the earliest stages of the process was a valuable element in the eventual success of the re-engineering effort. It was especially helpful in this instance since the unit had become so entrenched in historical routine and was so inwardly focused.

All-Staff Workshop

From the outset, it was evident that a unit comprised primarily of very long-term staff had to be provided with support to prepare for the radical changes ahead. There were two reasons for including the entire ULS staff in training about the nature of change: (1) Including everyone sent a clear message that change, even though it had been slow in coming, was soon to be an integral part of life in the ULS; and (2) all staff, not just those in TS, were going to be affected by the changes. Involving all staff from the beginning proved to be of great benefit.

In spring 1996, Ferketish conducted a half-day all-staff workshop titled "Change in the Workplace." Beginning with an introduction to the nature of organizational change that emphasized the necessity of *aligning organizational systems* capable of supporting long-term change, the workshop was intended to prepare attendees for the re-engineering of TS. Components of organizational systems to be aligned in such a change process include communications, recognition of achievements/celebration of successes, performance management, ongoing training and development for all levels of staff, setting out clear career paths for staff advancement and succession management, measurement of progress toward achievement of individual and organizational goals, and a compensation system that would reinforce top organizational priorities. Achieving this key organizational requirement (alignment of all systems) would move the ULS toward a culture of change (R. Miller and Ferketish n.d., slides 12–16).

Ferketish presented the following additional points:

- The dynamic interrelationship of organizational change to group behavior and to personal change.
- Drivers of change in the ULS: (1) inequities in budget allocations and the need to reassess personnel distribution; (2) the new strategic planning process for the entire ULS; and (3) the need to address and reduce or eliminate bottlenecks and inefficiencies in job designs, workflows, and work processes.
- The four phases of the change process, from initiation, through disorientation, to re-orientation, and finally to integration of change.
- The range of feelings and behaviors typical of staff experiencing change in each of the four phases of organizational change and the effects of such personal reactions on work (effort exerted, productivity, and morale).
- The normality of a temporary erosion of confidence and enthusiasm accompanying uncertainties endemic to organizational change and the range of negative emotions (loss, grief, anxiety, mistrust, alienation, and anger) that can surface in the initial stages of change in the workplace.

- Alterations in a person's spheres of influence (what one can control and what one can influence versus those factors that one can neither control nor influence).
- The roles that an individual can adopt in order to master change (i.e., choosing to act as a conduit rather than a victim) in order to solve problems and reemploy successful strategies (R. Miller and Ferketish n.d., slides 29–44).

Reactions to the Workshop

Not surprisingly, staff and supervisors alike benefited from the workshops only to the degree that they valued personal mastery and were open to the idea of change. Those interested in understanding change and working for the ULS's long-term goals of remaining a vital element of the university learning community were grateful to have their feelings legitimized and to learn to identify common behaviors and circumstances that mark different stages of the change process. (For example, in the phase characterized as "Disorientation," as the pace of change speeds up, it is not unusual to receive conflicting messages about what is going on or what is expected. Such circumstances need not be regarded as permanent or disastrous, however.) Staff members with open minds also valued information about how to think and act in ways that let them play a positive role, have a voice in change efforts, and avoid the victim mentality.

The staff members who ultimately never did "get on the bus" do not appear to have profited from the workshops. Unfortunately, in any change effort, a few persons inevitably remain adamantly opposed to and insist on remaining outside of the change process—adopting the victim stance, resenting change, denying the need for change, and even fighting a last-ditch effort to block any and all aspects of the change. Such attitudes and behaviors waste energy and generally damage any status or credibility these unfortunates may at one time have enjoyed within the organization.

By choosing to allow feelings of fear, powerlessness, confusion, and isolation dictate behavior throughout the change process, the few diehard skeptics among the staff of any organization ultimately condemn themselves to being marginalized in terms of their ability to contribute to the new organization being formed and thereby reduce their value as an employee. Staff members receptive to the idea of change, in contrast, appreciated being reminded that major disruption and confusion would be temporary and that by working through issues and problems associated with change, they could be part of the heady experience of forging a new and stronger ULS.

Short-Term Personnel Actions

A few ULS personnel members who either were not won over to the merits of the impending re-engineering or simply did not wish to wait for the eventual outcomes opted out in an acceptable way by moving into positions in other ULS departments and units. In April and May 1996, TS staff members were encouraged to apply for positions in other ULS areas as they became open and were assured that they would be given interviews for any open positions. Posting any ULS job outside the library would occur only if it could be determined that there was no TS person qualified for the position. The ULS director pledged that every effort would be made to avoid layoffs in the re-engineering process. But

he urged staff members to consider the goal of avoiding layoffs a *joint* responsibility, an unwelcome possibility that they could forestall if they were willing
to engage in rethinking what work should be the highest priority and how best
to institute changes (Kohberger n.d.b, under "Phase One"). Within a period of
a year and a half, no fewer than 20 individuals had been relocated from TS, a
staff cut of more than 50 percent as estimated by the department head (P. Kohberger memorandum to R. Miller, November 8, 1996). It must be noted that the
resulting disruption to TS in advance of revamping its processes and workflow
was immense. Remaining staff members made heroic efforts to keep essential
functions going and were committed to ensuring the eventual success of the
new unit. From the outset, there were those who embraced the notion of being
part of the change process. Their hard work and optimism went a long way to
ensuring a positive transition. The ULS administration anticipated a temporary
loss of productivity and made allowances. The focus from the beginning was on
the long-term positive benefits to be gained. Again, no re-engineering project
of this magnitude can be accomplished overnight or without some significant
short-term setbacks.

The Implementation Phase

The implementation phase of the re-engineering spanned the period from October 1996 to April 1997. A series of workshops on mastering change was given
to management personnel, a plan for the TS re-engineering was articulated, and
the Tech Services transformation was launched.

The Management Workshop

About six months after the first change workshop, Jean Ferketish was again
engaged to help prepare the staff—this time management personnel only—for
implementing the planned TS re-engineering. Firmly grounded in the concept
of the ULS aspiration to become a learning organization, the presentation urged
using systems thinking to make organizational patterns clear and then encouraging teams and individuals to recognize and intervene to deflect behaviors that
undermine learning.

Personal Mastery. Every individual's thinking is inextricably bound to certain
idiosyncratic ways of looking at the world and interpreting events (mental models
built from assumptions, generalizations, and images based on past experience).
Ferketish explained how managers could employ the learning organization
concept of personal mastery to guide subordinates in attaining a more objective
view of reality. By using one's abilities to test and refine his or her personal
vision, an individual is then freed to focus energy on transcending the personal
and finding common ground with others in the organization. By modeling
personal mastery and using consensus tools, supervisors could influence staff
to work toward a shared vision, a mutual idea of the ULS's future that would
lead to more than lip service and grudging compliance with change (R. Miller
and Ferketish n.d., slides 51–53).

The Organizational Leader as Change Manager and Coach. According to
Ferketish, the leader as change master fills a multiplicity of roles from Tea Leaf
Reader, Ambiguity Artist, Translator, Floodgate Manager, Celebration Catalyst,

Encourager/Challenger, and Humorist to the person who invokes the power of symbols. Ferketish then explained the dynamics of the dialogue process and illustrated the gamut of behaviors ranging from negative and obstructive tactics that inhibit team learning (politicking, interrogating others, abstaining, and tacitly withdrawing from the discussion) to constructive behaviors that enhance team learning (true dialogue, skillful discussion, clarifying what has been said, and interviewing others to fully understand their thoughts and reasoning). She also explained a variety of tools that can be helpful in gaining consensus: the affinity diagram, the nominal group technique, the impact effort grid, and the prioritization matrix (R. Miller and Ferketish n.d., slides 55–57).

Formulating the Technical Services Reorganization Plan

Starting in October 1996, TS supervisors drafted a reorganization plan for the department. With input from Younger, it was revised and submitted to the ULS administration in December 1996. In accordance with standard process improvement theory and practice, the definition, description, and analysis of core functions of the TS Department comprised part one of the plan. These were succinctly stated as "the essential functions that need to be done so that TS can order, receive, pay for, and make accessible in an organized manner, material and information that the ULS needs for its users" (Kohberger et al. 1996b, 2).

Guiding Principles. The eight guiding principles of the plan to alter TS were listed as follows:

1. Grouping associated tasks and functions and placing them in units with personnel best able to accomplish them effectively (to maximize benefits to library users).
2. Reducing the number of processing steps whenever possible without unduly sacrificing the quality of records, in order to get materials out of TS and into the hands of users as expeditiously as possible.
3. Eliminating any processing steps that could not be shown to add value in terms of specific benefits to library users.
4. Eliminating separate processing streams for items in nonbook formats (i.e., serials, microforms, electronic materials) and instead organizing the work flow by (a) methods of acquisition and (b) type of processing needed upon receipt.
5. Taking advantage of vendor-supplied services, aka "outsourcing," whenever practicable (i.e., when services that meet quality standards and are cost-effective either already existed or could be developed).
6. Substituting automated processes for current manual ones.
7. Using student employees rather than permanent staff as much as practicable.
8. Extending the role and responsibilities of TS staff to managing more complex tasks rather than performing low-level repetitive processes: articulating and communicating standards and policies for creating and maintaining an integrated library system database easily interpreted by staff and users alike; and coordinating staff training in database use and maintenance (Kohberger et al. 1996a, 1–2).

These principles were reinforced by the following statement embracing the need for continuous change:

We believe that these concepts, if applied intelligently, thoroughly, and honestly to the work we do, will represent a basis for a true rethinking and reengineering of Technical Services. Our organizational structure and our need for resources will continue to evolve as the University and the ULS continue to articulate and prioritize their needs, and our discussion with our colleagues and our continuing application of these concepts to our work will enable us to continue to fulfill our mission. (Kohberger et al. 1996a, 2)

New Configuration of the Department. The new TS organizational structure called for in the plan consisted of three units (Acquisitions Payments, Acquisitions Management, and Cataloging) with six professional librarians and 21 classified staff members to replace the former structure. The old organization had staffed these functions with a hierarchy of two departments (Serials/Acquisitions and Cataloging) and eight subordinate units—as noted in a preceding section an operation employing more than 60 staff members—plus a number of in-house employees on temporary contracts for special cataloging projects!

Shifting Non-Core Functions. Part two of the proposed plan recommended shifting functions not integral to TS core responsibilities out of the new department. Examples included gift and exchange processing, periodical check in, and University of Pittsburgh dissertation and thesis processing.

Implementing Technical Services Reorganization

With the approval of the ULS's administration, the plan was distributed to the ULS at large and to the Strategic Planning Steering Committee. Then work of putting flesh on the proposed new departmental structure and changing work processes began.

Filling New Positions. The processes for filling classified staff and faculty librarian positions were comparable. New job descriptions giving the qualifications for all proposed TS positions were written in consultation with the ULS personnel librarian and the University of Pittsburgh's HR department. Besides listing the skills and qualifications for each position, these job descriptions enumerated new responsibilities and outlined revised methods of performing the tasks retained within the new department structure.

For the first time, position descriptions in the ULS contained explicit behavioral expectations. Traditionally in the ULS (as in most academic libraries up to that time), behavioral performance expectations had been tacitly understood to be a requirement for Public Services staff to ensure positive interactions with users. But only in the new organization were such expectations acknowledged as an essential component of *everyone's* work life. Again, this brought the ideas about change expressed in the training into everyone's job responsibilities in a tangible way.

New Classified Staff Positions. Of the dozens of original staff positions, only four classified staff positions were *not* appreciably changed; and the incumbents remained in these slots. In addition to rewriting position descriptions, the ULS sent all positions—both new and existing ones—to HR for reclassification, a necessary and long-overdue project. This action not only contributed to the success of the re-engineering effort but also brought about change in ULS personnel management. The process of auditing position requirements, expectations, and salary ranges in connection with re-engineering TS demonstrated the organizational benefits of revisiting the work being done by personnel across the system on a regular basis. This practice has now become an integral part of the ULS routine.

Rather than reassigning staff via backroom deliberations limited to supervisors and administration, as is sometimes done in a reorganization, the ULS conducted a formal recruitment and interview process. With the exception of the four positions that were not altered, all TS positions were declared open and were posted for recruitment. TS staff members were invited to apply for any new positions that interested them and for which they felt qualified. There was no limit placed on how many open positions they could apply for. They were encouraged to ask questions about the jobs and/or about the recruitment process. Once again, open communication was an essential element in the eventual success of the process.

All applicants were interviewed by faculty librarians in the TS units where there were openings as well as by the interim coordinator of that department. Then supervisors from other ULS areas met to match candidates' abilities and preferences to the job requirements of the open positions. Most interviewees, but not all, were appointed to the positions that were their first preferences. Some agreed to accept a position of interest that had not been their highest preference. All started their new positions in April 1997 and completed a probationary period before being designated permanent employees in their new capacities.

Although most applicants qualified for a position within the new ULS organization, a few were not reassigned. Two ultimately withdrew their applications in favor of pursuing other options: one chose to retire instead of taking a new position; and one who had an MLS accepted a professional position outside of the Pittsburgh University Library System. One staff member was terminated because of performance and attendance problems unrelated to the reorganization.

New Faculty Librarian Positions. In a process parallel to that conducted for classified staff openings, the five available faculty librarian positions in the new department were filled by librarians from the old TS units following candidate interviews with ULS administration, the interim coordinator, and the heads of the hiring units. Faculty librarians with legal expectations of continuing employment who were not selected for TS positions were offered positions elsewhere in ULS.

One of the side benefits of this action was that people with years of technical services experience and expertise were placed in units where they brought new insight and a "behind the catalog" way of looking at things. In what had been a very compartmentalized library system, this infusion of new views and boundary-spanning approaches into several departments was invigorating. In April 1997, all began in their new positions within and outside of TS.

First Steps toward Outsourcing

Indisputably the most innovative aspect of implementing the TS plan was the pioneering partnership forged between the ULS and the Yankee Book Peddler, the vendor then supplying the ULS with current domestic imprints. The library set parameters for vendor-supplied cataloging, including quality guarantees for bibliographic records supplied by the vendor. And the library negotiated pricing for value-added services from the vendor, including cataloging, electronic invoice receipt, and physical processing for the books (e.g., labels, security strips). The contract provided for a per-book processing charge and also a bulk discount on guaranteed book purchases, since the ULS had converted from an approval plan with the privilege of returning unwanted items to a tightly crafted selection profile with the understanding that *all items sent* would be accepted automatically and added to the collection.

Transition to an Automated Environment

In early spring 1997, TS supervisors worked with the vendor's technical staff to specify requirements for computer programs enabling the full interface of NOTIS (at that time the ULS's integrated library system) with the vendor's computer systems. Protocols were developed for the following groundbreaking value-added vendor services for processing current domestic imprints:

- Creation of purchase orders by ULS staff in NOTIS and the subsequent electronic generation and delivery of corresponding acquisitions records from the vendor.
- Encumbrance of estimated per-item costs against various fund allocations tied to the materials budget.
- Matching acquisitions records in the catalog with vendor-produced bibliographic records and automatically overlaying the former with the latter.
- Delivering online invoices that reflected actual costs upon receipt of materials.
- Full physical processing of materials.
- Automated monthly upgrading of inferior bibliographic records via purchased files of full Library of Congress copy.

A contemporary article points out that most libraries at this time were merely "working at the margins" (Renaud 1997, 87) of what was possible in library cooperative efforts through Interlibrary loan, bibliographic utilities like OCLC, and fairly conservative on-campus partnerships and eschewing the close relationship necessary for electronic data interchange (EDI) with vendors and the degree of risk inherent in working out such a partnership. "EDI does not require human intervention" (87); therefore, a high degree of both detailed planning and trust between both partners is required. This being the case, "the slow rate at which EDI has been absorbed by academic libraries illustrates a reluctance to enter into deep and transformational partnerships, and a failure to reap the corresponding benefits" (87). The University of Pittsburgh was the exception to this rule.

A Positive Verdict on Outsourcing

Ultimately, both partners in this innovative venture found the outsourcing of many TS functions an unqualified success.

Benefits to the University of Pittsburgh: James Mahler, University of Pittsburgh provost and vice chancellor is on record as approving the outcomes of the re-engineering of TS:

First it demonstrates good performance of a crucial unit [the library] on which all units of the University depends. Second, the change was made in a cost-effective way, and the emphasis was on improving performance. It was so cost-effective that we didn't spend any money on the reorganization. (Bates n.d., 3)

Benefits to Vendor

- Yankee Book Peddler gained a secured revenue stream —20,000 books at a cost of more than $1,000,000 (Kohberger n.d.a).
- Yankee gained a reputation for innovative partnering with libraries.
- "For Blackwell's [a book vendor enlisted subsequent to the partnership with Yankee], the relationship led to the development of a new value-added service to introduce market-wide, a win-win situation all around." (Bates n.d., 3)

For a period of time, the ULS forged a similar partnership with Blackwell's as their principle vendor. However, as a result of ongoing cost-benefit analysis of vendor services, in 2005 the ULS came full circle and returned to Yankee (its original partner in innovative outsourcing) for domestic imprints.

Benefits to ULS

- Better workflow (redundancies eliminated) and greater efficiency because of technological developments—e.g., notification slip book processing reduced from 42 manual steps to 17 automated steps without sacrificing quality checks (Kohberger n.d.a).
- Improvement in cycle time from TS to shelving (Kohberger n.d.a).
- Cost efficiencies in that vendor discount partially offset annual service charges (Kohberger n.d.a).
- Changing staff roles/responsibilities: shift from repetitive tasks to *managing* the technical processes (e.g., acquisitions, payment, cataloging, and physical processing) (Kohberger n.d.a).
- Changing staff roles/responsibilities: "Staff energy and expertise can be redirected to new initiatives" (Kohberger n.d.a, under "Vendor Partnership Advantages").

Rebuilding Phase

The rebuilding phase of the TS meant taking the new organization structure and the new work processes for a "shakedown cruise" to learn what worked and what might still need modification.

Operational Changes. Starting in April 1997, three monumental changes were implemented in TS. First, staff members were trained in new procedures for accepting cataloging for English language books on receipt of the material; and the long-standing practice of warehousing masses of new books became an artifact of the "bad old days." Second, the existing backlog of monographs in all languages was frozen in anticipation of finding a way to free staff from this burden. At the same time, TS supervisors began to implement the third change—the migration of non-core functions (most notably periodical check-in) to other ULS departments and units.

Gradual Improvement. Since vendor services were phased in over time, anticipated processing efficiencies under the new TS structure and procedures were realized gradually rather than immediately. An initial target for throughput pegged at 500 volumes per month proved unattainable. The ULS administration made allowances for temporary lapses in productivity. Still, it is understandable that the staff members were overwhelmed at times by the mandate to catalog all materials manually upon receipt. And it hardly is surprising that stress levels remained high until the full array of vendor services was in place (P. Kohberger, head of TS, University of Pittsburgh ULS, in a conversation with the author, January 2005). It makes sense too that—despite the best intent to embrace change—an enormous effort of will was required to bolster morale among TS staff during this transition period. Even the most dedicated and positive person-nel in the unit couldn't help but feel a bit overwhelmed at times. Such tempo-rary frustrations did not derail the re-engineering at ULS because the change initiative was a robust partnership between administration and front-line staff. Tech Services staff demonstrated great perseverance and loyalty throughout the change process, and ULS management was grateful for their unflagging profes-sionalism and productivity. Lientz and Rea warn that when management *fails* to make allowances for temporary setbacks, the "pressure to keep process per-formance up during change" (2004, 25) can lead to resistance to changes and sometimes reversion to old processes.

Organizational Outcomes of Re-Engineering

Despite having undergone the disruptions and privations endemic to any such major personnel reorganization, ULS emerged from the process both stronger and much more agile. The TS department represented an enormous step forward for the library system with three important outcomes: (1) The re-engineering addressed an inevitable budget crunch without slashing services to the bone or damaging the libraries' political position among campus constituencies; (2) it served notice to ULS staff and university administration alike that the ULS administration was dedicated to true systemic change, and in so doing it set the stage for the ULS to develop into a change-centric organization; and (3) this colossal upheaval secured breathing space for the ULS to position itself to play a vital role in the University of Pittsburgh teaching and learning community and to plan ways and means of achieving its vision of a vibrant future.

Short-Term Gains

The immediate effects of the TS re-engineering were impressive as well:

- Processing time to get books into the collection was reduced by weeks and in some cases months.
- Cataloging costs for English language books were reduced to $2 to $3 per item.
- Salary savings amounted to a net reduction of $954,012 (47 percent of 1996 TS person-nel costs).
- Total savings associated with the re-engineering are estimated at $1.1 million.
- Within 5 years, all backlogged items (some having been warehoused for more than 20 years) were outsourced and processed.
- Staff members were freed from repetitive low-level tasks to undertake new responsi-bilities.
- The mandated giveback to the university was accomplished without layoffs.

- Processes developed during the re-engineering have proved robust enough to migrate to a new integrated library information system (EISI) and a new book vendor (Blackwell) without disruption to basic services.
- Based on a variety of estimates at the time, nearly $700,000 of the savings was invested in new research databases and journal subscriptions. The ULS saved more than $1 million altogether from the re-engineering, with $400,000 being used to self-fund library raises (to compensate for an insufficient pool of university funding for that purpose) and about $100,000 being allocated for outsourcing cataloging backlogs until they had been eliminated.

As noted earlier, examining and improving entrenched processes was a long-neglected area within the ULS. Perhaps the greatest single benefit of the re-engineering process was that it freed up time, money, and personnel—enabling the ULS to move forward aggressively in the acquisition and eventual creation of electronic resources. No longer was the emphasis on internal processing, but rather on the very visible user-centered creation of a robust digital environment that would rival any in the country.

Long-Term Gains

Looking back at the progress made, the long-term positive effects on the ULS and the university community served were spectacular. In following through with such a large-scale radical change following years of status quo thinking and ineffectual management, this ULS administration lent truth to the phrase, "Our only constant is change." The vital step of re-engineering TS, together with the implementation of strategic planning and the fact that the entire staff was engaged in a process of systemic change, positioned the libraries for flexibility in the future.

A Change-Centric Organization. Staff had been served notice that—undaunted by pockets of individual resistance to change and unavoidable temporary disruptions—this ULS administration was committed to continuous strategic change throughout the organization. By providing training about organizational change and conducting an ongoing dialogue with interested staff, ULS leaders clearly and unequivocally signaled that subsequent change would be effected in partnership with staff, as opposed to their having unilateral change imposed upon them.

Redefinition of Priorities. One notable example of the ULS's redefinition of priorities was the eventual withdrawal from OCLC's Enhance cataloging program and the CONSER project. It was clear following the process improvement effort in TS and the subsequent restructuring of the department that the organizational philosophy had shifted from technical quality at any price to putting a premium on tangible benefits for ULS library users. As mentioned previously, the two most visible and most well-received improvements for users were the timely processing of materials and access to an unprecedented array of electronic resources.

Consolidation of Support from Faculty. The campus community was shown that library budget cutting can be a win-win situation. Instead of the rancorous political infighting usually associated with slashing the list of serials titles needed for teaching and support of faculty research, the ULS reinvested money from the re-engineering in databases. This decision addressed perceptions of inadequacy in ULS serials holdings by increasing the amount of electronic access to the full text of periodicals. Nothing was taken away from users in order to follow this new strategic direction. Indeed, a subsequent series of major budget increases—brought on in no small measure by the credibility established in the re-engineering project—resulted in the purchase of more books than ever at the same time that the ULS was building one of the nation's largest and most comprehensive arrays of digital resources. This focus on first determining, and then securing, what customers value in order to get their patronage is sometimes referred to in the marketing literature as "buying customers."

The original investment of approximately $700,000 in databases has grown to a whopping $5 million-plus per year in the budget line dedicated to online resources. In addition to purchasing an impressive array of research databases, eliminating the backlog, and giving well-earned raises, the ULS also invested in a technology infrastructure including 110 servers (in addition to the online public catalog) located in and managed by the library system as well as a state-of-the-art wireless environment, more than 700 public workstations, a Digital Research Library Department managing dozens of digitization projects, five Open Archive Initiative discipline-based repositories, a campus-mandated Electronic Theses/Dissertations environment, and many other technology projects, some with federal funding. A large and varied staff including 12 systems analysts, several web designers, digital project managers, and other technology specialists support digital initiatives in the ULS. This support network undergirds the University of Pittsburgh's continuous development of digital collections and technology-based services of all types.

A Pledge to University Administration. The TS Reorganization Plan that came from the re-engineering effort acknowledged that the ULS was not alone in anticipating possible future financial pressures: "Now these circumstances [scarcity of federal, state, and student tuition funds] have forced us [academic libraries] to create and maintain our own internal support" (Kohberger et al. 1996b, 1). As mentioned previously, the re-engineering proved to the university administration that the ULS—unlike many of its academic library peers—could think and act strategically. Unwilling to be perceived as the perpetual bottomless pit of demand for university resources, the ULS avoided asking the university for more money to throw at existing problems. Instead, it demonstrated both the willingness and ability to honestly evaluate current operations and reallocate existing monies as necessary. And rather than conducting the safe but ineffectual holding action of across-the-board cuts, the ULS made an uncompromising analysis of its strengths and opportunities and invested in activities most likely to (1) pay off, in terms of advancing its mission in the short term, and (2) put the ULS into position to meet the future needs of its users and to serve the priorities of other stakeholders.

The ULS has continued to manage its budget carefully, "growing" funds to meet inflation in collection costs by factoring such increases into annual planning. This contrasts sharply with the brinksmanship practiced by all too many academic libraries—those that turn a blind eye to inflationary trends until a fiscal crisis develops and then threaten cancellations unless the university antes up an infusion of funds. In addition to keeping a close eye on monies allocated by the university, the ULS has assiduously pursued and secured *outside* funding from grants and major gifts fundraising. (The ULS routinely raises $1 million or more in fund raising; and in one recent year, it obtained more than $1 million in outside grants.) These funds have been dedicated to implementing new and innovative services of all kinds.

This unflinching commitment to pulling its own weight within the University of Pittsburgh system has garnered the ULS a remarkable degree of credibility and support among all campus constituencies: students, faculty/staff, and university administration. The goodwill and confidence evidenced by LibQUAL+™ ratings and other types of positive feedback is perhaps most dramatically documented by the ULS's prominence in the university's annual budget priorities.

Progress in Becoming a Learning Organization. And finally, in focusing on user needs, the ULS moved closer to its ideal of becoming a learning organization. Without exception, users benefited from the re-engineering in two ways. The first and most visible benefit was elimination of the backlog of thousands of older materials. A second and continuing benefit is that users began gaining access to new imprints within *days* of their arrival in the library, rather than weeks, months, or years later. This shift from library-centric thinking to a focus on customers paved the way for countless other organizational changes and signaled that the ULS was now much more outwardly focused.

A Positive Organizational Development Mode. The impact of what the ULS accomplished in re-engineering TS went far beyond their home campus and their own region. In involving more than 100 employees in an open, communicative, and "bloodless" restructuring, ULS's TS re-engineering accomplished one of the largest-scale change processes in the environment of major research libraries. The University of Pittsburgh ULS experience comprises a model of how to manage fundamental and wide-ranging changes in any complex organization.

6

Change Becomes a Given

MAKING CHANGE THE NORM

Any organizational change—no matter how impressive it may have been initially—can end up as an isolated footnote to an organization's otherwise mediocre history unless a support structure for continuous change is put into place. Absent a nurturing environment created by alteration of organizational processes, values, and structures, the single change effort sometimes leaves no more lasting a mark on the organization than a stone thrown into water. The collective will to embrace change can be a fragile thing.

There are countless reasons why change may not "take" in a lasting way. The leader or leaders who drove changes may decamp in search of more interesting challenges, better pay, or a wider scope of influence. If management broke faith with employees somehow during the change effort, the rank and file may actively resist any subsequent movement away from the status quo. Knee-jerk responses to budget difficulties can leave organization members hamstrung and unable to think beyond daily crises to what would benefit them in future years. Many change-resistant staff members learned in infancy that it is not necessary to display any overt resistance in order to defeat change. These folks know that simply by keeping a low profile and waiting for the first flush of enthusiasm to fade, odds are that in time they will be allowed to revert to old, cherished ways of doing things. Other staff members who bought into the need for change and took on extra responsibilities in order to make it happen may be too tired to sustain further progress. Thus, fundamental organizational change must be undertaken as a process and not an isolated event. Re-engineering of Technical Services (TS) was a good thing for the ULS. But it would be necessary for change to become the *norm* if this academic library were to have a chance at the future envisioned for it.

PLANNING FOR THE FUTURE

As noted previously, urgent necessity sometimes dictates taking the isolated strategic action (like re-engineering of a department or operational unit) in advance of the completion of a formal strategic plan. To mount the kind of powerful, unified, focused effort likely to achieve significant progress toward the library's vision, however, a formal plan is needed. "Strategic planning ensures that all activities are orchestrated so that their contribution to the vitality and long term viability of the organization is maximized" (Wood 1988, 100). This being the case, the ULS did not delay the re-engineering of TS, but it did begin a strategic planning initiative that was conducted concurrently with the re-engineering of TS and was implemented effective June 1996, two months after TS began operating under its new structure and procedures.

Preparation for Strategic Planning

Late in 1995, a Strategic Planning Steering Committee was appointed by the director. A two-day retreat was held the following January to inaugurate the strategic planning process, to orient a cross-section of ULS staff to the planning process, and to identify core values of the ULS. Attendees included the Director's Advisory Council of library faculty and staff managers, the ULS Planning and Budget Committees, and Jean Ferketish, at that time director of the University of Pittsburgh Human Resources Department's Organization Development Office. Maureen Sullivan from the Association Research Libraries (ARL) Office of Management Services facilitated the sessions.

The ULS management group understood that having objective outside parties facilitate the planning process would be critical to success in introducing strategic planning. They believed that considerable understanding of group dynamics and substantial persuasive ability would be required to ensure that all ULS staff involved begin to think beyond the traditional way of doing things; begin to focus on the entire library, rather than working from a narrow departmental frame of reference; and begin to trust that strategic planning might offer sufficient benefits to offset the hard work of learning to think differently and the risks of abandoning time-honored ways of operating. Management members knew too that enlisting outside experts usually helps to disarm initial resistance and/or any suspicion attached to new ideas espoused by people within the organization. This strategy can be especially important when dealing with a system in which there has been little staff turnover and few operating procedures or policies have been changed over time.

Organizing the Foot Soldiers

Task forces were appointed to pursue the following seven strategic directions: Building a Balanced Collection; Creating an Agenda for Diversity; Targeting Opportunities for Special Collections; Reassessing and Updating Information Technology; Creating a Positive Workplace; Delivering Quality Services; and Educating Users. Membership was comprised of not only representatives from all employment classifications and different parts of the existing organizational chart but also of staff with varying levels of experience (a mix of veteran employees and neophytes). A concerted effort was made to ensure that the task force membership was as organizationally diverse as possible, and not based on existing unit assignments. For example, the Education Users Task Force was chaired by a librarian from TS and drew members from several units outside of Public Services and Instruction. This provided the group with a variety of viewpoints and levels of experience and forced the group to look at long-established methods of user education from a fresh perspective.

Each task force had a liaison to the Strategic Planning Steering Committee, the group responsible for coordinating the planning effort in tandem with the ARL consultant. Yet—in keeping with best organizational development principles—it was made clear in each task force's charge that its deliberations and conclusions were *not* meant to be shoehorned into any set of predetermined outcomes. "The members of the task force should feel free to express their thoughts and ideas, and not labor under the impression that the Steering Committee liaison will be guiding the process toward a particular end" (ULS 1996f, under "Charge"). As stated previously, the very deliberate selection of task force chairs with no vested interest in the outcome supported this goal.

Sullivan would return to the University of Pittsburgh in May to assist the task forces in gaining the skills and knowledge to commence work and again after 10 weeks to work with the task forces and the Steering Committee in assessing progress and identifying areas of overlap in task force efforts.

The Central Question

Essentially, task force members and the ULS staff at large were asked to consider the question "What should the University of Pittsburgh Library System of the future look like?" within the framework of the strategic directions listed previously. Task forces were directed to use the foundation documents drafted by the Strategic Planning Steering Committee (mission statement, vision statements, planning assumptions, and other information defining general areas of concern and strategic directions) as an overall framework for their discussions.

Foundation Documents

A mission statement broad enough to stand the test of time yet specific enough to guide the planning process was crafted by the Steering Committee:

The mission of the University Library System (ULS) at the University of Pittsburgh is to provide and promote access to information resources necessary for the achievement of the University leadership objectives in teaching, learning, research, creativity, and community service and to collaborate in the development of effective information, teaching, and learning systems. (ULS 1997b, under "Introduction")

Although on the surface this appears to be a simple statement, it was arrived at collaboratively in meetings involving staff from across the ULS. Once articulated, it served to drive all future progress in the strategic planning process. The collective soul searching and wide-ranging discussions that go into crafting a mission statement typically are some of the most significant learning experiences of the process and are key to developing a sense of shared values and a common strategic direction for the organization.

Bryson (2004) claims some very significant organizational benefits from the process of clarifying the mission statement of non-profit entities—chiefly increasing employee buy-in and legitimizing the organization's existence in terms of "socially desirable and justified purposes" (104). He also makes a tight connection between such legitimacy and ongoing support. "Unless the purposes focus on socially useful and justifiable ends and unless the philosophy and values themselves are virtuous, the organization cannot hope to command indefinitely the resources needed to survive, including high-quality, loyal, committed employees" (103). This was the case at the ULS in the initial stages of strategic planning as it has been at other academic libraries. A well-crafted mission statement is a powerful tool for enlisting both staff and outsider support.

In addition, as part of the strategic plan, the ULS Steering Committee developed a lengthy narrative vision statement with separate "vignettes" from the perspective of an undergraduate student and that of two teaching faculty members. Then followed two paragraphs foreshadowing how the ULS of the future was likely to differ from the current entity.

Task Force Support and Guidance

In accordance with accepted practices for supporting groups and teams, the task forces were given both general and specific parameters for carrying out their respective charges.

Planning Assumptions

Eleven planning assumptions laid the ground rules for task force deliberations:

- Significant organizational and services changes were a given.
- Personnel training and resource development to support a reorganization would be made available.
- The new organizational structure must be flexible and responsive to user needs.
- University of Pittsburgh students, faculty, and staff were identified as the primary users of the ULS.
- Pursuit of new technologies would not mean abandoning traditional services or collections.
- Collection strengths that had earned the ULS the rank of twenty-eighth among 108 ARL peers would be maintained and further developed.
- Alternative means of funding must be developed to supplement university allocations to the ULS.
- Space planning would be excluded from the strategic planning charge, and departmental libraries would remain separate entities.
- ULS policies must be made to reflect the university's growing emphasis on undergraduate education while continuing its support for the university's scholarship and research missions.
- Diversity in every aspect of ULS operations would be a high priority.
- The NOTIS library management system would be scheduled for replacement by the end of 1999 (ULS 1997b).

Process Guidelines

The following broad process guidelines were given to each task force:

1. Each task force was to examine relevant internal and external documents and data. Environmental analyses must be conducted, including examination of the ULS, scanning important developments and trends in the fields of higher education and academic libraries, and gathering information about best practices in the seven strategic areas under study.
2. The focus of the analysis of ULS strengths and limitations for each task force was to consider the following key elements of the organization in light of the task force charge: "organizational structure, staffing patterns, policies, allocation of resources, and especially communication and decision-making structures" (ULS 1996f, under "Charge").
3. Each task force should compare areas of strength in the ULS and areas needing development were to be compared with opportunities and threats or barriers in order to find the best fit between what ULS was prepared to do surpassingly well and what was wanted and needed by stakeholders (i.e., various groups and individuals interested in the ULS and/or able to significantly influence its operations). Following strategic planning dictums, the areas of best fit would indicate the highest probability of success for investing ULS personnel and financial resources along with the library administration's energy and effort.

Task Force Charges

Boilerplate instructions in the section of each task force charge outlining the process for recommending changes were couched in classic strategic planning language:

- Identify resources needed to achieve the goals.
- Prioritize each of the goals and recommendations.
- Consider what presently held institutional values may need to be strengthened or changed in order to attain these goals (ULS 1996f).

In accordance with best strategic planning and organizational development practices, the generic section of each charge mandated soliciting targeted input from individual staff members, departments, and committees as needed and gave task forces the option of conducting open meetings as well. As was true in the re-engineering process, there was an overarching and unwavering commitment to open, honest communication.

Specific Task Force Responsibilities

In addition to general guidelines, each task force had a set of parameters and responsibilities unique to its specific purpose.

Building a Balanced Collection Task Force. Given the prominence of collection strength and collection volume as benchmarks among ARL libraries, together with a growing recognition of the importance of access to information sources beyond those owned by a given library, responsibilities outlined in the charge for this task charged were multifaceted:

1. Gathering and reviewing general collection development policies.

   - Making the policies representative of the needs of all academic programs at the university—both undergraduate and graduate levels—yet flexible and responsive to changing university priorities.
   - Soliciting comprehensive input, including user populations from whom input had not as yet been obtained.
   - Suggesting ways to monitor and modify approval plan parameters to reflect evolving collection development policies.

2. Reviewing and recommending enhancement of nonprint selection policies and procedures.

3. Investigating current methods for the acquisition and management of electronic databases and articulating a policy incorporating the following elements:

   - A library-wide decision-making forum.
   - Formal criteria for database selection.
   - A means and recommended frequency for monitoring database use.
   - A process for determining appropriate platforms for databases according to use data.
   - A mechanism for keeping database access methods flexible and representative of current conditions.

4. Reviewing policies and procedures for replacing lost/missing materials and for weeding collections as well as recommending how to communicate findings (actions needed and/or actions taken) to all ULS units involved.

5. Investigating the option of inventorying the collections and recommending when and how an inventory might be conducted.

6. Comparing unfilled requests from ULS patrons to regional campus holdings and recommending whether to purchase such items or to publicize inter-campus borrowing among University of Pittsburgh libraries.

7. Investigating the pros and cons of all past, current, and planned cooperative collection development agreements between the ULS and libraries outside the Pitt system, including but not limited to the Oakland Library Consortium, and making recommendations regarding ULS participation in such agreements.

8. Investigating the merits of comparing ULS collections to those in peer institutions, including the option of using a conspectus tool for benchmarking (ULS 1996a).

Task Force on Creating an Agenda for Diversity. Recognizing the potential benefits accruing to any campus entity that values diversity and reflects the growing diversity of this country's population to the fullest extent possible, the ULS charged the Task Force on Creating an Agenda for Diversity to work with an existing diversity committee to foster an even stronger diversity presence in the following ways:

1. Maintain ties with the ULS Diversity Committee.
2. Building on the committee's work, prepare an action plan with strategies to achieve greater diversity in the workforce, collections, and services.
3. Propose ways to incorporate into the strategic plan means of strengthening and/or changing the ULS's current diversity strategies.

4. Propose a mechanism to foster within the ULS an atmosphere of appreciation for and commitment to diversity (ULS 1996c).

Task Force on Targeting Opportunities for Specialized Collections. The first paragraph of this task force's charge deftly set out the strategic role of any special collection within the complex academic library environment, pointing out that—of necessity—a considerable amount of resource support is dedicated to the operation of special collections.

The specialized collections in a research library are those collections which, by virtue of their uniqueness, comprehensiveness, or format, make an outstanding contribution to the library as a whole. The very nature of these materials make such collections problematic; they may serve a limited audience and be expensive to maintain, and are thus difficult to justify as an expense. This does not detract from their importance, rather it serves to underscore it; the variety of specialized materials increases their value to the user. (ULS 1996g, under "Charge")

The overall charge for the Task Force on Targeting Opportunities for Specialized Collections was to develop a framework to guide development efforts, one specific enough about collection strengths and unique resources to facilitate decision making regarding (1) which fund-raising opportunities to pursue and (2) the amount of resources needed to manage, showcase, and provide access to the treasures held in each collection (ULS 1996g). The details of this committee's charge are as follows:

1. Identify additional specialized collections to consider for acquisition via donation or purchase. The primary criterion for such new acquisitions would be their potential to advance the ULS's mission of supporting research and teaching.
2. Identify existing specialized collections whose character and strengths make them good candidates for fund-raising and external grant application efforts.
3. Identify which operational aspects of particular specialized collections could benefit from an infusion of outside finds (including but not limited to preservation, access, and user support) and articulate how such needs might be matched to the aims and interests of potential funding sources.
4. Review current fund-raising/development processes for ULS specialized collections and recommend process improvements, including administrative support for such efforts if appropriate.
5. Investigate the possibility of forming financial partnerships or collaborative efforts to both support the growth of specialized collections and increase their use (ULS 1996g).

It is worth noting that the report of this task force stresses keeping a *balance* between emphasis on specialized collections and other ULS priorities, an important library management principle. "Collections that can be targeted because of the availability of opportunities should not dominate the development effort inordinately, but should be evaluated against other development and collection priorities" (ULS 1996g, under "Summary Report").

Task Force on Information Technology. Given the diverse meanings that the phrase "information technology (IT)" can have in different contexts, the introductory paragraph of the charge is essential to understanding the focus of this task force:

Information Technology is defined as those technologies that are applied in the library directly for users ... including information databases, electronic resources and the infrastructure (e.g., hardware, software, network, etc.). (ULS 1996f, under "Charge")

In recommending a framework (mission, goals, and focus) for meeting technology needs within the short term, the task force was constrained by the library management system in use at the time. The charge set forth the following important issues for consideration, putting the task force on notice that the list was not exhaustive:

1. Identify the most advanced knowledge about the research process along with best practices in the IT field for supporting user needs.
2. Identify the kinds of programs the ULS should put into place and the kinds of technologies suitable for accomplishing the aims of such programs.
3. Articulate the library's role as "content provider or publisher of information" (ULS 1996f, under "Charge"), addressing the following issues and concerns:

   - Adoption of an intellectual framework to guide the ULS entry into content publishing, with the primary criterion for development projects being the applicability of the material and resources to the University of Pittsburgh's teaching and research missions.
   - Identification of unique resources of potential interest to the academic community that is beyond the confines of the University of Pittsburgh's campus itself.
   - Recommendation of ideal methods for making available those resources judged interesting to the broadest segment of the internal and external research community.
   - Recommendation of a design and a strategy for implementing access to digital resources developed by the ULS.

4. Identify a means of continuous assessment of ongoing IT projects incorporating input from the widest group within the ULS with a stake in the outcomes.
5. Develop a mechanism for evaluating current IT projects and for screening proposed new ones that ensures input from users and other members of the learning community.
6. Identify a set of core IT competencies for all ULS personnel and share the list with the Creating a Positive Workplace Task Force (ULS 1996f "Charge").

Task Force on Creating a Positive Workplace. Having defined "the staff" as inclusive of all levels from student employees through librarians and classified staff and having affirmed the critical impact of staff attitudes and staff commitment on the provision of high-quality service to users, the introduction to this task force's charge described a positive workplace as one in which individual and institutional goals are congruent and as "an environment that is highly satisfying to the employees and is highly productive for the institution" (ULS 1996b, under "Charge").

As with other task forces, there were a few issues beyond this group's purview. Setting aside space, ergonomics, and salary considerations, the task force was charged with examining and making recommendations regarding the following aspects of the working environment: staff morale, staff recognition, communication, helping individuals and groups adapt to change, training, professional development, and finally the goal of moving the ULS organizational culture toward that of a learning organization (ULS 1996b).

The charge consisted of the following six specific elements:

1. Identification of ways to aid staff in adapting to rapid and continuous change.
2. Proposing specific means of moving ULS toward an organizational culture that perpetuates the ideal of a learning organization including continual learning and active participation of staff at all levels in training and professional development activities.
3. Suggesting a mechanism to recognize achievements of ULS staff.
4. Formulating a process for the review of new and innovative ideas and the implementation of the best ones, along with a mechanism for encouraging and rewarding the sharing of such ideas.
5. Identifying characteristics of the proposed new work environment and listing expectations for core staff skills and competencies supportive of such a workplace.
6. Recommending ways to develop and maintain a unity of purpose and direction and a sense of common values among ULS staff to replace the existing territoriality between departments and units (ULS 1996b).

Task Force on Educating Users. This task force's charge foreshadowed the twenty-first century emphasis on the library's opportunity to become central to the university's teaching/learning mission. The introduction to the charge alludes to the fundamental tenets of the emerging discipline known as information literacy: teaching library skills, guiding acquisition of knowledge of the research/information seeking process, and inculcating the skills and independent learning behaviors that prepare library users for lifelong learning (ULS 1996e).

Four main elements of the charge fleshed out the aforementioned concepts:

1. Identify information seeking and evaluation skills critical to users in the context of a growing shift to remote access and self-sufficiency.
2. Identify and recommend ways to develop such skills and to maximize user expertise incorporating the following considerations:

   - Established and emerging technologies that can enhance the effectiveness of library instruction.
   - Diverse learning styles and user group needs.
   - Targeted instructional modules.

3. Develop ways to monitor user needs in order to effect continuous adjustment of instructional programs in light of such needs.
4. Recommend strategies to integrate library instruction and information literacy concepts more closely into the university's teaching mission (ULS 1996e).

Task Force on Delivering Quality Service. The charge of this group was put into a strategic planning and marketing framework with the following words about the needs of two important constituencies of the ULS—individual users and the campus community: "Providing good service is one of the best ways to make a favorable impression on library patrons, and helps to assure that our community of users recognizes the importance and value of the University Library System" (ULS 1996d, under "Charge").

The introductory paragraph of this task force's final report did not mince words when describing the shift of fundamental values necessary for fulfilling its charge: "The goal of the Delivering Quality Service Task Force is to recommend ways of improving our service with an emphasis on client-centered philosophies, which means effectively performing all service with the needs of the client as the primary focus, rather than the ease of the ULS colleague" (ULS 1996d, under "Charge"). As discussed previously, the re-engineering had made it evident to personnel throughout the system that a shift in focus had occurred. The ULS was now committed to honoring the needs of the community of users, and these needs would drive this now outwardly focused system.

The charge consisted of the following five specific elements:

- Accountability: Recommend a mechanism to ensure that all departments and units of ULS are working in concert to provide users with prompt, courteous, and accurate service.
- Bibliographic access: Recommend a mechanism to deliver accurate, complete, and up-to-date cataloging information about all ULS collections.
- Problem reporting: Recommend a mechanism for addressing and resolving problems reported by users (e.g., missing items, inaccurate holdings information) as quickly as possible.
- Overcoming organizational barriers to quality improvement: Recommend a means of ensuring regular feedback and interdepartmental discussion of any problems in delivering quality service.
- Rational, user-centered design of the physical layout for service interfaces: Develop an action plan for locating both public service points and collections in a manner logical to users and clearly identify such locations (ULS 1996d).

Implementing the Strategic Plan

Implementation responsibility was vested in an Implementation Working Group chaired by the ULS director and comprised of managers ultimately responsible for strategic plan outcomes. As at every previous point in the strategic planning process, it was recognized as essential that this group be representative of the ULS across units and that all members encourage communication and feedback from staff members in their units as the process unfolded.

The Implementation Document

The beginning of the implementation document affirms the ULS's commitment to becoming a full-fledged learning organization by listing the following characteristics:

Individuals focus on key issues, base decisions on objective data, respect one another and give value to the natural diversity inherent in the organization, chart directions which are in the best interest of users, and engage in learning and growth as a central component of meeting the mission of the library system. (ULS 1997a, under "Introduction")

Core Values

This document also lists core values central to developing a culture supportive of learning organization ideals and practices:

- Client-centered: A focus, taking into account both external clients—ranging from University of Pittsburgh students, faculty, staff, to library consortia and the international academic community—and internal clients, meaning ULS front-line units such as Reference that depend on other behind-the-scenes units for support in meeting user needs.
- Growth: Continuous learning and continuous growth for both individual employees and the organization itself.
- Humane: A working environment that nurtures growth and development by embracing fairness, equity, and respect for the contributions of all members of the organization.
- Accountable
- Networked: Collaboration with partners both within and outside of the university
- Excellence: Providing top quality services and collections to meet constantly-evolving user needs
- Appreciation of the benefits that an organization stands to reap from religious, ethnic, political, and other kinds of diversity (ULS 1997a).

New Structure

Aspirational language in the document about improving communication, decision making, agility, and coordination throughout the organization set the stage for the description of a new organizational structure to be implemented effective July 1999. A flatter upper administrative structure would be supported by a middle management group and numerous cross-functional groups—both short-term, project-specific groups and ongoing working groups with responsibility for information gathering, problem solving, articulating policies and procedures, and similar tasks. Responsibility for making decisions and charting directions for the ULS was vested in an administrative council comprised of the director, senior staff (an associate director and two assistant directors), and middle managers (ULS 1997a).

Assigning Responsibility

Broad responsibilities are outlined for each of nine working groups charged with fostering consistency in dealing with issues and solving problem throughout the ULS. For example: "The Library Instruction Working Group will develop, coordinate, facilitate, and expand the teaching of information literacy and library research skills" (ULS 1997a, under "Working and Project Groups").

Next, responsibility for addressing the 48 specific and detailed strategic plan recommendations for achieving the shared vision of the ULS's desired future was assigned to the appropriate level of the new organization—the respective working groups, Administrative Council, all staff, and sometimes a specific library department (ULS 1997a).

Affirmation of Continuous Organizational Change

The Implementation Plan document concludes with a final statement unequivocally placing the strategic planning effort in the context of ongoing organizational change:

The ULS Strategic Plan represents a bold departure from the way the ULS has operated in the past. The specific recommendations are not the primary and lasting value of the plan. Rather, the plan's lasting impact will be a cultural change and the foundation for a more collaborative and healthier organization. By carrying out the implementation plan and continually moving toward the ideals and values in the overall plan, the ULS should become an improved organization for our users and ourselves. (ULS 1997a, under "Conclusion")

Strategic Planning Outcomes

Following the re-engineering of the University of Pittsburgh's TS and the initial strategic planning effort, a number of noteworthy projects were planned and implemented in order to build on the library system's strengths and preserve the momentum gained in this initial organizational development effort: high-density storage, a digital archive, consolidation of formerly independent regional libraries under the leadership of the ULS, an enormous deacidification project with a projected 10-year time span, and groundbreaking partnerships to help libraries in East Asia embrace modern academic librarianship.

Consolidation of Regional Libraries

In 2002, libraries at the Bradford, Greenburgh, Johnstown, and Titusville regional campuses of the University of Pittsburgh were brought into the ULS fold. This organizational development extended the following advantages to these small regional academic libraries: administrative and planning support from the ULS dean and administrators, standardization of promotion and tenure procedures for library faculty at these campuses, document delivery, and training and professional development resources. Sharing budget increases awarded to the ULS became critical to these units in preserving key services and addressing emerging customer needs.

Library Storage Facility

With no chance of library expansion on a venerable urban campus where for some years space had already been at a premium, in 2001 the library administration conceived of, brokered financial support for, and created the first high-density storage facility in Pennsylvania and named it the Library Resource Facility. Measuring 16,600 square feet, this environmentally controlled unit boasts a capacity estimated at 2.7 million volumes. Since books are shelved by size instead of by subject, there is virtually no wasted space. When needed, stored items can be located in the ULS online catalog and retrieved for on-campus users with an average delivery time of 24 hours during the regular semester.

Office Space. In addition to transferring lower circulation materials, several non–Public Services ULS staff operations were also moved to a renovated university building joined to the new storage facility: TS, the Preservation Unit, the Archive Service Center (manuscripts and materials documenting the history of the university, state and local governments, the labor movement, and a collections of 626 materials centered on the history of nineteenth- and twentieth-century urban industrial society, in which Pennsylvania was a major player), and the Digital Research Library.

Repurposing Space to Accommodate Users. Moving low-circulation books and staff offices out freed up space in the Hillman Library for long-neglected student-centered activities from reading, studying, and checking e-mail to conducting research. In addition, the reclaimed space was used to house services including library instruction and accessing course reserves—both paper and electronic—as well as a public services area for the East Asian Library, located within Hillman.

Space freed up was intentionally used to make the library more welcoming to users. One of the first such changes was opening the Cup and Chaucer coffee bar and cybercafé in Hillman Library, with not only e-mail access but also some 5,000 volumes of popular reading material. There library users can be observed relaxing, interacting with friends and acquaintances, and even meeting informally with professors. This setting seems more conducive than the classroom to the give-and-take that is characteristic of a higher education environment, in which students are expected to be full partners in their academic development rather than passive subjects of the educational process.

The Digital Research Library

Begun in 1998, the Digital Research Library's (DLR's) eclectic collection of web-based materials has become a treasure trove for both local and far-flung researchers. The popular Nineteenth Century Schoolbook collection is one noteworthy collection simultaneously preserved for posterity and made available for thousands of researchers to use each month via the DRL. These textbooks are used to shed light on many aspects of the 1800s—its cultural identity as revealed in textbooks, pedagogical practices in that period of the history of education, expectations of literacy, and what can be gleaned about textbook publishing. Some pieces date back as far as the sixteenth century.

Historic Pittsburgh, the centerpiece of the DRL, includes maps, books, photos, clipping files, and census data. Formerly housed in a labyrinth of different sites not all open at the same times and each with its own arcane system for finding and viewing the materials, these resources now complement each other in a seamless collection enhanced by keyword access to the content of any and all of its elements.

This flagship collection of images was brought together in a two-year collaboration between the ULS Archives Service Center, the Historical Society of Pennsylvania, and the Carnegie Museum of Art that began in 2002. The result is a stunning collection of visual images of Pittsburgh.

Additional examples of DRL collections run the gamut of textual collections, images, and preprint and grey literature archives. Two especially unique ones are the Thornburgh and the Parallax collections. The first is a rich archive documenting the career of Richard Thornburgh—who variously served as Pennsylvania governor, U.S attorney general, and undersecretary of the United Nations. The Parallax Project, which provides access to years of data from the Allegheny Observatory, is a world-class collection of material for identifying and measuring stars. According to a brochure highlighting unique collections and services within the ULS, "The data is highly regarded as one of the best ground-based parallax measurements of stars in the world" (*Boundless Connections* 2005). More recent additions to the DRL include the Stalinka collection of nearly 340 images supporting the study of Stalin and Stalinism (posters, photos, banners, sculpture, chinaware, pins, and more); the Clinical Aphasiology collection (an archive of papers presented at a conference dedicated to the study of brain disorders connected with the loss of the ability to turn thoughts into speech); the text of 64 song lyrics by Stephen Foster as well as images (musical notations, doodles, scribbles, signatures, etc.) digitized from 113 leaves of a sketchbook that Foster created over some nine of his most productive years as a song writer; the Minority Health Archive; an electronic archive for distribution of preprints in the philosophy of science; the Jack B. Yeats Broadsheets collection (broadsheets illustrated by the brother of William Butler Yeats); documents in George Washington's hand or bearing his signature; a collection of more than 3,000 high-resolution images documenting the sculpture, stained glass, and architectural features of the renowned Cathedral of Chartres in Notre-Dame, France; and more. The list of unique and valuable collections grows continuously.

R. Miller notes in a 2002 *Journal of Academic Librarianship* article that developing, maintaining, and administering local digital collections is both expensive and fraught with a complicated set of decisions. Although many criteria for selecting material to digitize are just common sense (e.g., choose original content that is pertinent to local interests and has lasting appeal for researchers), "there is almost no element related to the use of digital libraries that is not problematic" (100). Cost is formidable. "Our overall cost per page is roughly $1.50 to $2.00. An average book in the Historic Pittsburgh project costs $400 to mount" (102). And large-format material is especially expensive to scan. A key part of the ULS's success in digitizing plat maps for the Historic Pittsburgh collection was the opportunity to partner with a local architectural firm that supplied high-quality scanning at an affordable cost. Predicting and managing use is difficult. "As soon as we mount such collections, the constituents for them change dramatically, and we will then owe an obligation to meet the needs of persons we would never dream of serving directly otherwise" (103).

Preserving Threatened Print Materials

Provision of funds for a massive deacidification project was a mark of the provost's confidence in the ULS's good stewardship of university resources. Like all libraries, the ULS had observed that over time books published from approximately 1850 to 1950 were inexorably deteriorating—becoming yellowed, with dark, burned-looking edges, and crumbling badly—because of high concentrations of acid in the paper on which they were printed.

The scope of the acidification problem and the high cost of arresting further damage to any large collection are such that many libraries simply have resigned themselves to this decimation of their resources. Because of a proven track record of using resources wisely through re-engineering and other organizational efforts, however, the ULS successfully made the case for an infusion of funds for the preservation of the nearly 100 years of publishing output owned by the ULS. An outside contractor expert in neutralizing the acid in paper by applying an alkaline coating to each page was located and signed on to preserve the approximately 30,000 imperiled volumes. As of 2005, more than 13,000 books had been treated and safe guarded for future generations of users.

Adding Value through Special Collections and Partnerships

Collection strengths in Latin American, Eastern European, and Western European materials dating from the late 1960s and the middle 1970s have been maintained through a combination of university funding, judicious enrollment in exchange programs with other countries, and an active library development effort.

Evolution of an Outstanding Specialized Collection. Building on its strengths as a one-of-a-kind collection, the East Asian Library, originally founded to make materials available during the Cold War era, has through a number of partnerships evolved into a model of East–West library cooperation and collaboration. In support of the university's Center for Asian Studies, the increasing number of undergraduates specializing in Asian Studies, and the burgeoning international community of scholars and researchers interested in China, Japan, and their neighbors, several initiatives to strengthen access for Asian and U.S. library users have been instituted.

East–West Academic Library Cooperation. Three cooperative programs serve as exemplars of this unique partnership between ULS and the Far East:

1. The Japan Information Center, established in 1996 in connection with the Japanese Center for Intercultural Communication in Tokyo, connects businesspeople and researchers with information about Japan. Typical questions answered range from crime rates to poetry texts to census data.
2. To facilitate professional development for Asian librarians, the ULS sponsors an exchange program that brings each Chinese librarian in the program to Pittsburgh to work for six months in the ULS East Asian Library, bolstering their technical skills and increasing their familiarity with U.S. academic library resources. It also sends ULS librarians and staff members to work in Chinese university libraries. Each person is abroad for several months.
3. Through a combination of grant support and funds from a Chinese foundation, in 1996 the ULS unveiled its highly successful program of document delivery for U.S. and Chinese researchers. Within days of a request being placed, the Gateway Service Center obtains from Chinese libraries the full text of Chinese language journal articles unavailable in the United States. The Center reciprocates by supplying requested English language materials to researchers abroad via its Far Eastern partners.

An Invaluable Lesson

Perhaps the most instructive and enduring lesson of the first ULS change cycle is this: It is better to initiate change of your own volition and within your own time frame than to wait until change is mandated and the timetable is driven by circumstances completely beyond the library's control. In voluntarily pursuing strategic planning and process re-engineering, the University of Pittsburgh's ULS has become a model for academic libraries whose directors and staff members believe in being proactive about change. Besides significant cost savings and improvements in its internal operations, the ULS gained a tremendous amount of political capital at the university level by cleaning up its act before ordered to do so.

When the ULS was in the final stages of implementing its organizational development initiatives, the University of Pittsburgh's Board of Trustees was finding it difficult to persuade other departments and units of this venerable institution to rethink their operations or their respective organizational structures in response to growing fiscal challenges and pressures. Consequently, the ULS was hailed by a grateful provost as an early adopter of the re-engineering process and a division that other—somewhat reluctant—university entities should emulate. By taking its place in the vanguard of process re-engineering and strategic planning, the ULS had contributed enormously to developing enough momentum at the University of Pittsburgh to break the status quo and to institute badly needed fundamental change.

Things came to a head at the University of Pittsburgh in 1997, when a sustained economic downturn prompted the university administration to tighten its belt and to require significant cutbacks from all divisions. At that time, the ULS was assigned a sizeable amount to give back to the university. This mandate for the libraries to slash $200,000 from two successive annual personnel budgets (a total cut of $400,000) might easily have ended the ULS's prospects of maintaining its position as a world-class academic library. Indeed—although the library system probably could not have predicted the mandated across-the-board budget reductions—the folk wisdom about an ounce of prevention and a pound of cure seems quite apropos in this case.

The ULS had already begun rethinking its purposes through strategic planning and fine-tuning the efficiency and effectiveness of its work processes in 1995 (two years before the university's budget crisis). Therefore, when the financial crunch came, the library system found itself in an enviable position vis-à-vis other campus entities. It had in hand not only the $400,000 in personnel savings required by the university administration but also enough additional savings (approximately $700,000) to purchase an array of electronic resources unprecedented for that time and still among the largest in the nation. As mentioned previously in this chapter, these savings also made it possible to fund well-deserved raises for staff and to eliminate the cataloging backlog without making any additional claim on an already hard-pressed university administration. In large part, the re-engineering fueled implementation of the first strategic plan's recommendations. What a success story!

7

Looking Beyond Technical Services: The Second Change Cycle at ULS

Building on the momentum created by the re-engineering of Technical Services (TS) and the creation of the Strategic Plan, the ULS was committed to instituting a system of ongoing change. Implementation of initial strategic plan priorities set the stage for the ULS to address a variety of emerging academic library issues and challenges. The ULS decided to focus next on improving service for users—having defined its primary clientele as the University of Pittsburgh community—and intent on determining specifically on how all public services units could "ensure maximum benefit of Library resources and services to the university community" (Knapp, Miller, and Thomes n.d., under "Introduction").

THE SECOND CYCLE BEGINS: RETHINKING PUBLIC SERVICES

The introduction to the ULS's final report about restructuring public services points out that by the close of 2002, many goals of the 1996 strategic planning process had been fully met and others were in the process of being implemented. The ULS was ready for another major cycle of change and moved forward with Public Services as the focus for the next round of strategic planning.

As in the re-engineering of TS, the ULS deemed it essential to find an objective outside expert familiar with evolving national trends and best practices to assist in rethinking public services. Thus Association of Research Libraries consultant Julia Blixrud was enlisted to help develop a process for identifying unmet user needs and for "designing new products and services that go to the heart of ... customers' needs" (Knapp 2004, 165), as those needs continued to evolve and to reflect changes in society at large. The consultant's report advised that in order to be ready for the ULS's next annual budget request, the rethinking process would be "concentrated and intense" (Blixrud n.d., under "Background"). Blixrud's recommendation took the form of a narrative together with a chart showing activities, inputs, outputs, and persons/entities involved in the process, along with specification of the type of support to expect from the Association of Research Libraries Office of Leadership and Management Services (ARL/OLMS) for each stage, and another chart showing the time line for the process. She recommended a six-stage process for the rethinking effort: Preliminary Stage (planning the project, establishing the study team, and preparation of ULS staff) from October 2002 through the end of that November; Stage I (data inventory) conducted simultaneously; Stage II (literature review and identification of best practices) from October through December 2002; Stage III (focus groups and analysis of data); Stage IV (goal-setting based on Stages I through III and articulation of recommendations regarding appropriate goals, objectives, and budgetary support) from December 2002 through the end of February 2003; and finally Stage V (staff training in assessment theory and practice along with identification of unit objectives and creation of measurement tools for assessment) to be conducted from March through April 2003 (Blixrud n.d.).

The first step in this second cycle of change within the ULS would be forming a small task force to (1) determine the areas within Public Services needing improvement and (2) develop strategies for moving forward. This group, dubbed the Rethinking Public Services Team (RPST), was composed of librarians from various units within Public Services, including the head of reference, the coordinator for library instruction, and the head of the Engineering Library. Its charge was developing a road map for immediate and long-term change within Public Services and to "provide enough information for the development of a budget to achieve the stated goals" (Knapp, Miller, and Thomes n.d., under "Rethinking Public Services"). The group's initial task would be to determine what was working well and what needed improvement.

The Rationale for Change

As the final report of the RPST makes clear, in large part the raison d'être of all public services units and staff is to serve as a human interface that bridges the gap between the rich (and inescapably complex) information environment comprised of library resources and services and the limited experience, skills, and abilities of many would-be users of this wealth of information. "It is the role of public services personnel to facilitate the use of Library resources and services, to help ensure their maximum utility to faculty and students and to the University community" (Knapp, Miller, and Thomes n.d., under "Introduction").

This document drives home the importance of reference, instructional, circulation, and allied services in complementing the collections and cataloging that have long been considered hallmarks of distinction among ARL libraries. "Excellent collections and sophisticated systems of description and organization in combination with sufficient numbers of competent, knowledgeable, and service-oriented personnel create a world-class library. Without any one element, the others cannot function at a sufficiently sophisticated level to be called 'world-class'" (Knapp, Miller, and Thomes n.d., under "Introduction").

At the inception of the new initiative, Public Services was not ideally positioned for the new challenges that any such large-scale process would inevitably entail. This critical part of the ULS had basically remained at steady state for some time. "Public Services in the library system had experienced no significant administrative or functional change in several years," aside from incorporating appropriate new technologies into reference, circulation, and Interlibrary loan service points (Knapp 2004, 165).

Based on the consultant's recommendations, the task force embarked on a three-pronged approach to gathering data: inventory all locally available data, review relevant national data, and gather additional local data in the form of focus groups with users.

Initial Data Scan

The next step for the team was to determine what data were available and what would need to be collected. Traditionally, libraries have done a good job of collecting statistics that are easy to collect—that is, data such as the number of people entering the physical facility, the number of books circulated, the number of reserve items circulated, and so on. What hasn't been captured or documented nearly as well via traditional data collection tools is user satisfaction with the facilities, services, and collections. The team composed a list of obvious sources of internal data, which included data collected for the Association of Research Libraries annual statistics report, data reported to other regional and national entities, data collected as part of the ULS strategic planning process, and data gathered as part of a previous Public Services study, the Quality Services Survey (QSS) of all public services units conducted in 1997. Additionally, the team compiled a list of data that was available from various units across the ULS but not necessarily reported outside. This list included data on reshelving, building/user counts, the number of requests by hour at various desks, and so on.

As is the case in any study, what the team discovered as part of the background research process proved useful to the ULS in a broader context. The team's review of local data proved beneficial, not only for the Public Services restructuring but also as an indication of areas within Public Services where data collection techniques could be improved. What the RPST found overall was a lack of consistency, centralization, and standardization and generally the need for more thorough review of the data collected. Often it is not until a large project such as this one is undertaken that the quality and quantity of data is closely scrutinized in academic libraries. One of the tangential benefits of rethinking the reference process was that it contributed to the formation of a ULS-wide group to inventory and regularly review data collection procedures and reporting.

Review and Evaluation of Local Data

After a brief preliminary review of Public Services data, the team was ready to undertake a more thorough analysis of the nature and quantity of data available to inform their process. One of the first steps of the process was to inventory all existing Public Services data and to examine closely the process for the collection of the data. This review was carefully constructed to ensure inclusion of any and all areas within public services articulated in the previous strategic plan and thus to provide a good foundation for the new strategic plan due by March 2003.

Alignment of RPST Efforts with the Existing Strategic Plan

In a complex organization such as the ULS, it is sometimes difficult to know precisely which units and functions fall within specific departments. Before the RPST could even begin the data inventory process, they believed it essential to specify which units and corresponding functions fell within the purview of the study. These included the following:

Units Comprising Public Services

- Reference
- Instruction
- Circulation and reserves
- Document delivery
- Interlibrary loan
- Government publications
- Distributed public services (departmental libraries, archives, regional libraries)

Key Strategic Plan Issues

The team also felt it important to look at implementation of the current strategic plan to see what, if any, specific issues had been highlighted as key to the optimal functioning of the units outlined previously. These issues included:

- The paramount need to configure the organization and deploy staff in a way that would optimize the ULS's ability to meet client needs.
- The desire to enhance cooperation among library units and to mobilize the resulting synergy in delivering more effective service.
- The perception that the library-centric tendency to "harbor complexity in our processes" (J. Miller, Thomes, and Knapp n.d., under "Strategic Plan") must give way to a new simplicity that would benefit patrons.
- The need to "nurture and encourage responsiveness [to client needs] and creativity [in meeting those needs] in [front line public services] staff" (J. Miller, Thomes, and Knapp n.d., under "Strategic Plan").
- The conviction that staff must be empowered to cut through layers of bureaucracy to "do the right thing for users" (J. Miller, Thomes, and Knapp n.d., under "Strategic Plan").
- The necessity of continuing to serve two masters, in developing and supporting exemplary collections of both print and non-print materials (J. Miller, Thomes, and Knapp n.d.).

QSS: An Early Benchmark

Although somewhat dated, the 1997 Quality Service Survey (QSS), another internally produced document, was significant to the RPST's work primarily for two reasons. First, it represented one of the earliest ULS efforts to determine a percentage of users accessing ULS services and resources remotely. Second, now that more data had been collected, it served as a baseline for longitudinal analysis of changes in remote access. That said, its findings had to be considered in context. It was conducted before migration to the Voyager library system and before other significant changes were made in the ULS (J. Miller, Thomes, and Knapp n.d.).

Initial Hypotheses from Local Data

After reviewing all the available local data, including earlier user surveys and the findings and recommendations of previous studies, the team was able to make a few preliminary observations related to patron use of ULS physical facilities, resources in print and electronic formats, and emerging user expectations. This information was valuable because it gave the group something of a foundation for its work and a place from which to move forward. An exhaustive examination of available local data regarding on-site reference—library entrance gate counts, in-house circulation of materials, and statistics for remote use of electronic resources—was coupled with data gathered as part of the QSS, which was primarily qualitative rather than quantitative in nature

One conclusion was obvious immediately: In-library use by ULS patrons remained fairly stable across time, while virtual use was increasing exponentially (J. Miller, Thomes, and Knapp n.d.). This was a fundamental consideration that the team had to keep in mind as they moved forward, and it ultimately informed much of the process. Additional analysis produced several preliminary conclusions that were the starting point for further investigation:

- On-site and off-site visits appeared to be linked and to drive each other.
- Remote users might be underserved in terms of instruction and reference assistance.
- Public services should be extended to remote users as well as made available to on-site users (J. Miller, Thomes, and Knapp n.d.).

National Data Sources

Although early observations of the RPST formed a good basis for the group's thinking, it was evident that an examination of several national studies would likely be helpful as a way of identifying needs and characteristics common to most academic library users. On a national level, the team reviewed the 2002 Online Computer Library Center (OCLC) White Paper titled *Information Habits of College Students,* as well as a report issued by the Council on Library and Information Resources and the Digital Library Federation titled *Dimensions and Use of the Scholarly Information Environment* and LibQUAL+™ data.

Council on Library and Information Resources Report

Administered in 2001 and published in 2002, this report was a joint undertaking of the Council on Library and Information Resources (CLIR) and the Digital Library Federation. It surveyed more than 3,000 faculty, grads, and undergrads at public and private universities and at liberal arts colleges with the intent of determining "the relevance of existing and possible future services … [and the] library's value in the context of the scholarly information environment" (J. Miller, Thomes, and Knapp n.d., under "CLIR Data Collection"). The following findings from this survey proved useful for the RPST's study of public services trends and in particular contributed to better understanding of user expectations in a changing online environment.

Print versus Nonprint Collections

- For research and teaching, heavier use was made of print collections than electronic resources.
- Electronic resources were seen as supplements to print materials, rather than as a replacement for them, and users expected there to be a mix of print and nonprint materials in library collections.

User Behavior and Attitudes

- Forty percent of library users were increasing the amount of time that they worked and studied away from campus.
- Undergraduates gravitated to online resources for all assignments and research projects.
- A lack of training in how to search was regarded as an impediment to doing good research.

The Position of Libraries in the Information Environment

- Although nearly one-third of respondents rated the library as the most important source for information, the majority of respondents considered the library as *one of many* important sources of information.
- Academic libraries were trusted as an authoritative source of information.
- The way libraries collected and organized information was regarded as an important part of the research process.
- Then, as now, libraries operated within complex institutional and information environments characterized by heterogeneous user populations with varied levels of sophistication and support needs (J. Miller, Thomes, and Knapp n.d.).

OCLC White Paper

Another document that provided the team with a wealth of information about user behavior was the OCLC's *The Information Habits of College Students*. Because the report examined information seeking needs and habits of students from a variety of different academic institutions, it proved instrumental for the team's work. The following are some of the most useful findings:

User Values, Perceptions, and Characteristics:

> [Students] value accurate and up-to-date information.
> [They] value face-to-face assistance.
> [They] regard faculty as key resources [for information].
> [They] lack awareness of library resources and services.
> [They] recognize [that] they need some assistance to search print and electronic resources effectively. (Knapp, Miller, and Thomes n.d., under "OCLC White Paper")

Additional insights presented in this national survey that the RPST found valuable included the following:

User Values and Needs

- Both students and library staff value accuracy.
- Remote users need open access to the library's electronic resources.
- An academic library's electronic resources should be tightly integrated with other campus web sites.

Library Imperatives

- Navigational guides should be clear and readily available.
- To be effective, libraries must be "relentless" about instruction, promotion of their services and resources, and customer service (J. Miller, Thomes, and Knapp n.d., under "White Paper Recommendations").

LibQUAL+™ Findings

Another key source of user data, both local and national, was LibQUAL+™. The task force analyzed LibQUAL+™ data collected since the ULS first participated in the 2000 pilot of the LibQUAL+™ instrument. This data provided comparisons over time between the ULS and its ARL peers in several key public service areas. Amassed over several years, a significant amount of data from this ARL project had not yet been thoroughly analyzed until the RPST took a closer look at it. This wealth of data was an invaluable source of additional information for rethinking public services, particularly data enabling Pitt to benchmark its survey responses against national averages for the same dimensions among ARL libraries. These data continue to represent a unique opportunity to compare national trends to local phenomena. On an ongoing basis, LibQUAL+™ data give the ULS a foundation for (1) assessing the impact of changes already implemented and (2) identifying what remains to be done in terms of improving public services and other aspects of library operations.

It is instructive to look at LibQUAL+™ data both in the aggregate (e.g., all respondents, all those reporting library use, and all classifying themselves as nonusers) and within demographic segments (undergraduates, graduates, and faculty). By doing that type of detailed analysis, the RPST harvested a great deal of useful information.

Undergraduates. Among undergraduates, Pitt had a higher number of nonusers than the ARL average at the time the RPST was looking at the data: Undergraduates reporting that they never use on-site facilities was 1.4 percent for ARL libraries in the aggregate, versus 3.5 percent in this category at Pitt. Similarly, the number of Pitt subjects in the "never use" category regarding electronic resources was 11.4 percent, compared with the ARL average of 8.4 percent. These findings concerned the RPST greatly and were the focal point for development of several new services targeted at undergrads.

On a more positive note, University of Pittsburgh undergrads were satisfied with individualized attention in the library, the web site's usability and content, turnaround for Interlibrary loan requests, the library as a place to study, and the willingness of library personnel to help. Despite the apparent satisfaction with the ULS's Web presence as indicated by LibQUAL+™ data, user testing by the ULS revealed that the Web's functionality could be improved. (For more detail, see the section of this chapter labeled "Institutional Change.") Users were consistently highly satisfied with the willingness of staff to help them with any request. This was a great asset to the team's work, as it indicated that staff's user-centeredness had been communicated to users over time.

The LibQUAL+™ dimension of least satisfaction for undergraduates at the University of Pittsburgh was the library as "a haven for quiet and solitude" (Knapp, Miller, and Thomes n.d., under "Undergraduates"). As mentioned elsewhere in this chapter, the ULS interpreted this negative rating as an opportunity to make improvements. It was later concluded that what users found most off-putting was the policy of "no food or drink" in a facility that was open nearly 24 hours per day. This policy seemed excessively restrictive, and of even greater concern was the fact that the job of "policing" fell to the reference librarians, the people who at the same time were attempting to seem friendly and approachable. In response to this negative feedback, the library began permitting covered containers of liquid throughout the library, opened a café, and reconfigured the public spaces with soft furniture and more flexible work stations. These changes resulted in the libraries becoming both more functional and more welcoming to users. These measures also relieved the public services staff of the burden of enforcing an unpopular and difficult-to-effect policy. Knapp (2004) credits these measures with "soaring assessments of the library as place in subsequent LibQUAL+™ surveys" (165) and also with positive strides made in making the librarians and staff seem more approachable.

One of the best ways to utilize the data in rethinking specific areas of operation is to examine the data, not just in total, but by user group. This perspective suggested some of the most effective changes that the ULS implemented.

Graduate Students. Not surprising for an academic library supporting many acclaimed graduate programs, the ULS scored better than ARL averages for on-site graduate library use: At only 1 percent reporting nonuse of library premises, Pitt graduate students significantly undercut the ARL average of 1.29 percent respondents who identified themselves as nonusers of on-site facilities.

Graduate students were most satisfied with individualized attention and employees who instill confidence—with ratings well above national averages for these dimensions. Like Pitt undergrads, they indicated approval of the web site, Interlibrary loan, and general willingness of staff to help. They were more appreciative of the library as a place for "quiet and solitude" as well as for "reflection and creativity" than undergrads were (Knapp, Miller, and Thomes n.d., under "LibQUAL: Graduate Students").

In contrast to the substantial amount of positive feedback about employees and the building, the University of Pittsburgh grad students expressed dissatisfaction with the completeness of journal runs and with remote access, findings consistent with ARL findings for the same demographic group. Of greater concern was their reported use of electronic resources, significantly lower than ARL averages. Among graduate student survey respondents, Pitt had 6.84 percent nonusers of digital resources, versus the ARL average of only 4 percent. These findings, like the few negatives reported by undergraduates at the University of Pittsburgh, were addressed by development of new services mentioned later in this chapter.

Teaching Faculty. The University of Pittsburgh faculty reported lower than national on-site use, with nonusers at 2.44 percent as compared with the ARL average of 1.87 percent. This finding should be considered, however, in the context of use of electronic library resources that far outpaced national averages: Only 1.22 percent of those surveyed at Pitt responded that they never use the library's digital resources, versus a whopping ARL average of 3.37. So much is available digitally that Pitt faculty members are spared unnecessary trips to the library.

Areas of satisfaction among teaching faculty mirrored those for grads (dimensions of the library as place) and areas of general satisfaction for both graduate and undergraduate students: the web site, Interlibrary loan, and service qualities associated with staff. Like faculty the world over, they were highly critical of collections and access—indicating dissatisfaction with completeness of journal runs, the lack of comprehensiveness of print collections, and insufficient desktop access to electronic resources at home and at campus offices. At first blush, these findings might seem odd, considering University of Pittsburgh teaching faculty 's higher-than-ARL-average use of digital resources . But faculty members throughout academe know that more can always be done to serve them better. What else can be expected from a group with such finely honed critical thinking abilities and such overwhelming demands on their time?

Aggregate Ratings across All LibQUAL+™ Groups

After reviewing the data by demographic segments, the team turned its attention to patterns in user responses across user groups. To recap, in all groups, the ULS received the highest LibQUAL+™ respondent ratings on three dimensions of service within the category Affect of Service: (1) willingness to help users, (2) giving users individual attention, and (3) employees who instill confidence. In many ways, this was the most positive news the RTPS group could have hoped to receive. As no doubt most academic librarians will agree, effecting positive change with regard to the service commitment of your staff is much more difficult than correcting deficiencies in collections or facilities. A high degree of user satisfaction with "Affect of Service" revealed a fundamental strength upon which the ULS could build. This high level of satisfaction held true across user groups at Pitt but particularly with respect to graduate students.

However, in two aspects of service quality, the ULS failed across the board to exceed user minimum expectation by a significant margin: (1) dependability in handling users' service problems and (2) employees who have the knowledge to answer users' questions. In addition, as mentioned previously, analysis of faculty and student responses revealed several aspects of service that needed closer scrutiny. Accordingly, the RPST extracted from LibQUAL+™ general findings about the need for improvement in four areas of ULS operations: (1) customer service, (2) instruction, (3) in-person assistance, and (4) document delivery of physical items (Knapp, Miller, and Thomes n.d.). This analysis of LibQUAL+™ patterns was subsequently confirmed and refined by information from focus groups.

Responses to User Data

All of the aggregate and demographically segmented user data from LibQUAL+™ with national research into user preferences and user behavior provided the RPST with a great road map for rethinking public services within the ULS. Before any changes could take place, however, it was essential that the organization be prepared internally for significant change and moving forward with recommendations from users.

As Knapp points out in an article about using LibQUAL+™ findings to make decisions and guide policy, staff resistance to negative survey findings is common and completely understandable: "It is easy ... to become defensive and say 'They're wrong' or 'they aren't aware of ... ' or 'we already do that.'" Still the user remains the final arbiter of his or her own perceptions; and the academic library needs to address poor ratings, regardless of whether those perceptions reflect reality or merely document a user's inexperience or lack of sophistication about library systems and processes. "Your challenge in the library is to address these perceptions and come up with ways to increase user satisfaction" (Knapp 2004, 161).

Knapp (2004, 161) then lists several ways to address issues and bring LibQUAL+™ scores up: Do more and better customer service training for all levels of staff; do a better job of promoting services with which patrons are not familiar; and finally design new services to address issues about access or collections which have emerged from user input.

It should be noted that the last strategy Knapp (2004) mentions as a means to change perceptions—new services—will sometimes be the critical factor in improving user perceptions of library service. This is because of the possibility that the library can come up with a new service that will meet the client's needs *much better* than a current service that seems adequate or even exemplary to staff. Not all legacy services must be abandoned or even changed significantly. But library personnel can't *make* people want or value something that does not benefit them. And library personnel lack the power to set the priorities by which users will judge library service. For these reasons, librarians are well advised to steer clear of a selling mentality until they have completed other steps in the marketing planning process, particularly gathering open-ended information about user needs and preferences.

Chapter 2 of this book discusses some of the ways to customize the elements of promotion, including fine-tuning the type or types of promotion (e.g., personal selling versus advertising, or demonstrations, or contests, or giveaways), the message connecting your service or product with benefits for the user, the chosen medium or media best suited to reach the target market, the timing and frequency of promotional events, and other aspects of promotion. Any of these strategies would be consistent with Knapp's advice about improving user perceptions. The University of Pittsburgh's ULS takes such promotional issues extremely seriously, having engaged a professional marketing firm to assist ULS staff in this critical dimension of interaction with users and potential users of the libraries.

Further Collection of Local Data

In addition to examining national studies and trend data, it was essential to verify how well local survey data and other information about ULS users conformed to or departed from national trends. Only if University of Pittsburgh users closely aligned to the national averages would it make sense to implement changes based on findings and recommendations from these larger studies. Moreover, whereas LibQUAL+™ collects a significant amount of data at the local level, its scores and comments often are useful only as an indicator of broad concerns or general areas that need further investigation. Typically there is not enough specific information in LibQUAL+™ responses to identify the fine points of user dissatisfaction with a service or collection. Such details are critical to addressing user concerns and improving negative aspect of their library experience. It is often necessary to meet with people individually or in groups to coax out a sufficient level of detail.

After synthesizing key data from national studies with existing local data, the RPST had a solid foundation from which to begin identifying where they needed more details before they could articulate specific recommendations for change. One of the most natural places to begin this process of collecting additional specific local information was via open staff meetings.

Staff Input from Open Meetings

In any library, the most significant source of current and historical data regarding local users, library facilities, and library resources is, of course, the staff. As the re-engineering of Technical Services had demonstrated, not only does asking for staff input elicit valuable firsthand knowledge, the resulting dialogue also promotes staff engagement and buy-in, increasing the chances of successful implementation of recommended changes. The value that ULS staff input contributed to the overall success of the process cannot be overstated. Not only did they prove the best source for validating the data gathered via LibQUAL+™ and other surveys. They also affirmed that much of the national user trend analysis was relevant to ULS user needs and expectations.

To ensure that all staff had the opportunity to contribute, the team sponsored two open meetings. Open-ended discussion topics at these meetings included the following questions: (1) What do users say they need from the library? (2) What existing services could meet user needs better if changed? (3) What new services should be developed? (4) What are users doing in the library (research, recreation, socializing, etc.)? (5) What is important about remote interaction; how have interactions with users changed since two years ago? (6) What does "public service" mean in the context of an online environment? and (7) How should public service be assessed?

On the whole, staff comments revealed fairly sophisticated observations about user behavior and user needs as well as superb understanding of the fundamentals of good customer service and assessment. The following lists give selected examples of marketing and assessment concepts implicit in staff comments.

Examples of Marketing Concepts

- We need to [better] understand what users need. Not what *we* think they need.
- User need survey should be a normal [part of] work in library.
- How to survey users who don't use the library as to how we can bring them in?
- Find the causes of frustration of the patrons and accommodate these: [the photocopy system, real-time reference, adequate access to computers].
- Multiple ways to assist patrons: phone/in-person/e-mail/chat?
- The understanding that there is no separation between [libraries units]. ALL ULS is *public services.*
- Users need seamless access to all resources in [the] ULS and licensed by [the] ULS.
- Mailroom service more accurate (sending [library notices and announcements] to correct places) [internal marketing].
- Better communication between libraries, awareness of what is offered in other collections [internal marketing].
- Create teleconferencing classrooms between campuses for training [internal marketing]. (Knapp, Miller, and Thomes n.d., under "ULS Personnel Input")

Examples of Assessment Concepts

- Assessment tied to outcomes needed … [for] example: assess impact of electronic services on user behavior.
- Need to systematically track and analyze weblogs and other metrics of use.
- Collect reference stats automatically and all the time. (Knapp, Miller, and Thomes n.d., under "ULS Personnel Input")

Important Staff Observations about Users

In pulling together all of the ideas discussed in the meetings, three especially important observations surfaced: (1) Many clients need assistance in identifying and using information; (2) they also need a broad range of other types of assistance from public service staff; and (3) they do not understand or simply are not aware of many library policies and procedures. The fact that these observations predominated in all the open meetings was a good sign of staff readiness to initiate positive changes. It showed that staff were cognizant of the issues that had been raised in early studies and collected user data and that as a group they realized that the ULS would have to tackle these thorny issues. Best of all, these comments indicated that the staff would commit to the hard work ahead in addressing the issues and concerns of their users.

Using Focus Groups to Gather Data

In any library, one of the fastest, cheapest, and most convenient ways of gathering detailed user data is via focus groups. If constructed in such a way as to be truly representative of the population represented, focus groups can provide the library with rich user data. In accordance with the ULS's nonprescriptive approach to gathering user information, focus groups were employed by the RPST to gather specifics about areas of general concern extracted from analysis of LibQUAL+™ responses. This practice has been incorporated into ULS operations, so that a continuous stream of information about user preferences and perceptions is available to guide ULS planning and operations. In preparation for making changes in public services, the ULS conducted 12 one-hour focus groups comprised of faculty, undergraduates, and graduate students from all disciplines potentially served by the ULS—some users and some nonusers—for a total of 123 participants. They invited a random sample of individuals from the pool of frequent users of the library identified by ULS staff and a random sample of the general population of the Pitt campus.

Areas to Probe. One of the keys to successful information gathering with focus groups is identifying those key areas where more detailed data collection is needed and asking specific open-ended questions to elicit more robust information. Based on areas where LibQUAL+™ showed that respondents had issues, the ULS crafted 10 focus group questions in order to probe for detail about exactly what dimensions of service were and were not up to par, "additional substantive, specific information on what aspects of our services our users were most satisfied with, what services worked for them, and most importantly, what we could do to improve their perceptions of our services and resources" (Knapp 2004, 166). Areas examined included how (for what purposes) people used the library; from what locations they performed library tasks; how frequently they used ULS facilities, resources, and services; and what they found frustrating versus what things met with their approval and satisfied them.

Participant Responses. Focus group comments ran the gamut from suggestions for improvements in the physical environment (e.g., cleaner bathrooms, less cigarette smoke from outside the doors, incandescent lighting and soft seating to create a warmer environment) to the need to better accommodate known library use patterns (e.g., work stations and other spaces configured so that people can study and work together on small group projects) to the need for greater accuracy and functionality in PITTcat to proposing better support of remote users via extending research assistance to outside the library (e.g., providing trained help in places like residence halls) to the desirability of more fluid on-site reference assistance via roaming librarians equipped with PDAs and other wireless devices.

Focus Group Themes. Major themes teased out of faculty/university staff/ student focus group perceptions by the RPST included the following:

The Library's Value: Users expect library resources to be accurate and current.

Public Service Staff's Role: Competent and knowledgeable in-person assistance is important.

Formats

- Users value electronic resources and especially appreciate desktop access.
- Most patrons indicated that they continue to use both print and electronic resources and expect seamless access to both.
- Humanities users tend to rely more on print sources.
- Number of patrons who use electronic sources exclusively is growing, particularly in the applied science disciplines.

Research Skills:

- Teaching faculty members feel that their grad students lack the skills to do effective library research.
- Users are concerned about the pace at which new information is added to ULS collections and about their ability to keep up with the flood of information.
- Users admit to a lack of awareness of library resources and services.

Synthesizing the Data

The RPST now faced the task of synthesizing data from the various national studies with local user input and statistics along with library staff input and then extracting key information to guide the change process for ULS public services. They found that many observational data pertaining to ULS users were consistent with data from national sources. The following general conclusions about the Public Services environment within the ULS were supported by multiple sources of data:

The Library's Value: "Libraries are expected to contain high-quality information and accurate and accessible finding aids" (Knapp, Miller, and Thomes n.d., under "Consistent Findings").

Public Service Staff's Role: "Competent assistance from library personnel is highly valued" (Knapp, Miller, and Thomes n.d., under "Consistent Finding").

Research Skills: "Users lack awareness of many library resources and skills" (Knapp, Miller, and Thomes n.d., under "Consistent Findings").

Formats

- Both print and electronic resources are highly valued and used.
- Increasingly users are beginning the research process online.
- Research practices differ greatly by discipline and status (faculty/student). (Knapp, Miller, and Thomes n.d., under "Consistent Findings")

User Expectations/Attitudes

- Both physical and virtual library space is important to patrons.
- Seamless transition from identification to retrieval of information is important. (Knapp, Miller, and Thomes n.d., under "Consistent Findings")

FOLLOWING THROUGH ON RPST'S WORK

Having thus melded available information about national trends, local user patterns and expectations revealed by LibQUAL+™ findings, and other data examined together with information gleaned from local sources (open meetings with libraries staff, focus groups, the ULS strategic plan, and the QSS), the team was ready to complete its report. This report would include suggestions for the modification of existing services, the introduction of several new services, and a renewed emphasis on regularly scheduled Public Services training, as well as recommendations for organizational and structural change within Public Services. Again, the goal was to focus to as great an extent as possible on emerging use patterns and user expectations. The report was to be as user driven as possible and to demonstrate that the ULS was committed to listening to users and responding as appropriate.

Recommendations of the Rethinking Public Services Team

After thorough analysis and synthesis of available information, the RPST identified four broad areas that had presented themselves as the focus of the team's recommendations for implementing changes intended to bring public services into closer alignment with user needs and expectations for service. The final report notes that—although the strategic plan put a formidable technology infrastructure and an unprecedented array or print and digital resources into place—further effort and commitment of personnel and other funds would be required to "ensure that the resources are used to their full research and educational potential" (Knapp, Miller, and Thomes n.d., under "Recommendations"). In order to best meet user needs, the RPST recommended that the ULS:

1. Develop targeted instruction programs for undergraduate and graduate students and work proactively with [teaching] faculty to integrate library research skills training into the curriculum and at the course level.
2. Develop a creative outreach program to promote library resources and services in both the physical and virtual library environments.
3. Focus on customer service training to develop an agile, savvy, and effective group of public service staff to facilitate patrons' use of the libraries.
4. Establish an ongoing evaluation and assessment program for Public Services. (Knapp, Miller, and Thomes n.d., under "Recommendations")

Acceptance of Key Recommendations

As in the reorganization of TS, the ULS administration's response to the RPST's recommendations modeled the cardinal rule of strategic planning: Take stock of your best and most unique strengths and put resources behind your best opportunities—those closely aligned with your organization's fundamental purposes and also the needs of your stakeholders.

What is more, in each of these instances (re-engineering TS and rethinking Public Services), the ULS established its commitment to systemic and ongoing change management. Appropriate action from the leadership to back up rhetoric about change is critical to forging the true organizational *partnership* that is a prerequisite for establishing a change-centric organizational environment.

Instead of (a) shelving the staff committee or team's careful study and thoughtful recommendations for improvements or (b) making cosmetic changes that would avoid ruffling anyone's feathers, the ULS administration stepped up to the plate, providing the funding and other resources needed for implementation of meaningful change. Any other action would have seemed dismissive of the staff's work and likely would have sounded the death knell for any future change initiative within the organization.

INSTITUTIONAL CHANGE

The final report of the RPST contained several specific recommendations for revising older services and implementing an array of new user-friendly services to address customer needs and wants. Based on subsequent user studies, implementation of these recommendations has proved highly successful. Even more significant in terms of organizational change was the RPST's recommendation that the ULS not implement any new service without having designed a mechanism and time line for the evaluation of the new service was adopted by the administration. This policy has ensured that all new services proposed since the completion of the task force's work are subject to timely and appropriate review before they are instituted. It also ensures that in the future there will be a substantial amount of comparative data for the evaluation of existing services and implementation of new services.

Bringing Remote Users into the Fold

Ask a Librarian

As discussed in the national studies, remote users constitute a growing and underserved constituency of most academic libraries. Local surveys and focus groups confirmed the applicability of this observation to the ULS user community. In response to this identified need, the RPST's report suggested the development of several new services. In fall 2004, a new distributed reference service known as *Ask a Librarian Live!* was launched. It was intended primarily as a means of delivering research assistance to remote users.

For some time, remote users have had the option of contacting the ULS via e-mail reference, which during the regular term is monitored seven days a week by librarians who answer basic question and refer specialized queries to the library unit or person best able to answer them. A response within 24 hours is guaranteed to users of this service.

Building on the success of e-mail reference, the newer interactive digital (aka chat) reference service is staffed at peak hours (Monday through Friday). It lets Pitt users "chat" with a librarian online and in real time. In addition, the traditional reference options of getting face-to-face help at the reference desk, making a phone call, or scheduling an appointment for a research consultation offering in-depth individual assistance are still very much alive at the ULS.

Web Usability

Another user-centric outcome from the RPS initiative was a usability study of the ULS web site in order to align this very public face of the library with user expectations and to incorporate new web design practices where appropriate for Pitt users. Rather than being library-centric and stopping short at giving users what professionals felt was best for them, the ULS conducted extensive and painstaking tests of the web architecture's effectiveness.

Librarians sat with users and observed them searching in order to see firsthand how they interacted with the web pages and to learn what would work best for them. The following were key conclusions from the observations: Users expected a transparent "Google-like" interface that they could use without a steep learning curve; some searches were general (interdisciplinary) but others were discipline-specific; and both novice and experienced searchers desired a

Figure 7.1
Zoom mouse pad

federated search capability that would allow searching across multiple databases simultaneously and weeding out duplicate references.

The result was *Zoom!*, a federated search tool delivering significant benefits to all users but especially those with remote access and those on-site users reluctant to request assistance. Its quick find feature, located on the ULS home page, puts neophyte users into a number of the largest research databases provided by the ULS, where they are likely to find information relevant to their topics. Alternatively, the sophisticate can use this federated searching tool to simultaneously search any combination of online resources provided by the ULS: databases, electronic journals, PITTcat, and other digital resources. The graphic in Figure 7.1 shows the logo used on mouse pads and other promotional material.

Removing Barriers for All Users

Outcomes of the RPS initiative epitomize chapter 2's advice about combating barriers to library use with benefits for users. A number of new ULS services were designed in order to make using the library as seamless an experience as possible for the University of Pittsburgh teaching and learning community.

Wireless Access

Wireless access is another great new service. It accommodates the nonlinear nature of research—in which following up one good source may lead the user down a different path and back to the library catalog to forage after additional call numbers and locations. It also facilitates the eclectic list of tasks users want to perform in the library (checking e-mail, completing course requirements, etc.). And finally, it frees users from the constraint of having to depend exclusively on fixed work stations in arbitrarily designated physical locations. Installed first in Hillman, wireless capability is being extended across the Oakland campus and will soon be available in all libraries.

Some users bring their own laptops and other digital equipment to the University. But the ULS also purchased 30 laptops for use by those who don't come in with a personal portable electronic device. By fall 2004, more than 200 students had registered to use these laptops, which are equipped with storage drives (for CDs, zip disks, etc.) and which have the capacity to search the catalog, to browse the Internet and Web for amusement or to complete class assignments, and to send, receive, and read e-mail from any location in the library. Individuals use them for projects or study groups as well. This greatly facilitates collaborative work in library locations where there may not be a regular work station.

Electronic Reserves

Another new service designed to eliminate barriers and expedite service is electronic reserves, a very useful addition to the suite of digital products and services offered by the ULS. Notorious for slow turnaround times, insufficient numbers of copies, long waits for large classes, and inexplicable losses from its closed stacks, the traditional paper-based reserve room has long been a source of frustration to teaching faculty and students alike.

Recognizing the greater convenience and reliability of electronic reserves, the ULS piloted e-reserves as one of the first products of the RPS effort. As of fall 2005, professors teaching more than 200 courses had used electronic reserves to give students access to course-related materials: links to full text articles contained within ULS-licensed databases, articles scanned as PDFs, book chapters, and links to ULS-held electronic books. Once posted in the e-reserve space, this course-related content can be accessed via the library catalog's reserve module, through Blackboard, or as a link from any web page by simply inserting the course site's URL. Access is controlled by a unique password associated with a specific course. Course material is available to students for the duration of the term but not beyond the end of the term. Not surprisingly, the evaluations of the electronic reserve service have been positive and the number of paper reserves has decreased dramatically.

HelpHub

Cognizant that not all barriers are tangible, the ULS instituted the student-staffed peer counseling service known as *HelpHub* to address several emerging user expectations. First was undergraduate students' desire for in-person assistance in study areas outside the library. Second was the tendency of some users to seek help from other students. Having heard repeatedly in focus groups that some undergrads were more comfortable asking a friend for library assistance than approaching a member of the professional staff, the ULS decided to incorporate this input into designing a new service instead of taking the library-centric tack of fighting to change user behavior. The ULS inaugurated *HelpHub* in concert with Pitt's university-wide commitment to enhancing the undergraduate learning experience.

The result was a highly successful (and relatively inexpensive) peer-to-peer instructional service staffed by graduate student assistants from Pitt's School of Information Sciences, Department of Library Science. *HelpHub* staffers are trained to answer simple informational questions, introduce the ULS home page, and refer more complicated queries to the appropriate full-time staff member. They work at various locations outside the libraries in wireless zones around the campus where students like to study. The logo used to publicize the *HelpHub* service is shown in Figure 7.2.

Figure 7.2
HelpHub logo

Filling Collection Gaps

One of the areas of perceived user dissatisfaction was inadequate access to journal articles. In both the LibQUAL+™ and focus group sessions, users argued that after identifying appropriate sources of information, they were frustrated by the difficulty of locating appropriate and timely full-text information. LibQUAL+™ results from teaching faculty and graduate students were unequivocal about the desire for access to the full publication archive of journals and about dismay at gaps in the ULS serials holdings. Accepting this challenge, the ULS has channeled resources into a number of convenient new options for obtaining the content of articles, books, and other materials needed for papers and projects.

Electronic Backfiles. In response to concerns about gaps in the collection, the ULS has begun systematically purchasing electronic back files to fill gaps (six such packages were acquired in 2003–2004 alone), rather than taking a giant step backward by pouring great quantities of its person power and materials budget into filling gaps with paper-based copies. Unlike paper, electronic content is not subject to vandalism, being misplaced, or being damaged by the lack of control over humidity, natural and artificial light, or other preservation problems. Even better, the digital content of an article can be read and printed out by many users simultaneously and from either an on-site or a remote work station.

Links to Article Content. Of course, in and of themselves, electronic back files are a mixed blessing if users have to search multiple databases to find the text they need. But the ULS has removed this barrier as well. All users benefit from the implementation of software (Serials Solutions), connecting them seamlessly to the full text of periodical and journal articles in any database from which Pitt users are licensed to retrieve articles. Instead of having to guess or ask a librarian where to find the archive for a given article, Pitt users need only click on a live link to one or more sources of that article text. By fall 2004, use of full text at the University of Pittsburgh's libraries had already increased an astounding 500 percent. It continues to grow by leaps and bounds.

Enhancing Physical Access

Document Delivery. In addition to supplying more electronic access to content, the ULS has unveiled a premium document delivery service called *Libraries to Go!* This service gives faculty an alternative to the laborious process of traveling to the main library to personally locate, check out or photocopy, and lug around the material not yet digitized. Started in summer 2003, this exceedingly popular service provides more than 300 registered faculty users with physical delivery of books and electronic delivery of articles scanned from hard copy formats. As of the fall term 2005, more than 9,000 items had been delivered either physically or virtually at no cost to the user.

Although originally conceived for delivering material from place to place on the main campus only, whenever possible this service has been extended by locating and delivering to main-campus professors what would otherwise have been classified as a "no-fill" request. Whenever a request cannot be filled at Hillman or another main campus library but the item is available from the Oakland campus, another Pitt regional library, or the Pennsylvania Academic Library Consortium, the *Libraries to Go!* service goes the extra mile to obtain and deliver the item. Even faculty outside the prescribed service area benefit, in that faculty on the Oakland campus can request ULS materials and pick them up at the ULS service point nearest to them.

Reading Room. In addition to implementing document delivery, Pitt has enhanced direct physical access to the existing print serials archive and to the low-circulation monographic materials still vitally important to many researchers by (1) adding a reading room at the storage facility where these volumes are housed and (2) implementing a shuttle service between this location and the main campus. These new services have restored to researchers the option of paging through a single volume or browsing multiple volumes.

Digital Microform Readers. And finally, again with the goal of enhancing access to materials, digital microform reader-printers were purchased to replace unwieldy and unreliable antiquated machines. The new reader-printers greatly simplify access to content held in microfilm or fiche; and most importantly, they facilitate alternatives to printing out the text of documents — namely, downloading large files to portable storage devices or copying/pasting small portions of text into word-processed documents. These new machines have been enthusiastically received by users, especially faculty who are now much less reluctant to design assignments that require the use of resources in microformat.

Additional New Initiatives

A significant benefit of the work done by the RPST with regard to local user and national trend analysis was that the ULS could use this data to implement several attractive new programs. Responding to the recommendations of the RPST that were affirmed by additional data, the ULS looked at a select number of new services and operations to undertake. It should be noted that some of these activities were not totally new but were augmented and enhanced by some of the ideas and recommendations of the Rethinking process. Clearly, another benefit of the process is that — besides identifying new service areas to develop — it also reaffirmed the validity of many long-standing service commitments within the ULS and indicated which were worth supporting more fully. One of the assumptions verified by the Rethinking process was that increasingly users were beginning the search process online and they expected more and more full text data to be available.

Figure 7.3
Digital publishing postcard, front and back

Scholarly Publishing

It is by now a truism that digital publishing is one of very few workable options for circumventing the vicious inflationary cycle in scholarly journal prices—doubly vexing when, in effect, academic libraries are paying a premium for access to scholarly work produced by colleagues at their own institutions. Although virtually all academic libraries decry this problem, the University of Pittsburgh's ULS is one of a very small number of libraries actually doing something about it.

To date, there are five substantial open archives initiative compliant online collections under the ULS's electronic publishing umbrella, a program that has not only "made thousands of vital academic resources ... significantly more available" but also "opened doors for researchers to immediately share their findings, to give and receive feedback on their research documents, and also to reduce publishing costs" (*Boundless Connections* n.d., under "Improving Research Through Electronic Publishing"). The postcard used to publicize the digital publishing program to faculty who might benefit is shown in Figure 7.3.

One of the first scholarly publishing initiatives of the ULS was the Archive of European Integration, an archive and repository for two types of material: (1) the text of official European Community/European Union documents not already accessible through the European Research Papers Archive (ERPA) and (2) independently produced (copyright-free) research material submitted by authors focusing on European integration and unification.

The second noteworthy scholarly publishing project is the PhilSci Archive of preprints, supporting the University of Pittsburgh's Center for the Philosophy of Science and used by scholars throughout the world. This mechanism for rapid dissemination of scholarly thought is a model of how libraries can circumvent the commercial publishing establishment to provide access to the output of scholars on their own campus at an affordable price.

Third is the Electronic Theses and Dissertations (ETD) Collection, providing access to and free downloads of theses and dissertations produced at the University of Pittsburgh. Initially implemented as a voluntary pilot project, this collection became essential in 2005 when electronic submission of theses and dissertations became mandatory at the University of Pittsburgh. This repository serves much the same purpose as the PhilSci Archive, albeit for disseminating the work of fledgling scholars, rather than established authorities in their respective disciplines. Additionally, it provides for much earlier access to these materials than was available in traditional formats. A unique feature of this service is that ULS personnel work with the student to create their electronic document and offer assistance with conversion as necessary.

Yet another example of scholarly publishing within the ULS is the Clinical Aphasiology Archive, a repository of interest to practitioners and researchers concerned with acquired neurological language disorders. It contains the text of more than 1,000 published papers originally presented at the Conference of Clinical Aphasia.

The final scholarly publishing project to highlight is the Minority Health Archive of more than 200 documents (published articles, pamphlets, and more) submitted by registered users of the repository. It supports the Center for Minority Health at the University of Pittsburgh's Graduate School of Public Health. Full launch of all search engine capabilities with a larger collection of documents is planned for 2006.

Extending Diversity within Academic Libraries

For the first decade of the twenty-first century, one of the ULS's strongest commitments has been to diversity. The ULS is deservedly proud of both the strides it has made in this area locally and the impact its contributions to diversity efforts have made to the library and information science profession nationally. Recruiting and retaining staff from the small pool of underrepresented ethnic and racial groups, in order to reap the benefits of cultural diversity for the organization and for its patrons, is a perennial challenge for libraries. Beliefs and behaviors typical of women and minority groups (aka "co-cultures") have much to offer the predominantly male, European-based culture that has been the defining characteristic of both profit-making and non-profit organizations in the United States for hundreds of years.

What's at Stake? Examination and incorporation of feelings, intuition, and qualitative indicators into the one-sided picture resulting from relying exclusively on quantitative measures—an orientation formerly more associated with women and non-European cultures than with organizations dominated by the cultural majority—is one such multicultural value that enlightened organizations are beginning to add to their repertoire of behaviors. Nonlinear reasoning is a mental model that had to jump gender and cultural barriers in order to gain wider acceptance in organizations as well. It is worth noting that—though women have long swelled the ranks of library employees—until very recently, that gender's values have not necessarily prevailed in our organizations. Who among us can name a historical female librarian with the stature of Dewey or other male librarians? Who, for that matter, can name more than a handful of women who occupied dean or director positions in academic research libraries before 1980?

In addition to the previously mentioned co-cultural values, many characteristics now sought in team members came into organizations via the "back door." Sensitivity to relationships as well as to achievements, paying attention to process or "means" as well as the desired outcomes or "ends," a focus on group skills and achievements as much as on the individual, and the greater efficacy of cooperation over competition in many situations all are examples of important values originally infused into organizations by members of nondominant cultures.

The Need for Strategies that Work. For academic libraries, it is just as important to provide to library users a public face reflective of diverse cultures as it is to cultivate alternative cultural values and perspectives and to integrate them into the fabric of the organization's operations and value system. To some extent, this more-inclusive public face can be achieved by reflecting co-cultures in collections of library resources. But hiring minority staff and student workers in numbers roughly proportional to their presence in the general population is without question a far more powerful signal to patrons that people, ideas, and achievements of nondominant cultures are valued by the library in question than merely building a collection that includes authors outside the canon of mainstream writing and that reflects the thoughts and values of diverse cultures.

Like the vast majority of organizations, the ULS was able to move toward its goal of becoming more diverse but at a slower pace than desired. The will to make swift progress was never lacking. But the problem of identifying, attracting, and retaining minority candidates is complex. Finding the right combination of financial incentives, prestige, latitude in the scope of job duties and organizational involvement, a nurturing atmosphere to ensure success, an attractive geographical area, a large enough community of like-minded people, and proximity to family and/or familiar cultural necessities (food, entertainment, and other elements of cultural identity) is difficult for all academic libraries. The ULS is no exception.

The best and the brightest minority graduates from underrepresented groups may simply opt for a career in politics or law or show business, rather than academic libraries. They are greatly in demand in virtually all professional fields and not enough of them are called to our profession. Therefore, there is fierce competition to hire those few Hispanics, African Americans, Native Americans, and Asians who *do* pursue a library and information science degree. And there are many challenges with regard to retaining those who academic libraries have successfully hired.

The most qualified applicant for a midlevel or upper-level position—the one whose background, skills, and abilities are the optimal fit with requirements (e.g., head of an Asian Studies collection)—may be a fast-tracker who, shortly after coming to a place like the University of Pittsburgh, soon moves on to a more responsible position in another library or in a more diverse demographic area. Or to an area more conducive to competitive rowing or pursuit of a similar passion. Or to a region with a faster growing economy where a spouse or partner has a better chance of finding employment opportunities commensurate with his or her dreams and abilities. The newly minted graduate ideal for an entry-level position, in contrast, may have legitimate reservations about some other dimension of the hiring decision—perhaps doubts about setting up housekeeping too far from the circle of friends and family that sustained him or her throughout graduate school.

Early Diversity Efforts within the ULS. Over the years, the ULS has pursued its diversity goals in various ways. Early efforts, sparked by the chancellor's 1994 report *Diversity and Inclusion on Campus* along with growing awareness of the value of diversity, started with a ULS diversity committee whose mission statement reads in part as follows:

The committee is entrusted with the mission of working to create an atmosphere that values diversity in the ULS workforce and services, recommending strategies for accomplishing increased diversity and mounting programs to achieve those goals. The Diversity Committee invites all ULS employees to join together as we strive to create a workplace environment in which employees of all ages, beliefs, disabilities, genders, heritages, and lifestyles are welcomed, valued, and respected. (ULS, 1996h, 5)

This committee and its successor, a staff development working group, programmed activities such as a film festival with informal discussions to raise staff consciousness of diversity issues. The intent was that the committee should work with the ULS personnel librarian, the director, and other groups (Faculty Affairs Committee, Faculty Peer Review Committee, Staff Advisory Committee, and others) to implement a support system for increasing diversity.

In its final report, the committee made recommendations related to five different areas of concern: (1) Demographics (i.e., reflecting in ULS staffing demographic changes projected for the country); (2) Employment and Personnel (e.g., training for supervisors in how to manage diversity in the workplace, programming aimed at increasing appreciation for and understanding of diversity, a system of incentives for pro-active employees, and committing financial resources to enhancing diversity throughout the ULS); (3) Public Services Recommendations (including making all service points more welcoming); (4) ULS Collection Recommendations (including increasing the amount of material reflecting diversity and also developing "more sensitive subject headings than the LCSH [offers]"; (5) Programming (including communicating with diverse user populations, networking with appropriate campus entities to foster diversity, and "taking a national leadership role" in advancing diversity), and—perhaps most important for a learning organization—Assessment ("establish a multi-level assessment plan for the diversity program") (ULS, 1996h, 15–16).

Breakthroughs in Advancing Cultural Diversity. The most notable signs of progress toward greater diversity at the ULS are two to date: (1) internship programs and (2) creation of an administration position dedicated to advancing diversity as an agenda.

First, a Minority Librarian Fellowship and Residency Program was established in partnership with the University of Pittsburgh School of Information Sciences. Starting in 1996, students eligible by virtue of their acceptance into the Information Sciences degree program, their membership in an underrepresented racial/minority group, and their qualifying immigration status (U.S. citizen or permanent resident) could be hired as graduate assistants with a full tuition scholarship for three terms plus a stipend and full benefits package in return for working 20 hours per week in the library. Upon graduation, recipients receive a 12-month appointment with the rank of Librarian I at the prevailing entry-level salary. Having experienced academic librarianship through work assignment in public services/reference, technical services, and collection development, graduates are placed in an area of interest in the ULS where additional staffing is needed.

The second internship program (implemented in 2005) is targeted at public service and specifically at gaining experience as a reference and instruction librarian within the Information Sciences departmental library. A two-year appointment, this position is intended to attract persons of color or minority status who seek experience at a large academic research library and entrée into the profession. Graduates of any American Library Association–accredited master's program who are African American, Asian American, Latino/Hispanic American, or Native American and who are citizens or permanent residents of the United States qualify. Starting salary and benefits are the same as for graduates of the Pitt Information Science program who have served a year as a graduate assistant in the Minority Fellowship and Residency Program and are being placed in an entry-level position within the ULS.

The second significant step toward placing the ULS in the vanguard of academic libraries committed to diversity occurred in 2005: The ULS and the Graduate School of Information Sciences jointly funded the director of diversity initiatives position. The incumbent of this joint appointment focuses on employing every means, including personal and professional networks, to identify and recruit a diverse group of highly qualified individuals to the degree program and to the ULS staff. A member of the ULS administration, she is involved in strategic planning, serves on all faculty search committees, and is privy to other planning and operational decisions. As such, this director is ideally placed to put teeth into every aspect of the ULS's efforts to enhance diversity. An initiative that reaped enormous rewards was the exhaustive environmental scan she conducted to assess the climate in the ULS with regard to diversity. The findings of this scan helped determine where best to focus her efforts. In fact, this position proved to be such an asset to the ULS that in 2006, the person in this split position was hired by the ULS full time; and she was given additional duties in the coordination of marketing and communication for the ULS.

Since accepting the full-time position, the coordinator has proven even more successful. She has formed strong partnerships with the ALA's Office for Diversity and ARL's Office of Diversity Initiatives. One of her most impressive achievements to date has been working with ARL to develop the "Divine Nine" Listserv. This online communication tool serves as a networking vehicle for members of the Black Greek Letter Organization (BGLO) in libraries, supporting them personally and professionally and solidifying their commitment to the field of librarianship. Her other ongoing activities include: recruiting minority ULS staff and interns via campus groups, such as the Black Action Society and the Asian American Alliance; coordinating diversity programs for the libraries; and the ongoing development of diversity training for librarians and staff members. A key to the success of this position is that the ULS recognized the need to be proactive rather than reactive in terms of diversity. From the outset, this position has been an asset to the ULS and the university, reaching out and collaborating with units throughout the ULS and across the campus.

The city of Pittsburgh is a culturally rich environment, attractive throughout its history to individuals from many different ethnic and cultural backgrounds and blessed with a philanthropic community that is far more well endowed than most cities its size. Both the city and the University of Pittsburgh value diversity. Although there is always more that can be done with regard to promoting diversity, the dedication of personnel funds to the director of diversity position plainly shows that—like the university and the community—the ULS values diversity and places a premium on building a welcoming and nurturing environment for all.

POSITIONED FOR ONGOING CHANGE

Clearly, the University Library System at the University of Pittsburgh is committed to ongoing organizational change and revitalization, has created internal support for it, and has laid a firm foundation for the continued growth of the libraries in the first decade of the twenty-first century and beyond. It is hoped that this account of their process and outcomes will be useful to others who are looking for ways to redesign their public services operations.

8

Standing Up to Scrutiny

LIBRARY ACCOUNTABILITY

At least one article attributes the long-standing disinclination of libraries to perform quantitative assessment to our professional values: "A profession that inherently believes that it is a 'public good' does not feel the need to demonstrate outcomes and articulate impact" (Lakos and Phipps 2004, 350). But there is an additional reason for the failure of academic libraries to welcome change and to adopt a culture of assessment. In past decades—compared to now—there was more institutional support to go around.

For decades, hardware costs to support the use of information, data, and images at any place on campus (libraries, registration and records, financial aid, art or chemistry faculty offices) meant little more than the purchase of slide carousels most years, a few microform readers every 10 years, and file cabinets or card-file furniture only every fifteen to twenty years. During this time—in contrast to now, when personal computers with a usable life of three years or less are needed in quantity for virtually *all* university staff and student activity—there was a much smaller gap between needs around campus and university resources.

The "Good Old Days"

For a span of years toward the beginning of many a practicing librarian's career, libraries were accountable primarily for building and circulating collections adequate to support teaching and research needs and for being good enough stewards of the budget to keep up with inflation. But in direct contrast to now, the library was not in intensive competition for its budget allocations with every department and unit from athletics to the registrar. Even in the 1960s, when library circulation operations and college registration began to automate via a system of punch cards and batch processing on a mainframe computer, costs were insignificant compared to now. And the bulk of the costs were borne by the university as a whole and not allocated to separate departments and units.

For years after libraries first started implementing automation, it was still true that a library's bibliographic records needed attention only when a new edition of subject headings came out or when catalog cards got ripped and dirty from use. There might be an OCLC terminal or two around, but much of the cataloging and Interlibrary loan processes were still manual in all except the largest academic libraries. Again, costs were nothing like the current dizzying succession of new hardware and software replacements and infrastructure upgrades (new hard-wired connections and/or wireless computer architecture) that require massive infusions of funds at every turn. And the only technicians needed in the library were catalogers and not computer programmers or analysts.

A Sea Change in Accountability

But in the 1980s and 1990s and the new millennium—with the spread of automation, the unceasing inflationary pressures, and the difficulty of competing for tuition-strapped college students—*accountability* became less of a buzzword and more of a mandate in higher education. Any facet of academic library operations—even administrative matters such as reorganization—can come under scrutiny from internal program review, from reaccreditation review, or simply in connection with the annual university budget allocation brouhaha.

DOCUMENTING THE EFFECTIVENESS
OF ORGANIZATIONAL CHANGES

Cohen (2000), a seasoned veteran of the OD arena, comments that the practice of instituting organizational change for lack of a better idea is centuries old. He quotes a military writer from 66 A.D. to make his point: "I was to learn that later in life, we tend to meet any new situation by reorganizing, and what a wonderful method it can be for creating the illusion of progress while producing confusion, inefficiency, and demoralization" (179–80).

In reviewing and comparing the philosophies of two OD professionals, Cohen (2000) points out that "both Galbraith and Hirschorn agree that [changing] structure alone is not enough" (177) because people's attitudes and skills must change in order to make a new structure work and because meaningful, productive work is a powerful incentive for embracing rather than merely acquiescing to change. Like Galbraith, Cohen advocates taking a wholistic approach to OD. Cohen cautions against viewing it merely as boxes and lines on an organizational chart or simply as the sum total of written rules and regulations. He alludes to unwritten rules—employee habits that persist until they have the force of official written policy—as one aspect of the structure frequently not taken into consideration when planning change. He points out that structure actually includes "the organization's prescribed roles, job assignments, rules for proceeding, decision-making powers, reporting relationships, communication channels, hiring and retention practices, career paths, and other practices that attempt to channel people toward organizational ends" (180). And he insists that all of these factors must be kept in mind when planning and implementing organizational change.

Cohen (2000) concludes by affirming the difficulty of negative interpersonal interactions and the tendency of some managers to use reorganization inappropriately in solving a specific personnel problem. "Instead of dealing directly with a problematic but established powerful individual, they invent a new structure to work around the person" (190). The end result is that "restructuring becomes a substitute for interpersonal courage, and the opportunity to build greater honesty and directness in the organization is lost" (190). He believes it is a mistake to assume that a direct but supportive approach will not work in addressing an individual staff problem.

Library administrators, like other managers, may at times be guilty of making organizational changes when they don't know what else to do—implementing reorganizations and other changes that don't make a dime's worth of difference in the library's long-term success. If, for example, an individual or a small group of unproductive staff just need to be transferred to a place in the organization where they will do less harm or put into a less-comfortable assignment and monitored more closely, sheltering behind the fig leaf of a comprehensive reorganization may not be a justifiable strategy. For such isolated personnel problems, it may be wiser to make a specific reassignment and then face the music by doing a better job of supervising and documenting performance so that the problem employee or employees ultimately are motivated to either shape up or leave the organization.

But even when more wide-ranging change has been implemented—change with broad goals for altering how the organization functions—evaluation and documentation of progress are necessary. Simply "declaring victory" and behaving as if substantive improvements have taken place may buy the organization some time. But ultimately key stakeholders—in the case of academic libraries, chiefly library users and the university administration—will call the library to account if promised improvements do not materialize.

So how can the positive impact of organizational changes be measured? Since business benchmarks like sales and profits do not translate well to the non-profit sector, for years libraries measured their effectiveness by input and output measures—numbers of books and other materials added to holdings each year, number of items circulated, number of Interlibrary loan transactions, number of reference questions asked, and number of people moving into and out of the library's doors. But these kinds of measures fall short of demonstrating library effectiveness in terms of specific outcomes or providing information on which to base decisions.

Portfolio Method of Evaluation

One useful model for judging the effectiveness of a non-profit organization's portfolio of goods and services offered to the public ("products," if you will) is based on three criteria: quality, centrality, and marketability (e.g., attractiveness to the market segments targeted by the organization) (Wood 1988, 160). Bryson (2004) praises the flexibility of this method of analyzing performance: "Portfolio methods are flexible in that any dimensions of interest may be arrayed against one another and entities then mapped on to the resulting matrix" (281). This process works at many different levels of the organization, from subdivisions of the organization to the supra-organizational.

Quality

The most strategic opportunities to pursue are those in arenas where the library is equipped to deliver quality or can gather the resources to do so. The quality component of this model can be measured against industry standards (in our case ACRL and/or ARL standards for collections, support of distance education, methods of measuring use of web-based informational and instructional objects, and the like) along with best practices in the field. It goes without saying that such regional, national, or industry benchmarks should be considered in light of local expectations and priorities as well as availability of resources.

Customer-Defined Quality. An additional word of caution here: It is not wise to assume that the customer thinks like a professional does or bases decisions on the same values that the professional holds. Well-meaning people who have not fully grasped customer service concepts often think they can be user-centered by deciding what the user needs, without verifying what users want. Such individuals are apt to push what *they* think of as quality and to waste resources trying to make people accept what really doesn't work for them.

One example of this phenomenon is that when a seldom-used database is on a list of possible cancellations, one or more librarians almost invariably will plead for more time to "educate" patrons about the database and to build up its use. They have assumed that they can "sell" the database quality to users, even when it may not be relevant to the curriculum, may not offer remote access, may not have the functionality of more-popular databases, may contain less full text, or may have some other characteristic that prevents all but the most diehard researcher from using it.

Other examples abound. It is a truism in academic libraries that too many students are happy with whatever they find on the Web, whether authoritative, up-to-date, and reliable or not. Those customers (and sometimes a few naive professors) have chosen speed and convenience over what librarians would define as quality resources.

Evidence of Customer Values. Reference librarians can also testify that—though more-complex questions do not lend themselves to the chat or e-mail reference formats—users cannot always be persuaded to forgo the convenience and anonymity of electronic assistance when told that they could get better help with their question in person at the reference desk. Again, what professionals consider the quality of answers or assistance is not always key to the user's choice of library products.

As OCLC reports and other recent analyses of user behavior show, the abstract notion of quality takes a backseat to enjoyment, convenience, and a host of other customer values in making decisions about libraries and research. The sidebar in a *Library Journal* article cautions, "Are you using space for collections that your community doesn't want? No matter the quality of the collection [as judged by librarians], if it isn't being used, it's wasting space" (Dempsey 2005, 75).

So for the quality component of the portfolio model of evaluation, think "customer benefits." Since only the user can say what is most important to him or her, *user-defined* is a much better term than *user-centered*. Among all of the literature about the customer service orientation in libraries, Dean Carla Stoffle is one of the few writers who makes this distinction. "Focus on adopting a user (customer) focus, committing to quality service with quality defined by the user" (Stoffle 1995, 6). Thus libraries must be mindful that conducting a survey, focus group, user-testing, or some other method of sampling user preferences is paramount to success in designing products or services.

An OCLC survey describes an interesting insight regarding how some library users judge quality of libraries versus search engines like Google: "Speed is not the only, and not the primary, reason search engines are the preferred starting point for today's information consumer. Quality and quantity of information delivered are the highest determinants of overall search satisfaction" (De Rosa et al. 2005, section 6, 5). Even more important, respondents to this survey feel that "search engines deliver better quality and quantity of information than librarian-assisted searching—and at greater speed" (section 6, 5). Members of all age groups surveyed trust information from search engines and from librarians equally, but this is particularly true of ages 14–24 (section 6, 5).

Centrality

The second criterion for good product development is that opportunities funded and most fully supported with other resources (staff, priority for information technology attention, etc.) should be central to the library's mission and annual priorities and congruent with the university's purposes and emphases. An example of how centrality tends to shift for academic libraries can be traced from the recent resurgence throughout much of the higher education community of emphasis on quality undergraduate education, in contrast to a focus on graduate programs prevalent during much of the late 1970s and 1980s. As priorities change in this way in a resource-poor period, typically there is a constant threat that a considerable portion of scarce university resources may be diverted from "support services" such as dining facilities, libraries, and the like to the academic side of the enterprise.

Aligning with Parent Organization's Priorities. In such an environment, libraries are scrambling to align themselves with the university's teaching mission. They must do so or else suffer a net loss of unfilled positions, receive less annual operating money, lose eligibility for capital funding, and/or be forced to dig deeper any time that university-wide cuts or givebacks from operating, personnel, or materials budgets are mandated. For example, in response to the renewed emphasis on all things academic, library instruction is now emphasized on any list of annual accomplishments and in requests for funding.

Renewed university-wide emphasis on undergraduate success is an example of when individual library departments and divisions in poorly funded academic libraries might consider realigning with changing campus priorities. In such an environment, the intrinsic value of collections and services (e.g., archives of photos, manuscripts, and other treasures from local history and culture important to faculty researchers and heavily used by the international community of scholars) may no longer matter as much as it formerly did. Accordingly, managers of collections unused or seldom used by undergraduates often find that they must reposition their collections, stressing their relevance to some part of the undergraduate curriculum and stimulating use of specialized resources for completing undergraduate assignments and projects. Should such efforts fail, these library units stand to lose out when the library administration allocates the few open positions and scarce collection monies available.

In well funded libraries, not all collections and services need be realigned. It may be sufficient to demonstrate a critical mass of resources and services supporting current university priorities. At the University of Pittsburgh's ULS, as at other leading academic libraries, the library administration has been successful in positioning many library services in alignment with shifting university priorities as a major component of success for undergraduate student. As a result, the ULS's funding has not been cut, and a number of new library programs targeted at improving the undergraduate experience have made a successful bid for university funding. Examples include the following: the implementation of an award-winning federated search engine; a program for replacing missing books dubbed "LUCI" (Library Undergraduate Collection Initiative); development of an electronic course reserves system; renovation of reading rooms; and the popular Cup and Chaucer Coffee Shop, with its inviting furniture and collection of popular reading materials.

A succinct way to illustrate centrality is to quote the folk wisdom coined by business practitioners: McDonald's didn't get where they are by selling vegetarian food. Although this company has added soups, salads, and other such health-conscious fare to its product lines, from the beginning its mainstay has been burgers and fries drenched in beef tallow. And it is doubtful that the company will switch to a menu emphasizing vegetarian dishes to the exclusion of meat any time soon.

Centrality: We're Catching On. The good news about centrality is that our library colleagues are getting much savvier about writing grants that fit in with and support the library's mission and overarching strategic directions. Rather than diverting staff's time and energy to a project so esoteric that it will not be sustainable at the end of the grant period, it is usual now to think of activities that advance the library's top priorities. One example is targeting grant writing to the acquisition of equipment to enhance library instruction such as smart boards (projection screens that permit the presenter to add a great variety of graphic enhancements to screens from the Web or other sources of content), laptops to add flexibility in the configuration of instructional venues, or poll takers (clickers that permit sending and instantaneous tabulating of answers).

Another example of centrality is enlarging the focus of grants to link them with more than one library priority. Rather than applying for funds simply to organize or preserve local archives or specialized materials, it might be possible to make relevance to the local curriculum a primary criterion for selecting grant opportunities to pursue. In addition, it would be good for libraries to ask for enough support to make digitizing possible so that they can use grant money to accomplish not only preservation but also greater access for users through indexing and electronic access to texts and images . An enterprising archivist might even tack on seed money for promotional activities such as a conference presenting scholarship based on locally held collections such as the history of flight, union activity in a given region, civil war manuscripts and diaries, female mystery writers, or rare examples of pulp fiction.

Marketability

The concept of market attractiveness was touched on earlier in illustrating that the user himself or herself is the final arbiter of what is a high-quality product. Although practitioners in any field *do* know to some extent what individuals in segments of their intended market need or could use, these professionals still need to explore the dimensions of user needs and preferences. Any of the four fundamental product characteristics—product design, price (both monetary costs and nonmonetary costs such as inconvenience or embarrassment), promotion, and place or manner of distribution—can serve as the basis for customer choice (Wood 1988, 7).

Library Use: Complex Motivations

In the past, problem solvers quite often jumped to the conclusion that more or better promotion and publicity were all it would take to attract more users to the library. Now, however, more academic librarians understand the complexity of a user's decision about whether to use the library or any of its services much better than in previous decades. Many of the things measured in LibQUAL+™, for example, are good examples of elements of distribution and price that are important to many users: the library as place, the completeness of the collection in a given field of study, and the competence and approachability of staff are just a few examples.

A Texas A & M a user offered the following comments and observations about the price (in both psychological and financial terms) of using traditional reserves. Copying reserve items cost the respondent $45. He had to do it himself on a machine "that basically Moses would have used" (Cook and Heath 2001, 573), and it took him four hours. He could have used the library photocopy center except that the cost of his job was too high—the center being limited to accepting checks in amounts no higher than $20. Neither cash nor credit card payments were permitted. And to add insult to injury, parking was not convenient. This highly frustrated patron concluded, "They're not trying to sell you something; they [the library] are trying NOT to sell you something" (573).

Most undergraduates manifestly could benefit from a librarian's help with research projects and would probably get a better grade with help than without it. But reference librarians know that all too often they sit alone at the desk like the Maytag repairman. Barriers to getting help with research can be wide ranging. Some examples include (1) the need to make an appointment for an extended consultation; (2) a disinclination to admit that help is needed; (3) a preference for working with other students rather than asking questions of full-time staff sitting behind a desk and wearing business clothes; (4) a personal or work schedule that prevents the patron from coming in while the desk or chat reference is staffed; and (5) a hot new romance that leaves little time for research, combined with a lack of awareness that librarian assistance often can save the user time.

Fight Barriers with Benefits

To increase market attractiveness, the library's task is to design and articulate to the potential user of its services a benefit strong enough to neutralize or overcome such barriers. Barrier number one (the inconvenience of having to wait for help) could be addressed by piloting walk-in consultations as a supplement to traditional appointment-based assistance. Then, too, libraries might consider implementing instant messaging between reference librarians and clients, a practice begun in 2006 by Ohio University at Athens, according to an OhioLINK announcement (M. Spernoza e-mail message to Chat Reference staffers [chatref@ohiolink.edu], February 21, 2006). Doubtless, other academic libraries will soon be considering and/or implementing this option. Some may have done so but not yet taken time to write about their experience.

Problem number two (also known as "jerk-o-phobia" or fear of appearing incompetent outside of one's normal sphere of operations) can sometimes be addressed via tutorials, class web pages, and other kinds of help that don't require admitting one's inadequacy to a person. Number three (lack of affiliation with older, professional-looking staff) might be addressed by instituting peer research counselors and/or adding student employees to reference service points in the library and sometimes in satellite locations such as computer labs or residence halls. (The ULS at Pittsburgh, like some of its peers, has addressed this subtle user reluctance to approach and "bother" regular staff by putting library school interns at service points in its HelpHub initiative. In addition, working with the School of Information Sciences, the ULS has created an extensive library interns program that places library school students in Public Services units to further promote the peer assistance concept.

Number four (conflicts with existing library service hours) could be addressed by such means as e-mail reference services or implementation of consulting hours with appointment slots outside the traditional nine-to-five Monday through Friday work week. Alternately, a library can contract with a vendor or share chat responsibilities with some other entity (e.g., a library consortium) in order to staff its chat reference service outside of traditional library open hours—thus making the dream of 24/7 availability of reference assistance a reality. The latter solution has the virtue of maximizing librarian flexibility by avoiding tying professional staff down to a specific location when the number of transactions fluctuates in unpredictable patterns. Or the user's home library can simply make staffing reference and/or chat more generously a priority. (At last count, the University of Pittsburgh's library chat service was staffed by 23 people.)

Barrier number five (pheromones) is a tough one. But sometimes word of mouth from a professor or a student colleague about how much time a librarian can save the researcher and how much our help can improve the quality of the research paper or project provides sufficient incentive to motivate even the romantically blitzed to get help. Generally, some type of wake-up call about falling grades and/or parental displeasure will aid in breaking down this barrier.

In short, to maximize marketability, librarians need to realize that services—and electronic services in particular—must be designed with the preferences and predilections of the intended clients in mind. The University of Pittsburgh's ULS is a good example. The strength of their Zoom federated search function is that it fully emulates a Google-type environment, the preferred search environment of most students. The same fit with user needs and preferences is characteristic of other ULS services and programs. Pitt has achieved the library core value of user-centeredness by consciously and formally evaluating each proposed new service to ensure relevance to users.

Not all academic librarians are as willing to cede power to users, however. Some are lax about user testing and give users what they "should" want. An example is screens designed with links to superfluous information that users *ought* to pursue but are not likely to look at. A society that aims to get through life and research with as few clicks as possible has little tolerance for extraneous information, no matter how educational or worthy. Veteran reference librarians know, for example, that—rather than follow a link to read about the content and scope of a particular resource—many patrons willingly waste time in trial and error exploration of a research database only marginally useful for their topic.

Another good way to ensure that users and potential users learn of library strengths and benefits is to dedicate a position or part of one to the task of marketing or public relations. The University of Cincinnati employs a full-time public relations professional. The University of Pittsburgh's ULS has a program for communicating with users and has designated a specific employee as coordinator of communication. These institutions certainly are not the only academic libraries to incorporate this important function into the organization in a formal way.

Additional Factors to Consider

Abell and Hammond point out factors (1979, 188) for which the portfolio model of analysis does not account. These factors must be examined—with respect to the organization itself and with respect to the chief competitor(s) within its industry sector—and they must be carefully considered before deciding on basic strategies for each product or setting out implementation details to execute the chosen strategies. Among those factors listed are barriers to entering the market (e.g., need for extensive technology training or the need for heavy capital outlays to get started); rates of technological change; social, political, legal, or environmental pressures; unions and related human resource considerations; management skills and capabilities; whether there is excess capacity or underuse; whether activity such as sales is cyclical or continuous; how much sales/use will fluctuate in response to changes in price, promotion, service levels, and the like; extent of "captive" business (e.g., Microsoft's long-time penetration of the PC software market through the domination of successive version of its Windows operating systems); opportunities to reconfigure processes or production mechanisms (e.g., off-shoring parts of the business); and the like.

Crafting Strategies from Portfolio Analysis Results

There are four basic strategic choices for allocating resources based on the portfolio approach to evaluation: building market share; maintaining (holding market share); downsizing, aka "harvesting"; and terminating or withdrawal from the market sector in question (Abell and Hammond 1979, 182–84).

Clear-Cut Strategy Options: Building, Terminating, and Downsizing

Both existing and new products ranking high on all three of the preceding dimensions should be fully supported financially and viewed as good prospects for strategically building the academic library's position within its industry. Conversely, products ranking low on all three aspects are candidates for downsizing or outright elimination, no matter how much they were cherished in the past. Hardcopy files of acquisitions invoices and paper-based finding aids for archives and special collections are historical examples of library artifacts that have been virtually eliminated.

Downsizing or weaning the public away from a product or service that does not rank high on all three criteria need not be painful. A good example is the demise of the fee-based or intermediated database search. Nobody mourns its passage any more. Another example is the paper-based union catalog for library networks that typically was updated only every couple of years and sometimes went a decade without comprehensive revision. Some librarians view the fixed reference desk as just such an anachronism, although the academic library community is far from unanimous in its views on that issue.

Termination of a product or service, in contrast, can be quite painful in the short run. Transitional stages in implementing the decision to terminate can be difficult—the period when a critical mass of users has not yet fully experienced the benefits of the replacement product or service and practitioners are still attempting to serve two masters. Closing the card catalog is a prime example of this phenomenon. There was trepidation if not outrage and public outcry when many academic libraries stopped running the card file and the electronic system in tandem. But as so often happens, within a few years the superiority of the replacement product became so evident that few patrons remember (much less yearn for) the legacy product; and successive generations of professionals cannot fathom why their predecessors agonized over the decision. There may still be drawers of catalog cards or invoices or piles of paper guides to manuscript and photograph collections under some ancient librarian's bed, but it's hard to find them any more in a well-run working library.

Nostalgia aside, online systems meet the needs of staff, patrons, library consortia, and budget administrators so much better. These systems transformed cooperative collection development from a rhetorical phrase, honored more in the breach than the observance, into a vital tool for supporting research in the face of increasing inflation. They also ushered in an era of unparalleled success with inter-institution borrowing, particularly where library networks or consortia have the infrastructure to implement patron initiation of transactions and timely delivery of materials.

Tougher Decisions

Midrange products are more difficult to judge. A library can sometimes continue to support a marginal resource or service—one that meets criteria for centrality and quality, let us say—while efforts are made to improve its rating on the third dimension of marketability. As long as it meets targets set for the two criteria where it is satisfactory and improves in the dimension in which has been deficient, its maintenance remains viable. Over time, such a product occasionally can be revitalized enough to rejoin the ranks of products considered good prospects for the building strategy. If it does not improve in the third criterion for portfolio management, then it should be relegated to the category of downsizing.

An example of a suitable candidate for the strategy of maintaining support over the short term is the local history archive. Occasionally, eliminating barriers of time and space and concerns about preservation by digitizing records of political groups or labor unions or old school books or maps or picture files or other archival treasures will transform a local collection into a resource that not only supports the curriculum but also attracts national or international attention. As use of the collection increases, the flow of local and sometimes grant dollars can transform the former liability into a real asset to the academic library.

Caution must be exercised, however, in making the decision to digitize. Although the scanning is relatively inexpensive once the equipment has been purchased, good management and maintenance of the digital archive or digital collection takes a lot of resources. Digitization takes a lot of person-power to design, implement, run, publicize effectively, and upgrade when equipment and software have reached the limits of their usability. The infrastructure (hardware and software) is a huge expense, as are the technicians needed to program and maintain public interfaces and personnel required to tag data features for retrieval. As hardware and software become superseded, there are sizeable costs associated with migrating to the next generation. The ULS at Pittsburgh estimates the full cost of digitizing to be close to $200 a book. No library can afford to expend resources on such a project without first doing a careful study of costs and benefits and a careful analysis of the expected audience for the final product.

The Biggest "Bang for Your Buck"

The implications of such portfolio analysis should be obvious. All resources, from operational dollars (telecommunications costs, equipment and supplies, allocation of space, etc.) to materials budget allocations to personnel (e.g., priority in information technology support) should be aligned with the results of such analysis. Bryson (2004) notes that, unfortunately, more organizations use the portfolio method informally than formally because of its potential to cause political fallout. "It creates comparisons that may be troubling for politically powerful actors" (281).

The stakes are high. Failure to make the hard decision to decrease or terminate resource support to a weak library program or unit moves the institution inexorably down the road toward mediocrity and marginalization, if not outright extinction. Conversely, supporting the most viable elements of the library can catapult the institution into the type of approbation and recognition that means a steady supply of dollars for maintaining current operations and moving judiciously into realms that will distinguish it in the future.

The trick is to communicate the benefits of backing the library's strengths and the consequences of *not* doing so. Again, the University of Pittsburgh is a model of what can be achieved when this challenge is taken seriously. By committing resources to a communications coordinator position, the ULS has elevated this task to the same significance as careful, responsible, and creative budgeting and other key management functions. The proof of the pudding is in their LibQUAL+™ results.

Hoshin Planning and Analysis

Hoshin planning, with its deep analysis of root causes among interrelated elements of a problem or barrier to success, is a particularly effective means of focusing resources on the organization's best opportunities. Its focus on drivers of the library's future success combined with specific performance targets dramatically reduces the human tendency to dilute the effect of strategic planning by giving a portion of available resources to every existing program or unit, in a misguided effort to avoid causing pain or provoking controversy.

ASSESSING AND MANAGING LIBRARY PERFORMANCE

Despite the rhetoric about creating a culture of assessment in academic libraries, many academic librarians are woefully lacking in the skills and background needed to handle quantitative data. Stoffle, Allen, and colleagues (2003) comment on this phenomenon: "Libraries and librarians do not have the values, experience, or skills to successfully implement assessment programs. Although we collect a lot of data, librarians have little experience with data analysis and use; and we are not always sure whether the data we collect is what we need in order to make good decisions" (368). Another academic librarian expresses a similar sentiment: "We [libraries] have traditionally captured statistics that are easy to capture, but not necessarily those that provide us with the information we need to evaluate and design services" (Knapp 2004, 159).

The principle ways that librarians can improve their handling of quantitative data in order to make a stronger case for whatever they are trying to document are (1) to use multiple measures and (2) to gain the skills they lack in using quantitative data—from how to design action research to how to code the data appropriately for the research design and the hypotheses chosen.

Assessment and Evaluation Issues

With the advent of the assessment movement focused on verifiable student learning outcomes in higher education together with the adoption of information literacy standards and the availability of tools such as LibQUAL+™ to measure customer satisfaction with various service dimensions, libraries have learned to use more sophisticated methods of demonstrating their effectiveness. New approaches to managing and documenting organizational performance (e.g., hoshin planning and balanced scorecard, discussed in chapter 2, along with customer relationship management introduced in chapter 9) cannot and *should* not entirely supplant traditional benchmarks for academic libraries. But new techniques and new measures *do* give a fuller picture of the academic library's role in supporting and advancing the teaching and learning endeavor than the old measures that were more suited to the era when libraries were a self-evident good with less need to compete actively for limited university funds.

Choosing Measures of Organizational Effectiveness

Customer data gathered via various means can shed light on areas of collections or services needing improvement, can help in anticipating future customer needs, and even can be used to test whether team members have achieved required competencies. Each of these measures is important. And each may be useful as part of a "suite" of measures to judge the library's effectiveness. Even the most enthusiastic exponents of LibQUAL+™ data concede that it is not the only effective measure of academic library effectiveness. "The comments we now get from LibQUAL+™ are yet another piece of customer feedback that can be used along with other information to gauge the needs of our campus customers and to plan new services and new approaches to meeting their needs" (Begay et al. 2004, 118–19). The same article notes, "For the most part they [conclusions drawn from LibQUAL+™ data] provide important support and verification for patterns already observed" (117), rather than offering epiphanies about previously unknown user needs.

No Clear Consensus

There is no clear consensus on what measures make the most sense for academic libraries to collect and use for evaluation. And—given the unique local environment influencing each library—there can be no simple answers beyond the obvious rule of mirroring the priorities and values of the parent body. No matter how enthusiastically academic libraries have enlisted in the righteous cause of customer service, each one knows that pleasing the provost and other stakeholders who influence allocation of campus funds is key to survival and long-term success fully as much as meeting expectations of end users.

Better Data Gathering and Analysis

There does seem to be widespread agreement, however, about the need for more sophisticated handling of any data under analysis. A case in point is LibQUAL+™ data. This treasure trove of numbers and comments reflecting user expectations can be used at a very simple level to guide library decisions. If a lot of respondents have indicated a lack of awareness of library open hours or remote access to digital resources or a 24-hour delivery cycle for resources housed in a remote storage facility, it seems obvious to make a greater effort to publicize these service aspects and to "educate" the campus community about the worthiness of current library offerings.

However, more astute libraries will add another layer of data gathering to pinpoint and capture pertinent details of broad issues and concerns suggested by LibQUAL+™. They will conduct focus groups to elicit concerns not brought out by survey questions or comments, they will interview users or they will administer a targeted survey to various academic disciplines and/or campus constituencies (e.g., graduate students and faculty) to uncover factors underlying user behaviors and user attitudes. And they will go beyond impressionistic analysis of the data.

Using Multiple Measures

Along with others who write about measurement, Bertot and McClure (2003) advise the use of multiple measures. "One evaluation method does *not* fit all types of libraries. The promotion of one particular method by some at the expense of all other methods does not reflect the complexity of situational factors as they relate to assessment in a library context." They go on to caution that any single, stand-alone approach is not likely to be reliable or valid: "There is a need for flexibility in methods and execution for libraries to engage successfully in evaluation activities" (607).

Among others, Arizona models the recommended practice of using multiple operational assessment measures to track customer needs and progress toward library goals. The Strategic Long Range Planning Team (SLRP) analyzed LibQUAL+™ reports and used them in combination with information from other sources to allocate funding for projects critical to supporting strategic plan priorities. Examples of other useful information sources include published information about national trends in academic libraries and higher education, information about the current campus situation at the University of Arizona, and customer data gathered from non-LibQUAL+™ instruments.

Along with LibQUAL+™, Arizona teams use a variety of additional tools to obtain customer feedback. Besides a web-based survey billed as "Library Report Card," the library periodically administers separate surveys. Teams might focus on a specific demographic subgroup. Alternately, aggregate data from all demographic segments can be brought to bear on an issue or question. In addition to LibQUAL+™ data and separate surveys, Arizona teams have used traditional assessment methods like citation analysis of dissertations and faculty journal articles and examination of interlibrary loan borrowing patterns for planning and decision-making. For examples, a Current Situation Analysis mentions using surveys, focus groups, and usability studies and gives a succinct report as to the findings of each method of gathering data. Most interesting, the document goes on to address the following pointed questions about impacts of the research findings in some detail:

- Based on the feedback, what are you doing to meet customers' needs (e.g. projects created, process improvements undertaken)?
- What products and services have been requested that you have not been able to provide? (e.g., *all* full-text journals online)
- What would need to change to be able to provide these products or services?
- Looking to the environment beyond the library, list forces that will change the way we serve our customers (e.g., electronic publishing, copyright laws, Campaign Arizona) (University of Arizona Libraries 2005a).

Giving a complete catalog of research methods and explication of their relative strengths and weaknesses for a particular situation is beyond the scope of this book and the talents of its authors. Cresswell and others are far more qualified to expound on this topic.

Grounded Theory

Grounded theory is a research method first articulated in 1967 (Cresswell 1998, 56) that is gaining in popularity among librarians and is worth mentioning here. The essence of grounded theory is that researchers extrapolate experimental hypotheses *from the data* instead of imposing on the data a structure dictated by a preconceived theory or theories and then shoehorning the data into said theories, whether it fits or not. Cresswell (1998) characterizes it this way: "The intent of a *grounded theory* study is to *generate or discover a theory* [emphasis added] … that relates to a particular situation" (55–56). He explains that data are processed first by open coding, in which investigators aggregate the data into different categories, each category spanning the "extreme possibilities" or range of highs and lows of responses. Then axial coding is employed to identify a "central phenomenon" along with whatever conditions seem to influence or correspond with variations in that phenomenon (Cresswell 1998, 57).

Texas A & M

As librarians at Texas A & M have observed, an important consideration in doing more sophisticated analysis of data is the need to preserve the integrity of data and to safeguard the multiplicity of perspectives commonly embedded in the range of user inputs. They quote the following observation by an expert in naturalistic inquiry methods: "Perhaps not every actor's perspectives can be discovered, or need be, but those of actors who sooner or later are judged to be significantly relevant must be imported into the emerging theory" (Cook and Heath 2001, 551). The grounded theory method of analyzing data is an excellent tool for showing multiple perspectives instead of smoothing results into a meaningless muddle by making the data fit preconceived categories.

As mentioned previously, in using grounded theory, the frame of reference for asking questions of the data in order to give it meaning is derived from either (1) the data itself or (2) a previously formulated grounded theory that seems applicable to the phenomena being studied. Any such theory adopted from earlier research is then further developed, "elaborated and modified as incoming data are meticulously played against [it]" (Cook and Heath 2001, 550). For example, instead of categorizing survey comments about service in some arbitrary way that makes sense to librarians and coding all responses according to a few one-size-fits-all criteria, the insightful researcher will first look at overall response patterns and derive coding categories from the data itself.

Participants in the groundbreaking 2000 ARL project to fine-tune the SERVQUAL instrument measuring gaps between customer service expectations and what respondents perceive as the *reality* of service found that quality expectations for several aspects of academic library service varied significantly by user group. Researchers conducted a series of 60 lengthy open-ended interviews at nine different ARL libraries including Texas A & M. After each interview, insights gained were incorporated into the next interchange until "saturation was attained and no new information was forth coming" (Cook and Heath 2001, 551). Although all SERVQUAL service dimensions were confirmed in the library context, three separate SERVQUAL dimensions seemed to be combined in responses from academic library users. "Responsiveness, assurance, and empathy seem to merge into a general need for a satisfying affective relationship between the library and its constituents" (Cook and Heath 2001, 581). Evidently, the old adage that for a reference librarian, being nice can be as important as giving a correct answer has some truth to it.

One of the strong findings that the nine ARL libraries uncovered is that "the definition of a satisfying affective relationship seems to change over an academic lifetime from an undergraduate to a full-fledged professor engaged in research and teaching" (Cook and Heath 2001, 581–82). The fact that undergraduates typically care more about library buildings than senior professors, for example, is old news to libraries currently using LibQUAL+™. But this kind of variation in response patterns across the data was a revelation to those attempting for the first time to identify dimensions of library service quality specific to ARL libraries.

The result of using grounded theory to adapt SERVQUAL for libraries was that the following three unique aspects of service quality in the library context—items now quite familiar to users of LibQUAL+™—were identified for the first time: "ubiquity and ease of access to collections, the library as place, subsuming dual concepts of utilitarian space and of the library as a symbol of the intellect, and finally, the overwhelming drive on the part of users to be self-reliant and confident in navigating the information world" (Cook and Heath 2001, 582).

University of Arizona

University of Arizona is another library that has used grounded theory effectively to analyze LibQUAL+™ comments. The library-wide planning group at Arizona (the SLRP) had 303 comments from the 2002 LibQUAL+™ survey—a richer source of detail than the numbers by themselves—coded in a process described in a *Journal of Academic Librarianship* article (Begay et al. 2004). In the initial step of analysis, Arizona used QSR's N6, a qualitative statistical software, to code responses demographically and to aggregate responses into the broad categories or themes of Library Access, Environment, and Service derived from actual language used by the respondents.

Reports derived from the coding yielded both basic and more complex information. Simple counts of the number of comments on a particular theme were isolated for analysis—for example, the number of responses about the broad topic Access as compared to comments about the topic Service (290 about Access versus 161 about Service). In addition, counts for subtopics such as Lighting (6 comments) versus Noise (38) within the broader category of Environment were shown.

Besides these simple counts, cross-tabulations were charted to facilitate comparisons of more than one variable at a time. One example from the article is a chart showing the number of comments about Access versus the Environment versus Service for various demographic groups (undergrads, graduate students, faculty, staff, and total). This report suggests the relative importance to respondents of different aspects of library work. Additional report options might include cross-tabulations comparing issues such as the importance of access to print resources versus electronic access for different demographic groups—graduate students/faculty and undergraduates.

The next step for Arizona was axial coding (Begay et al. 2004, 116). As explained previously in this chapter, this means classifying each response for a given category (e.g., staff competence) into a group representing one of the points on a continuum from highest to lowest (e.g., a scale from positive to neutral to negative or one from high positive to positive to neutral to negative to extremely negative) and showing variations over demographic group or over time or some other aspect of the data. As mentioned previously, the University of Arizona Libraries characterized survey responses according to "properties (characteristics or attributes)" extracted from the respondents' language (Begay et al. 2004, 116).

The article doesn't go into detail about what properties or characteristics were used for coding comments, but here's a hypothetical example to illustrate: Comments relating to staff knowledge and abilities (e.g., a statement about receiving assistance with library research for class projects/assignments) could be coded as positive or high positive if it contained words and phrases such as "always understand" or "know" or "very helpful" or the equivalent. The comment "Generally know what they're doing but had nothing pertinent to the percentage of unwanted births in third world countries" should be coded once for the positive element and again to record the negative content. An observation that "Google is faster; but the teacher marks down for Internet sites" would be coded as neutral or negative, depending on agreed criteria for each point on the continuum.

University of Arizona researchers next made some educated guesses (hypotheses) grounded in response patterns about some factors that might affect variations in customer opinions about staff competence. From the fact that several positive comments identified librarians by name and the fact that many of the negative comments were about part-time student employees, two hypotheses were formulated: (1) Does the personal relationship established between a librarian and a customer affect the customer's perception of staff competence? and (2) Does the level of training and experience of public services staff affect customer satisfaction with staff competence?

These questions in turn were tested against the data, providing feedback for another cycle of refining the hypotheses. A relationship between comments about staff competence and comments about service affect was noted: "The respondents many times started addressing staff competence, eventually commenting on their satisfaction with the services received" (Begay et al. 2004, 116). This connection could be incorporated into a final hypothesis positing that three or more factors affect customer perceptions of staff competence: namely, personal relationships, staff affect, and staff training and experience.

Successful Data Users

Four libraries are singled out in the Hiller and Self (2004) article "From Measurement to Management" as exemplars of intelligent use of data in planning and decision making (144–49). The University of Arizona is cited for its design and implementation of the well-known and innovative PEMS (performance effectiveness management system), which rates the performance of individuals and teams based on how well they address customer needs.

The University of Pennsylvania's use of a dynamic database to assess the use of resources and other aspects of organizational effectiveness is praised. The data (both items collected locally and items supplied by vendors) mounted on the "Penn Library Data Farm" is available to staff for a variety of uses including creating customized reports.

The University of Virginia made a formal commitment to data-based decisions when it established a Management Information Systems Committee to serve as a clearinghouse for deciding where data collection was needed to improve performance, identifying suitable programs to gather data, and educating staff about issues related to management of information systems. An early study investigated the relationship of reserve use to student grades. A later one used circulation patterns to change collection development policies and staffing. Having established the value of data, the library eventually replaced the committee with permanent staff in a Management of Information Systems (MIS) department staffed by three employees.

And finally, the University of Washington (UW) Libraries' commitment to collecting comprehensive data about user needs is described. Having instituted a continuous three-year cycle of user studies and dedicated one half-time position to coordinating library assessment, this institution has used a range of methods including "targeted surveys, focus groups, observation studies, usability studies, usability testing, guided interviews, meetings and both traditional and electronic suggestion boxes" (Hiller and Self 2004, 148) to gather data for monitoring existing services and resource use and for developing new ways to meet user needs and expectations. According to an article by UW Libraries staff, a reaccreditation review characterized the library leadership as "visionary" and applauded its having incorporated sound management practices into its administration of the library. "Planning, assessment, and continuous improvement are ongoing processes with broad staff participation" (Northwest Association of Schools and Colleges and Universities 2003, III-5–1).

The University of Pittsburgh's ULS—though not mentioned in the Hiller and Self article—is also gaining a reputation for its leadership in assessment practices, as is covered in some detail in previous chapters. Pitt employs a wide range of assessment tools on a continuous basis to ensure that all programs and services remain viable and relevant to users' needs. Focus groups are used regularly to gain user views on subjects from collection adequacy to web site usability to perceptions of specific services. Every new initiative has an assessment plan in place to review the pilot and then to follow up annually on how the service is perceived by users.

The approbation accorded these institutions should inspire academic library colleagues to consider good assessment a moving target instead of an unattainable goal. As better methods and practices become available, it makes sense to adopt them. In the meantime, implementing one of the newer types of assessment, no matter how imperfect, is preferable to using only the old input and output measures or wringing one's hands and waiting for the ideal assessment environment to materialize. As Lakos and Phipps (2004) put it, when libraries have fully adopted systems thinking, "appreciation of the need for assessment as an everyday, reflective, systematic activity" (358) will be the norm.

9

Positioning the Academic Library for a Vibrant Future

DIFFERENT PERSPECTIVES ON LIBRARY PERFORMANCE

In a *Journal of Academic Librarianship* article, Dugan and Hernon (2002) identify three perspectives from which libraries have long been and still are evaluated:

- Looking at operations from the library's perspective
- Looking at the library from the user's perspective
- Looking at the library in the context of its contributions to the mission of the university. (376)

Dugan and Hernon (2002) also give a good sketch of the fundamental complexities of assessment for academic libraries. Early on they state, "Clearly quality is a multi-faceted concept that focuses on collections, services, and the place of the library in the learning process occurring within the institution" (376). Consequently, these authors along with many others urge the use of multiple measures to piece together an accurate picture of how well libraries are doing.

TRADITIONAL EVALUATION METHODS: FOCUS ON THE LIBRARY'S PERSPECTIVE

Collection size, budgetary support, staff to student ratios, available seating, and later on access to electronic resources remain important criteria for ranking members of consortia such as the Association of Research Libraries. As well as qualifying a library for consortial membership and benchmarking its adequacy (both over time against its own baseline record and with respect to peers), these types of input and output measures remain an important factor in making operational and administrative decisions such as staffing, operating hours, and allocation of materials and equipment budgets.

These traditional measures do give a picture of how well at a broad level libraries are equipped to meet information needs on campus. What they do *not* reveal is the information about individuals critical to assessment. Dugan and Hernon (2002) state emphatically, "Outputs do not measure changes in skills or attitudes of the individual as a result of their interactions with the library" (377) and again "they [aggregate statistics] reflect what the institution has accomplished; they do not reflect what (or how much) students have learned" (378).

In their 2002 book, *An Action Plan for Outcomes Assessment in Your Library,* Hernon and Dugan touch on a range of assessment issues including requirements of regional assessment bodies, information literacy, the balanced scorecard method of performance analysis, and measuring service quality; they also include a chapter on research methods such as reflective inquiry.

Nevertheless, as Bertot and McClure (2003) point out, the lack of common definitions and workable measures for fundamental elements of assessment such as outcomes, quality standards, service quality, and other performance dimensions hampers the most well-intentioned effort (610).

They conclude that as of the time of publication, there was no good way to measure outcomes. "While there certainly is potential for developing outcomes assessment, much work especially empirical research is necessary" (610). They point out the lack of time and understanding as major stumbling blocks for libraries that aspire to do assessment. "A major difficulty with outcomes assessment is that understanding outcomes, developing approaches to use outcomes as an assessment technique, training staff to be able to implement outcomes assessment, and then using the results for decision-making can be time-consuming and difficult" (608). And they quote a workshop participant to the effect that "clear, practical, usable evaluation methods and approaches are not available to practitioners" (608). One is left to ponder what *does* work and to decide on a method or methods that—if not ideal—represent the lesser of several evils.

ADOPTING THE USER'S EYE VIEW

Any discipline that subscribes to user-centeredness or customer service ideals, to the extent that academic libraries would have the public believe they do, should be willing to grant that the customer has some of the answers and be eager to incorporate customer input into planning and operational decisions. Indeed, the phrase "customer-centered" is an oxymoron without fairly detailed customer input.

Libraries and Social Exchange Theory

The belief in social exchange theory is the basis for accepting numerical and textual data from LibQUAL+™ as reliable indicators of library performance. This theory holds that in any social or economic exchange, the customer is the sole arbiter of the value of any tangible or intangible benefit(s) received in return for surrendering time, money, or effort to another person or entity. For this reason, data about perceptions of gaps between the ideal library service and the realities of what is delivered are one good measure of performance.

Professionals can say what they think is good for customers; but they cannot decree how customers will rate various offerings or which things customers will ultimately choose. Some select a lipstick, for example, for its staying power over the course of the day. Other customers decide mostly on the basis of price or the hot, new colors or even shopping convenience. One cannot reiterate too often that the value of a thing cannot be dictated to a user.

It is dangerous for any profession or business to attempt to prescribe what is valuable to someone else. As mentioned previously, the phrase "user-defined" expresses this concept much better than "user-focused" or "user-centered." The makers of the better buggy whip, the better mousetrap, New Coke, the Edsel, and countless other marketing failures all learned the fallacy of working in a vacuum when attempting to become *customer-centered*.

Absent input from customers, virtually any strategy for meeting customer needs is doomed to failure. For example, prior generations of U.S. consumers frequently prized quality (product features such as solid materials and careful construction) above style, convenience, or affordability in what they bought and used. But today's consumers—much more mobile than their forebearers and subject to a virtually constant barrage of media input—may well select products on the basis of color, disposability, price, or even celebrity endorsement in preference to durability and other product attributes formerly associated with quality. The astute library marketer has this rule engraved on his or her heart and ignores it at his or her peril.

How does all of this talk about the customer's perspective apply to academic libraries? Librarians need to get better at viewing their entire operations through the customer's eyes. A *Library Journal* article about signage and other cues to navigating in the library lambastes librarians for not adopting the customer's perspective frequently enough. The author begins with this bold statement about what library users and indeed almost everyone else values: "In a society that jealously guards its time, our job—if libraries are to remain relevant—is to get patrons in the door and in front of the materials they want quickly and easily" (Dempsey 2005, 72). Then she launches into the importance of "information architecture," meaning "the view of the library from its users' vantage point" (72). Apparently this term is equivalent to what was called *semiotics* (signage plus other things that help a use interpret his or her environment) some years ago.

The thoughts of Karen Rossi, a first-floor manager at Pittsburgh's Carnegie Library, are paraphrased by the author in these words: "The best information architecture is one that is completely intuitive and predictable to the user" (Dempsey 2005, 72). Most damning, the author goes on to charge that instead of designing library spaces and signs "so that our users can find things and find help easily … our field [library and information science] organizes in a way that makes it simple for librarians to put their hands on materials but has left users on the outside" (72). She gives "reference desk" as an example of library jargon and the Dewey Decimal System as the quintessential example of how libraries use complicated numerical systems instead of arranging materials in ways that users would find easier to comprehend and to locate (72).

With a string of irreverent, insightful, pithy maxims "Launched after a discussion with a passionate young librarian who cares," Karen Schneider's 2006 blog posting "The User Is Not Broken" captures the difficulty that librarians have listening to and sharing control with the user. The following is a selection of her comments:

You fear loss of control, but that has already happened. Ride the wave.

The user is not broken.

Your system is broken until proven otherwise.

It is easier for a camel to pass through the eye of a needle than to find a library website that is usable and friendly and provides services rather than talking about them in weird library jargon.

You cannot change the user, but you can transform the user experience to meet the user.

The user is not "remote". You, the librarian, are remote, and it is your job to close that gap.

Not surprisingly, this posting provoked 84 comments (and counting) from this country and abroad along with four backtracks. Most respondents found Schneider's document a breath of fresh air (e.g., "Can I get a *hell, yes!* Here?" from dmw later the same day). Interestingly, however, quite a few responses vigorously disagree with the idea of moving with the times and/or making the user the center of the library enterprise.

Analysis from the User Perspective

Of equal if not greater importance to *gathering* input from users and potential users is *analyzing* data from a user perspective as well as from the library's perspective. It is critical that the researcher avoids interjecting his or her prescriptive idea of what the user needs into the solution to problems unearthed by data. Libraries must be open to tailoring the library's processes to what users find important, rather than explaining and justifying current ways of operating that already have fallen short of meeting user expectations.

As the following comment attests, there frequently is dissatisfaction about user ability to locate books that are supposed to be on the shelf: "Perhaps the most frequently-occurring complaint [from the rounds of interviews to fine tune SERVQUAL results] is the unavailability of books found in the catalog and noted as available" (Cook and Heath 2001, 572). If this complaint is encountered, then the tactic of relocating sorting shelves and putting up new signs probably is not the most effective thing to do. Improving public access to sorting shelves might seem to staff like a solution to problems in finding books on the shelf. But why on earth should users have to check *two locations*? Clearly a better approach would be to shorten lag time between when books are returned and when they are reshelved by rethinking how to schedule staff and revising shelving procedures to reduce delays. Users like finding books where the catalog says they are located.

Processing reserves is another familiar example of the tendency to look at data from the library's perspective and—instead of changing library processes to better deliver what users want—expecting users to accept the library's excuses in lieu of asking for outcomes that would make their lives better. For example, too many libraries respond poorly to user dissatisfaction with the time it takes to process reserve materials at the start of the term. Complaints often result in nothing more than an elaborate campaign of reminders that faculty should request needed materials well in advance of when classes need them. A truly user-centered library, however, will examine its processes and procedures to significantly reduce lag time, in the way that a team at Arizona did.

Having discovered that root causes of delays as indicated by out-of-control points in processing reserve materials were (1) batch processing of like types of materials, (2) not scheduling for peak workload times, (3) requiring that a single person (with multiple responsibilities and interruptions) must process each item from start to finish, and (4) the need to release and reprocess some material every semester, an Arizona team made dramatic improvements by suggesting changes rather than endeavoring to "educate" users to expect less of the library. Scheduling more workers at peak intake times, implementing a first-in, first-out system to replace batch processing of reserve books and articles, and empowering and training workers to perform all steps of the intake procedure instead of being responsible for only discrete parts of the process resulted in big gains in user satisfaction (Larson 1998, 56–58).

Thus libraries subscribing to the balanced scorecard concept and/or learning organization ideals supplement traditional and easily collected statistics with a hefty amount of data focused on the users' needs and their satisfaction with library resources and services. And they address user concerns rather than brushing them aside. What does it take to capture this user perspective? Getting back to the core concept of user-defined benefits treated extensively in chapter two, a robust branch of mainstream marketing theory and practice tied to what customers want is customer relationship management (CRM), a relative newcomer on the marketing scene.

Customer Relationship Management

Companies and other organizations that believe in CRM seek a relationship with customers in order to build loyalty to their products and services—to avoid commoditization or the market dynamic wherein offerings of different firms are seen largely as interchangeable (like coal or sugar or some other products not particularly distinguishable one from another). This practice can give them an edge in a competitive environment with many players.

Not an Add-On

Despite the growing popularity of the concept and its partial implementation by a good many firms, OD professionals warn that CRM cannot merely be grafted onto an existing organization without concurrent organizational changes. "Getting close to customers is not just a matter of installing a better CRM system or finding a more effective way to measure and increase customer satisfaction levels" (Gulati and Oldroyd 2005, 92). The process of building good customer relations "is not so much a problem that the IT or marketing department needs to solve as a journey that the whole company needs to make" (92).

Aligning All Strategy

To achieve good CRM, all strategy must reflect a customer focus. As mentioned in chapter 4, Galbraith advises aligning all elements of the organization—the organization structure, strategies, human resource policies and practices, the reward system, and information handling processes—around delivering satisfaction to the customer. He contrasts the product-centric organization with the customer-centric one and explains in detail how each element of a customer-centric company is grounded in and derived from what the customer needs, rather than based on a desire to increase sales or profits or growth of the company.

Product Design. In companies attuned to CRM, the most important customer is not necessarily the most advanced customer but the most loyal customer. Thus the optimal outcome for a customer-centric organization is not delivering the latest technical innovations but finding the "best" products, meaning the best solution for each customer. "The best solution will involve a customized and personalized package of reliable products, services, support, education, and consulting to make the customer more effective" (Galbraith 2005, 17). It follows that the value a CRM company seeks to deliver is not necessarily new applications or cutting-edge technology or more utility. Instead, much of its focus is (1) customizing existing products to craft the best total solution for the customer and (2) searching for more customer needs to satisfy by the optimal combination of old and new products for this customer (10).

Price. According to Galbraith, the CRM company's prices are not based on what the market will bear but on a share of the value it delivers to the customer and a share of its risk in diverting money from operations to training. For example, a business school offering courses to a corporate customer will charge not a flat fee based on the cost of developing and administering the course content but a percentage of the savings or increased earnings the company enjoys after its staff receives the training. If there is no improvement, the business school gets nothing. If there is improvement, it gets, say, 5 percent of the savings achieved or 5% of the increased earnings (17).

Organizational Implications of CRM

Galbraith goes so far as to assert that the company with a strong customer focus wants what is best for the company (profits, growth in sales, etc.) *only if* its strategies for attaining company goals are also in the customer's best interest and thus will make the customer more efficient and effective at the same that the company prospers. This being the case, the customer-centric organization's structure and processes will revolve around the customer. Instead of being organized into profit centers with product teams engaged in product reviews, the company practicing CRM will be organized by customer segments with customer teams; and its criteria for success will be helping the customer to function better. Its most important operational processes, therefore, will be customer relationship management and developing solutions, rather than constantly developing new products (18).

Finally, in the customer-centric organization, both the organizational culture and the reward structure will reinforce desired behaviors. The most powerful staff will not be innovators and product developers but those with the most in-depth knowledge of the customer's needs. Achievements will be gauged not by market share, percentage of total revenue earned by new products, or by the number of new products developed within the business cycle. Instead, the reward system will recognize the following outcomes: increases in the customer segment deemed most profitable and most loyal; increases in customer satisfaction; and solid performance in retaining valued customers, especially lifelong customers (22–23).

Moving toward CRM

One wonders, "How exactly can an organization transform itself into a customer-focused entity?" Gulati and Oldroyd (2005) have found that organizations that have made significant progress toward becoming customer-focused subscribe to three basic beliefs and model these principles in their operations: (1) Customer knowledge at the "granular" level—in other words, a comprehensive database of each customer's past, current, and future contacts with the company must be compiled; (2) the norm of sharing such information across the company must be instilled in employees and a mechanism for doing so created; and (3) the insights gained must be used to guide all aspects of planning and operations, "not only their product and service decisions but their basic strategy and organizational structure as well" (95). The key to such progress is coordination.

Over time the successful companies studied by these authors managed to "enable and enforce coordination between internal units at successively more sophisticated levels … [including finding] new ways to manage the flow of information … [establishing] routines for decision-making that incorporate customer preferences, and ultimately they shift the locus of their customer-focused efforts from a centralized hub to a more-diverse set of activities that spans the entire enterprise" (Gulati and Oldroyd 2005, 95).

Four Stages of Coordinating Customer Relationship Information

Through their work with 17 firms—including Harrah Entertainment, Continental Airlines, and the Royal Bank of Canada among others—Gulati and Oldroyd (2005) identified four stages in the transition to a customer-focused organization and mapped the organizational changes needed for such a progression. They characterize stage one as communal coordination, stage two as serial coordination, stage three as symbiotic coordination, and stage four as integral coordination.

Communal Coordination. The first step toward stage one, communal coordination, is establishing a database that records as many interactions as possible between the customer and the firm. (Note that these authors include in the definition of the customer other stakeholders with an interest in and/or the ability to affect the business. For example, the pharmaceutical industry might include in their customer database not only patients for whom medicine is needed but also their doctors, their families, insurance companies, and regulatory bodies.) Information gleaned from what the authors call "touch points" (95) where customers and employees interact must be coded in standardized ways and organized with the individual customer as the fundamental unit of analysis rather than the purchase details (price, time, etc.), the product, or the sales location. All company units contribute data to this central repository; and after the data has been cleaned up and made easy to access, any unit can draw information from the database as needed. It is advisable to give responsibility for maintaining the central repository to a part of the organization outside of any functional area, so that it remains politically neutral and can be expected to exhibit less bias than any unit affiliated with a given functional area. It goes without saying that this entity must have the requisite technical skills to maintain the information database.

The foremost advantage of a central repository is having a company-wide unified view of issues like who the most valuable customers are and what is important to them. This information can be used to find and remedy errors in customer service, to point out where processes can be improved to save time or cut costs, and to discover more sales opportunities. Most important, this development constitutes a milestone in moving toward a customer-focused organization as individual units begin to realize that customer information they have gathered is an important asset to be shared across the company and as ambiguities caused by data that cannot be compared have been eliminated.

Serial Coordination. In stage two, serial coordination, the company moves beyond collecting customer data to coordinating analysis of data and sharing of conclusions throughout the organization. At this stage of the transition to a customer-centric organization, the unit responsible for initial analysis of the data typically is either marketing or a separate unit staffed with experts in statistical analysis of business factors. The term *serial coordination* comes from the practice of handing the information from one department to another in succession to use in planning and executing strategy based on customer behavior and preferences. Various operational units (e.g., sales, marketing, finance, and product development) are asked to give input about how changes to key variables such as prices and scheduling might be expected to affect customer choices.

Symbiotic Coordination. Stage three, symbiotic coordination, requires a higher level of coordination as companies begin to shift from dissecting past customer contacts to anticipating and, it is hoped, influencing future customer behavior by answering the following types of questions. Which customers are likely to try a new product or service? Which might be lured away by a competitor? What incentives might forestall such a defection? And which customers represent credit risks? Answering such questions requires that "information and decisions flow back and forth between central analytics units, operating units, and marketing, sales ... and even laterally among the organizational units themselves" (98). (It is worth noting that the stage three process of determining what works with customers described by these authors is similar to the action research that libraries are urged to conduct.) Models are created to predict customer behavior, various strategies intended to influence behavior are carried out, the results are measured, and feedback from front-line staff is used to improve the models.

Not all staff members who must cooperate and coordinate their stage three activities in order to test such models are likely to be in the same department or unit. "Symbiotic coordination requires people in several units who have no formal reporting relationship to interact in spontaneous and unsystematic ways through a constant give and take. Work is not handed off serially from one group to another; people are learning together in real time" (99). This being the case, two approaches to fostering coordination of efforts are common: Either a new organizational unit is created to handle such coordination or the entire company is reorganized into "customer segments that cut across product, technology, and geographic boundaries" (99).

Integral Coordination. The objective of stage four, integral coordination, is to incorporate the new, more sophisticated understanding of the customer attained by the stage three "test-and-learn culture" (99) into every part of the business, in effect to "weave customer focus into the informal values and daily behavior of all employees [until] customer focus begins to define the organization and pervade its every aspect" (99). At this point, responsibility for initiatives to improve customer satisfaction is distributed throughout the company, rather than vested in one or a small number of units, as line employees "are given the autonomy and latitude … to focus on the customer in virtually every interaction " (99). The payoff is that this stage makes possible real-time responses to customer needs (97). The authors concede that stage three is difficult to achieve and to maintain because it requires changing the attitudes of a critical mass of employees. "Shifts in attitude cannot be forced. Employees can only be nudged, pressured, coaxed—and provided incentives" (101). They reveal that after changing the reward structure to reinforce desired behaviors, at least one company also took the drastic step of letting go "recalcitrant resisters" (101) to the customer-focused organization.

The degree of CRM exemplified by some of the most well-regarded commercial entities might seem like an impossible dream, given how academic libraries are staffed and funded. Yet it is a model libraries should emulate. Along with all other organizations in the service sector of the economy, academic libraries share the difficult task of ensuring that our entire outfit from top to bottom and sideways as well puts the customer first—communicating fully, putting the customer's interests above our own comfort and convenience, and empowering front-line staff to solve customer problems instead of passing the buck when formal policy seems inimical to the customer's interests. CRM is a tool that offers academic libraries a decent chance to compete successfully for customers in the rough and tumble information arena.

THE THIRD PERSPECTIVE FOR LIBRARY EVALUATION: THE HAND THAT FEEDS US

Taken by itself, neither the library perspective nor the user perspective constitutes a comprehensive assessment of library quality. Since opinions of *all* stakeholders (i.e., any persons or entities possessing an interest in or the ability to significantly influence the marketing enterprise) are pieces of the mosaic defining quality, expectations from publics beyond the library and its users must be addressed as well.

Assessing Student Learning Outcomes

Evaluation versus Assessment

Parent institutions have long required that academic libraries be trustworthy and competent managers of information as well as good stewards of financial and human resources, supporting campus information needs as comprehensively and as cost-effectively as possible. Since the advent of student learning outcomes assessment, however, an additional and very important dimension has been added to the factors by which library quality is judged.

Dugan and Hernon (2002) take a great deal of trouble to distinguish assessment of student learning outcomes from other forms of evaluation. Evaluation is intended to "measure whether or not a system does what it is designed to do in an efficient and effective manner" (378). The traditional notion of evaluation *assumes* a relationship between input statistics (e.g., materials budget), output statistics (e.g., volumes added annually), and general outcomes or results (institutional performance on some aspect such as retention of students), whereas assessment requires *proof*. It calls for qualitative and/or quantitative documentation that libraries along with academic departments and other campus entities have had a positive impact on the knowledge and/or skills and competencies acquired by students during the higher education experience.

Gratch, Dugan and Hernon, and others have pointed out that accrediting agencies increasingly require documentation of student learning outcomes when assessing quality in academic library operations—student learning outcomes being defined as documentation of changes in "attributes and abilities, both cognitive and affective, which reflect how the student experiences at the institution supported their development as individuals" (Dugan and Hernon 2002, 377).

Good Assessment: A Mix of Objective and Subjective Measures

Dugan and Hernon (2002) caution that it is not wise to rely exclusively on subjective measures for assessing either a specific instruction class or the library services as a complex of resources and services. "Student learning outcomes assessment involves more than just measuring student expectations (service quality and satisfaction)" (380). More robust documentation will include objective measures along with self-reporting.

This is particularly true of library instruction. While relatively easy to obtain, self-assessments about what concepts were learned in an instruction session or about incorporating new knowledge into future research strategies provide rather weak evidence of learning. How does one separate over-confidence and good intentions from real cognitive gains?

Administering an objective measure before dismissing an instruction class—for example, asking attendees to draw a diagram or a map showing relationships between key concepts taught in an instructional session or asking attendees to identify the three muddiest (least clear) points—should be effective in documenting what was and was not learned. Alternately, assessing learning some time after a given session by doing content analysis of student work or evaluation of source lists can also provide strong documentation. In an optimal assessment environment, a rigorous research design including pre-test and post-test results would be used to supplement one-shot measures of student learning outcomes.

In addition, employing both direct methods (e.g., examination of student products such as developmental portfolios) and indirect methods (reviewing curricula and class syllabi) is recommended when possible.

Correlation versus Causation

It is relatively easy to show correlation between some level of library use or library instruction and student learning. Between first year and senior year, most undergraduates do indeed show improvement in cognitive abilities such as critical thinking and attitudinal characteristics such as valuing diversity. But establishing causation is difficult. The observation that two things are true about a subject population in no way proves that one of the variables has caused the other.

Here's a hypothetical example to illustrate the difference between correlation and causation. Assume that an observer has noted from data about Swedish-American women that they not only attend church in higher numbers than women from other ethnic groups but also that they tend to have significantly larger feet than other women of all ethnic backgrounds. Despite the immutable truth of both observations, however, categorically stating that regular church attendance causes women to have big feet would be errant nonsense. This is a prime example of correlation where no causative relationship between the two variables can be said to exist.

Accounting for all variables is important in establishing causation. In documenting positive outcomes of library instruction, for example, it is desirable to control such variables as prior instruction (transfer students and students with transferable skills from high school), help from peers or faculty mentors, independent learning, and so forth to the extent that this consideration can be factored into the research design.

Performance Evaluation: Institutional Outcomes

When the entire library's performance is being evaluated, capturing significant and reliable information becomes even more difficult. Isolating the effects of library operations from other college experiences is difficult. "It is nearly impossible to quantify, much less isolate, a university library's contribution" toward outcomes like "development of student attitudes of openness, flexibility, curiosity, creativity, and an appreciation of a broad perspective" (Bertot and McClure 2003, 603). Like many other out-of-class aspects of education—faculty mentoring and advising, on- and off-campus dining experiences and living conditions, affiliation with the Greek system or with clubs, and a host of recreational/leisure pursuits— the library doubtless *does* contribute to such aspects of student learning.

Arguably, academic libraries play a role in advancing other university priorities such as student recruitment and retention as well as in achieving specific learning outcomes. But these authors maintain that it is a stretch to connect library resources and services to either student learning outcomes or other institutional outcomes, to say in what exact ways and to what extent the library's existence may have affected these types of institutional priorities: "To ignore other university activities that likely contribute to the outcome would yield an incomplete picture of library contributions ... at best and distort the library's contributions to outcomes attainment at worst" (Bertot and McClure 2003, 603).

In practice, rigor in documenting the library's contribution to campus-wide priorities is not necessarily demanded by the university. Good faith efforts to align library operations with university priorities and to assess the library's performance with respect to goals and priorities that fall under the umbrella of the university's mission and emphases will be appreciated despite any incompleteness and/or lack of a direct and demonstrable link between library operations and institutional outcomes. Since the library serves the entire faculty and student body, not as much data-supported proof of its contributions to institutional priorities is expected from the library as is required of specific academic disciplines and units. The best approach, therefore, is to measure what makes sense and to qualify any analysis by acknowledging that not all factors related to library support of the university mission, goals, and priorities can be directly measured or demonstrated.

The ACRL's *Standards for Libraries in Higher Education* (2004) offer some useful broad approaches to documenting academic library contributions to the university, particularly in the context of re-accreditation. Starting with the disclaimer that to be widely applicable, the standards must avoid being narrowly specific or prescriptive, the document goes on to offer "a comprehensive outline to methodically examine and analyze all library operations, services, and outcomes in the context of accreditation" (under "Preface").

This document defines outcomes as "the ways in which library users are changed as a result of their contact with the library's resources and programs"(ACRL 2004, under "Forward") and urges that outcomes should be used for assessing academic library effectiveness in addition to the traditional input and output measures. It points out that meaningful assessment takes into account *non-users* as well as current users. It provides points of comparison for gauging internal progress and the library's position relative to peer institutions. And finally, it gives both a summary of what is essential in assessing library effectiveness in various operational and administrative areas as well as specific talking points in the form of questions to address. The areas of endeavor covered include Services, Instruction, Resources, Access, Communication and Cooperation, Administration, and Budget.

The standard applicable to facilities reads as follows: "The library facility and its branches should be well planned; it should provide secure and adequate space, conducive to study and research with suitable environmental conditions for its services, personnel, resources, and collections. The library's equipment should be adequate and functional" (ACRL 2004, under "Facilities"). Specific questions cover mechanical systems for heating, cooling, and ventilation, ergonomic workstations and well-configured work space for staff, seating for users, signage and other mechanisms for navigating throughout the building, electrical and network wiring and connections, ADA compliance, and accommodation of distance learners.

IF IT'S SO HARD, WHY EVEN TRY?

No More Free Passes

If not required to do so, hardly anybody would choose to take time from the joys of serving people that called many to librarianship in the first place to do administrative chores such as budgeting. But most librarians have long since learned that they'll never again enjoy the kind of free pass to do good works that libraries enjoyed during the halcyon days when funds were more plentiful and library operations were relatively inexpensive. Thus a realistic annual budget request reflecting both library and university mission and priorities, preferably with room for pursuit of long-term aspirations, is the backbone of everything else that libraries do.

In the same way, librarians need to accept the new reality that marketing and organizational development tools now are necessities and not merely options for those who like to dabble in them. Librarians can equip themselves to deal with these disciplines now. Or they can wait until *driven* to adopting newer management philosophies and tools. The consequence of waiting, however, may well be working in marginal institutions where opportunities to do what one feels is important are diminished with each succeeding day.

How Do We Cope?

In the academic library milieu and beyond it, some of the literature would have the reader believe that defining organizational culture it is as straightforward as reciting the chemical formula for water. Indeed, a *Library Trends* article advocates using the library's organizational culture to recruit prospective employees—as if the essence of this elusive attribute were no more complicated to capture and articulate than the library's geographic location (Oltmanns 2004). In point of fact, however, reputable OD theoreticians view diagnosing organizational culture as a complex and difficult task.

A classic OD text identifies five different systems for measuring organizational culture, aka "organizational climate," singling out Likert's model as "the best known of these and also the most applicable in many situations" (Higgins 1982, 209). This system is based on four styles of management characterized variously as Exploitive Authoritative, Benevolent, Consultative, and Participative Group. According to Higgins, Likert rates organizational cultures based on the following dimensions derived from various management styles: (1) modes of motivation utilized and locus of responsibility for achieving goals; (2) the purpose, direction, accuracy, and completeness of communication; (3) the source of information for making decisions and the degree of participation from different levels of staff; (4) the method of developing organizational objectives and the degree of resistance/support from subordinates; and (5) details about the review and control mechanisms (211).

A later book about organizational culture offers an excellent picture of its richness and complexity. It describes how after subjecting 39 measures of organizational effectiveness to statistical analysis, two management professors found that organizational values extrapolated from descriptions of effectiveness clustered along two major dimensions. From this analysis, they developed the Competing Values Framework for assessing or diagnosing organizational culture.

The vertical axis of their model has opposing end points ranging from "flexibility, discretion, and dynamism" to "stability, order, and control" (Cameron and Quinn, 1999, 30–31). The horizontal axis represents a continuum between two other extremes in organizational values: "an internal orientation, integration, and unity" versus "an external orientation, differentiation, and competition" (30–31). They dub the four quadrants on one side or the other of these axes respectively as "clan," "adhocracy," "hierarchy," and "market" cultures. Although Cameron and Quinn claim a great deal of utility for their model and assert that it is predictive of organizational performance, they also concede that not all organizations fit neatly into one of the four quadrants.

About 20 percent of the organizations Cameron and Quinn (1999, 40) studied exhibited an almost equal balance of the four types of organizational values. The following statements these authors make about such atypical organizations are applicable also to many academic libraries:

- "Mature and highly effective organizations tend to develop subunits or segments that represent each of theses culture types" (48).
- "Those [leaders] rated by their peers, supervisors, and subordinates as the most highly-effective exhibit skills and abilities in all four quadrants" (42).
- "Organizational effectiveness in institutions of higher education was highest in organizations that emphasized innovation and change (adhocracy) and at the same time, stability and control (hierarchy) ... were supportive of and developed their employees (clan) but also demanded output and achievement from them (market)" (71).

Like the companies Cameron and Quinn studied, academic libraries are assessed by multilayered and sometimes contradictory sets of expectations. Indeed, this aspect of Cameron and Quinn's work goes a long way toward explaining why academic library cultures frequently seem somewhat schizophrenic. Judged by users, administrators, staff, and other stakeholders according to outcomes flowing from diametrically opposed belief systems and modes of behavior, academic librarians must make obeisance to many different deities. They are told by various stakeholders, "Save money but deliver more, better, and quicker service. Court prospective donors but don't neglect our bread and butter, the campus community. Store seldom used materials off site to relieve crowding but have everything users could ever want at their fingertips. Staff as many reference desk, chat, cataloging, and individual consultation hours as possible but keep personal costs low. Participate in library and campus discussion and decision-making groups. Lend as much energy as possible to endeavors such as changing the structure and practices of scholarly publishing but don't skimp on keeping computer skills current or polishing communication, decision-making, negotiation, analytical, and other skills critical to the smooth functioning of teams. And in your spare time, excel at teaching and join communities of reflective practice."

So how can academic librarians cope with such diverse expectations and begin to employ disciplines they may not fully understand, much less be in a position to implement? They can learn from the example set by Pitt, Arizona, and other progressive library colleagues, extrapolating to the local environment whatever theories, tools, and practices fit. It is essential to formally incorporate as many best practices from marketing, strategic planning, and organizational development into library planning and daily operations as possible. Librarians mustn't leave the higher order of management concerns to chance or give them a lesser priority than reference service, cataloging, systems development, or other library responsibilities. The following are some recommendations about how to get started.

Become Proficient in Quantitative Aspects of Operations and Planning

If possible, library administrators need to learn enough about quantitative theories and tools to take the lead in measurement and analysis of customer input, process improvement, and the like. Failing that, they must learn enough about quantitative matters to recruit others with the requisite skills and to be confident that subordinates are doing the highest caliber of work and not leading the library down a dead-end path. Then administrators need to empower subordinates (individuals or teams) to do this top priority work, support them with sufficient resources, and monitor their work without second-guessing or micro-managing.

Please the Holders of the Purse Strings (Administrators)

First, last, and always, academic libraries must please those who fund them. This does not mean flattering or bamboozling university administration, browbeating faculty colleagues into thinking the library's way, or playing campus politics in a cynical manner. (Virtually all people have a long memory for a slight or a betrayal.) Instead, "pleasing the holders of the purse strings" means demonstrating by actions as well as rhetoric that the library understands and embraces the university's values and priorities, makes thoughtful choices, uses resources responsibly, and is ready to play a positive and unique role in the teaching and learning community's present and future success.

Assess and Report Progress

No matter how timely or how popular an aspect of library operations is, it is unwise to declare victory without carefully measuring and analyzing outcomes and comparing what is with what will be most beneficial in the long term. Don't take anything on faith even if it represents the best thinking to date. Although what the library presently is doing may be worthwhile, there may be a better way. Don't represent the failed or marginal effort to the outside world as a significant improvement. It might be easy to pull the wool over the eyes of the public in the short term, but libraries inevitably are called upon to prove the value of their achievements and to justify retention of any increases in their share of university resources.

Avoid jargon and esoteric details. Couch report content in terms the intelligent lay person can understand and spare the reader interesting but unnecessary digressions. Where possible, refer to concepts and invoke values that are broadly familiar to the intended audience. It isn't hard to hide negatives behind obfuscation. But in doing so, one runs the risk of losing the reader's interest and failing to connect at any level. Any beleaguered administrator might confess, "I don't come in every day and decide which of the things on my to-do list are important enough to do. All of the items are critical, and I have the unhappy task of deciding which of them to defer." Take it on faith, such is the plight of virtually every denizen of today's fast-paced higher education world, whether anyone heard them articulate this sentiment or not. Write briefly. Find the "hooks" to grab their attention. Be succinct and make a graceful exit *before* you or your documents are given the bum's rush.

Keep Asking the Hard Questions

Library administrators cannot rest on their laurels or allow anyone else in the organization to labor under the misapprehension that the status quo is good enough. In today's milieu of blindingly fast environmental changes, the best one can hope for is to get ahead of the curve temporarily, consolidate lessons learned, and get ready for the next realignment with reality. There can be no sacred cows among library operations. Collections and services that currently are suboptimal can be given a temporary reprieve if there is a plan to bring them up to par. But they cannot be continued indefinitely based on nostalgia or reluctance to make hard choices.

This principle is as important in vetting proposed new projects as in reassessing established operations. The idea that an interesting and attractive new project will do no harm is not sufficient justification for approving it. Any aspect of operations that cannot be shown likely to make a distinct and sustainable contribution toward the library's long-term survival is a waste of precious resources and a luxury that today's academic library cannot afford.

Be Proactive

Librarians must anticipate and address changes in the environment instead of merely preserving the status quo or being responsive to changes that are mandated for them. Although it is necessary to start with what stakeholders need and want, beyond initial information gathering, it is unwise to be always asking permission to do what is in the library's and the university's best interest. When a difficult path has been chosen (e.g., closing a collection that is no longer relevant to curricular or research needs), it is best to forge ahead even where there is some resistance to the decision. Fallout will be much less prolonged and much less damaging if the library administration assesses the number and political strength of areas of support and potential resistance to its proposed action, outlines the consequences of *failing* to act, makes a cogent and convincing case for the benefits of what it feels is the best course of action, and then lets the chips fall where they may.

Reach Out

It is a truism that the heyday of the bricks-and-mortar library is gone probably forever. Yes, certain classes of library users—undergraduates (who typically live in cramped quarters and lack the funds to write and study in the comfortable atmosphere of a commercial establishment) and those few faculty whose early training and personality make them reluctant to eschew the serendipity of browsing the shelves and fondling the physical volumes in favor of online access—still affirm the importance of the library as place. And yes, certain classes of library materials still important to researchers may never be cost-effective candidates for digitization. But for most academic libraries, enticing users into the library buildings is at best a niche marketing strategy and cannot represent the totality of their operational effort. Gone forever is the efficacy of sitting complacently inside the library and expecting users to be drawn into the library's orbit. This holds true for virtually all aspects of library operations.

Instruction. Take library instruction out to nonlibrary classrooms where possible. If the facilities are as good as library connection and projection capabilities, the librarian faculty will be viewed as an outside expert instead of an interruption to the more important work of the class. Take publicity out of the library to where both users and nonusers are. Put up posters and hand out premiums (magnets, coupons, etc.) in the student union, the dorms, the recreation facilities, at sports events, and in faculty office areas as well as in library buildings.

Gathering Customer Information. Recruit survey participants not just on library pages but as much as possible from other sites within the university's information technology architecture. (If survey questions and data must be hosted on library space, then at least get links to them placed on upper level university pages.)

Providing Services. Give up on "educating" faculty about adapting to the convenience of library staff and the pace of library work. Provide them on-campus delivery of nonelectronic library materials and off-campus access to electronic library resources. Design services with their preferences in mind, rather than library limitations. Instead of scolding faculty for procrastination or nagging them to plan ahead, schedule reserve staff intensively at the beginning of the semester when faculty are ready to think about putting course materials on reserve. Instead of requiring them to provide the library with photocopies of reserve materials, find a way to pay royalties and digitize course materials as much as possible. Cook and Heath (2001) advise, "Access ... is not merely a substitution of electronic versions for print but rather the delivery of information when needed, wherever needed, in the medium of choice" (567).

Do 360-Degree Evaluation and Communicate Fully

Never forget to get input on important plans as well as current operations from peers at the same level, vendors/suppliers, subordinates, competitors, partners, those above in the university hierarchy, politicians who can help or hurt you, accrediting agencies, and others who can significantly influence the library's future.

There is never enough time to communicate; but it still is critical to assess strategic communication links and be intentional about communicating as broadly as possible and in the best manner to groups and individuals that matter.

Emphasize Recruitment and Training

Given the irrevocable pace of change, *all* organizations now are learning organizations, whether they know it or not. And the implications for academic libraries are considerable. Functional competencies—cataloging, reference/instruction skills, information technology skills, successful grant-writing experience—will be emphasized for the foreseeable future in position descriptions, job ads, and the interviewing process. Yet the ideal candidate will have not only functional expertise but also characteristics and qualities that suit him or her for the learning organization: team skills, leadership qualities, quantitative abilities, project management skills, software competencies, and a future orientation.

Such is the investment of time and funds in identifying and recruiting the best candidate for a position that no library can afford to ignore the importance of retaining productive employees and providing regular training and development opportunities to all staff. Training can no longer be considered a frill or implemented as an afterthought. It is essential for all organizations aspiring to remain current and competitive, not the least academic libraries.

The nature of the training can vary depending on the needs and learning styles of staff members as well as the resources available to support their training: user groups sharing applications, tips, and tricks of new software versions; reflective practice groups for reference librarians and instructors; formal course work; vendor training; telecasts; electronic tutorials; and the like. As much time and money should be earmarked for its support as possible.

In allocating financial support and/or released time for training, attention should be paid to intended outcomes. What skills and competencies does the organization need to develop? Are supervisors/teams requesting such training for staff or encouraging staff to make their own request? Which staff members actually use their training in their jobs and what are the benefits to the organization and/or to end users following staff training?

Are there staff members who appear to volunteer for any and all training simply because they prefer being anywhere except at their assigned work station? Are there those who have an appetite for learning and extensive curiosity but are more hobbyists than practitioners, making no attempt to apply the new skills or to keep them current? Training requests that appear to have marginal value to the organization can be approved or deferred on the basis of staff's brief rationale for how the training in question will enhance their performance. Specific, measurable outcomes may be asked for and follow-up must be done. Reporting "I went to the training on such and such a date" would not qualify an applicant for approval of subsequent optional training. Conversely, "I made an Access database to handle transaction statistics at the reference desk" would be an excellent training outcome and should incline the supervisor to approve subsequent training opportunities.

Establish a Safe Atmosphere

It goes without saying that in order to get anyone to stretch him- or herself, the powers that be and staff at every level must cooperate to establish a safe atmosphere. This does not mean giving anyone carte blanche to experiment without being held accountable. But it *does* mean that rather than punishing mistakes, the organization needs to consider failures part of the learning process and to mine them for chances to improve subsequent efforts. It also means that people must feel safe talking about ideas, questioning popular viewpoints, and proposing innovations. These principles are emphasized in teams can also be applied by smart managers and supervisors within more traditional organizational settings.

Maximize Planning Outcomes

Birdsall (1997) gives good advice about making the most of the strategic planning process in academic libraries. Prefacing his remarks by pointing out that—despite the amount of effort and time that typically go into an academic library strategic plan—"libraries typically are given scant mention in the strategic plan of the institution" (254), he offers to libraries three excellent tips for increasing the positive impact of the process: (1) recognize and build on diverse stakeholder interests; (2) form alliances and coalitions for support of the library among critical campus entities and individuals; and (3) market the planning document by involving campus decision makers in its formulation and by making its every aspect appealing (254–55).

In building upon diversity of interests, Birdsall (1997) counsels against the prevailing practice among many academic libraries of avoidance of "hot" issues. "Library administrators ... often skirt around anything deemed political in academe" (255). Instead he urges involving as many stakeholders as possible in the planning process, with the expectation that "in this way, differences can be recognized and conflicts mitigated, if not resolved" (255). Failing such a hopeful outcome, he says "general policies can be formulated to stand, in effect, as treaties among interest groups. Although such policies may not reflect a true consensus, they should approach a reasonable level of agreement among the parties" (255). Harvard is cited as a shining success at harnessing instead of dodging such diverse pockets of specialized interest and potential resistance to library plans.

He concedes that it is "more difficult to generate coalitions of support and advocacy among external campus groups" than to enlist library staff in supporting the strategic plan. Birdsall (1997) relates how some ARL libraries approached this challenge—each one going beyond communicating with the library advisory committee and the provost to establishing a dialog with "key campus officials" from vice presidents and other deans/directors to opinion leaders among faculty (256–57). Then he recommends posing three questions to campus planners, in hopes of making library goals important to the whole university. His paraphrase of Breivik's questions from her 1993 *Educational Record* article follows:

- How can information resources and technologies best support institutional priorities?
- How can we best organize our information resources and technologies to make the strongest contribution to the identified priorities?
- How can we best deploy our limited human and fiscal information technology resources so that all graduates are information literate? (258)

Finally, Birdsall (1997) advises employing every tool and tactic available to make the strategic plan persuasive, attractive, and inviting. From looking at 17 plans written by Association of Research Libraries members, he notes several features characteristic of the ones that he finds most effective in "conveying that the library is in control of its future and worthy of fiscal support" (258):

- Carefully thinking
- Avoidance of "pedantic" writing
- Consistent alignment of library directions with institutional goals and stakeholder interests
- Attractive layout that supports the text in conveying a positive impression
- "Simple but elegant" format to showcase "an articulate essay on the library's readiness to face the future" (258)

For This I Went to Library School?

At this point in the chapter, the long-suffering, traditionally oriented librarian reader—having had it "up to here" with talk of marketing, strategic planning, and organizational development—may be audibly muttering, "I didn't go to library school to muck around in stuff like this!" But guess what? By and large, the libraries many professionals prepared themselves to work in and lead do not exist any more. (Practitioners who graduated less than six months ago might be an exception to this broad generalization.)

Optimistic View

One contemporary view of libraries' future is fairly sanguine and could be applied to the academic library milieu. "Rejuvenating the brand depends on reconstructing the experience of using the library" (De Rosa et al. 2005, 6–8). Since libraries' role "as a place to learn, as a place to read, as a place to make information freely available, as a place to support literacy, as a place to provide research support, as a place to provide free computer/Internet access and more" addresses real consumer needs and since these services are distinct aspects of a vital library brand image, this study commissioned by OCLC says that libraries have a bright future as long as they can effect sufficient large-scale change to update their image with consumers from a purveyor of nostalgia (books) to relevance in today's "infosphere" (6–8).

Darker View

Writing for *EDUCAUSE,* the dean of University Libraries and chief information officer at University of California–Los Angeles paints a less certain future for academic libraries in their present incarnation. Campbell (2006) concedes that in the current period of transition from a hybrid of print-based and electronic resources to the preeminence of electronic content, academic libraries still have a value-added role to play on their respective campuses. "Simply put, even a revolution as rapid as this still requires a transition period—during which current library operations remain necessary" (16). But he admonishes that—since the Internet and Web turned the world upside down in "a scant decade"—libraries may not have as long as they might wish to come to terms with their changing roles. And he points out that there may be a fight for each of the nontraditional roles (18) to which libraries aspire.

Learning Space Role. Regarding the information commons or quality learning space role for academic libraries, Campbell (2006) cautions that even if universities decide they need "high-quality, library-like space for student interaction, peer learning, collaboration, and similar functions" (20) that space will not necessarily be under library control. "Thus, although it is highly likely that library space in prime locations will be utilized increasingly less for storing book collections, how such space will be repurposed is less certain" (20).

Metadata Provider Role. Of the library's self-appointed role as provider of metadata, Campbell (2006) questions to what extent librarians will be involved in the future. "Precisely what kind of organizing principles will eventually be employed [within the Web environment] and what role humans will play in the process are still being discovered" (22). And he says much the same about library interventions to make using the Web more intuitive and transparent to users. "There will be considerable need within the academy for the development of portals, tools, and strategies for precision research on the vast Web. But it is not clear how long this need will exist or whether such portals, tools, and strategies should be developed by librarians [since] most major developments in these areas have taken place outside of libraries, in the commercial database or portal world" (22).

Reference Guru Role. Campbell's (2006) take on virtual or chat reference is similar. He feels that the academic library's Achilles heel here is based on (1) "encroachment from increasingly sophisticated natural-language search engines" and (2) their "decreased patience with reference services based on personal response, even if they are Web-delivered and asynchronous" (22)—in other words, customer preference for impersonal and nonintrusive assistance.

Teaching/Training Role. As far as information literacy, Campbell (2006) mentions several potential challenges to any ongoing need for this type of training of users: (1) simplification of the complex information environment, reducing the need for explication; (2) increasingly sophisticated vendor marketing directly to readers, reducing dependence on librarian intervention; and (3) "maturation of the Web as a source of knowledge and as a knowledge-retrieval mechanism" (24), which he expects to need for personal help in navigating and using web-based information. Even if the need remains, he questions whether it will be sufficient to justify keeping academic libraries at full force.

Collection Management Role. Pointing out how approval plans have already revolutionized the role of librarians as selectors and collection developers, Campbell (2006) anticipates a continuation of this trend. As more material is issued digitally and less is published in print form, he sees the librarian's role shifting further from selector to manager of licenses and ponders how "large and how important this role will be" (25).

Digital Collection Management Role. Conceding that some types of archival material that have not been digitized still retain value for scholars and researchers, Campbell (2006) believes that the trend toward digitizing a *portion* of these archives and mounting them on the Web has revitalized the library's role as collector, preserver, and distributor of materials "essential for documenting major aspects of represented cultures" (26). He asserts that the resulting increase in use of archival materials has both (1) "given new value and impetus" to the importance of archival collections and (2) possibly provided "a significant opportunity" for future librarians/archivists (26).

Affirming the value of digitizing archival and scientific material (such as that mounted by ULS at Pitt, Massachusetts Institute of Technology, and a number of other institutions), Campbell (2006) opines that the need for institutional repositories (IRs) remains robust and comprises a compelling role for academic libraries. "This [the capacity of IRs to host faculty publications and data sets as well as archival materials like photos and local history] is exceedingly fortunate because of the growing need for a long term preservation of the datasets originating from the computational sciences, sciences, social sciences, technology, and medicine" (28). Urging libraries to acquire necessary technical skills to manage and maintain IRs, he is guardedly optimistic about IRs being a significant role in the academic library's future. "Even though the management of IRs goes well beyond the skills of most senior librarians and even of some more recently educated librarians, to the degree that IRs become the responsibility of libraries, they may provide a solid foundation for the future of academic libraries" (28). Again, that nagging doubt about whether librarians can capture responsibility for IRs or whether they will lose this turf battle to another campus or commercial entity surfaces.

Many academic librarians will want to debate the points Campbell makes and dismiss out of hand the issues he raises—asserting that, *of course* libraries are doing good and *of course* their place in the academy is assured and unassailable. But is it really? And can librarians afford to brush aside Campbell's challenge to face these issues head on and to engage the rest of the university in a robust exchange of ideas about the continuing role of the academic library in higher education?

The Handwriting on the Wall

Campbell (2006) points out signs of "financially triggered draconian responses" to financial pressures on institutions. These have prompted layoffs of librarians in places as close as Philadelphia and as far flung as Wales; the closing of the Salinas, California, public library system; and the proposed withdrawal of state support for Mississippi's 60-member library consortium (28). To forestall similar actions in academe, he says that to contend successfully for roles that will utilize their unique skills and consolidate their value to the public, academic libraries must initiate a lively discussion about such issues. Since "neither academic librarians nor others in the academy have a crisp notion of where exactly academic libraries fit in the emerging twenty-first-century information panoply," he warns that librarians "must … understand that *not* raising such questions abrogates a crucial professional responsibility: helping the academy recognize the implications of the changes taking place" (28).

Campbell's (2006) conclusion is well-balanced as well as provocative. He is generous in praising the library's historic role: "Because of the fundamental role that academic libraries have played in the past century, it is tremendously difficult to imagine a college of university without a library" (30). But he contends that the library's role is sure to change beyond what anyone can envision at this time. "Considering the extra-ordinary pace with which knowledge is moving to the web, it is equally difficult to imagine what an academic library will do and be in another decade" (30).

Some interesting ideas about what librarian roles and behaviors, technological developments, and the library's function might be in the future were published in *D-Lib Magazine*. The winning essay by two library school professors portrayed librarians of the future as "communicating through Virtual Reality helmets and V-mail, and utilizing diagnostic tools to customize resources to individual profiles [in the course of delivering] effective support for problem solving and discovery groups" (Marcum 2003, 2).

Changing Nature of the Internet

Indeed, the very idea that the Internet as we know it (usually free of charge for content once access has been gained, chaotic, and largely untrammeled by regulations or hierarchies) will still exist a decade from now is far from assured. There already is a challenge to equal access in the form of the Internet II, which gives priority in transmissions to heavy hitters in the scientific and technical community. One reads about Google (along with Cisco Systems and Microsoft) capitulating to pressures to restrict and censor its services in order to do business in China (Schatz 2006). Perhaps most disconcerting for libraries, an article by the executive director of the Center for Digital Democracy about cable, telephone, and telecommunications company planning and politicking warns, "The nation's largest telephone and cable companies are crafting an alarming set of strategies that would transform the free, open, and non-discriminatory Internet of today to a privately run and branded service that would charge a fee for virtually everything we do online" (Chester 2006, 1).

Volatility of Academic Library Environment

There may be a few remaining ivory tower setups where the academic library is inviolable and impervious to pressures of the marketplace (stakeholders, competitors within and outside the academy, political forces, and public opinion). But at this juncture, virtually all entities in higher education need to pay attention to such forces. Librarians who do not want to "play that game" should make plans for early retirement from the library or—if retirement is not an option—they should explore changing careers altogether at the earliest opportunity. The majority of academic librarians will be embracing the forces of change and abandoning the "lifeboat" mentality. It's a lot more satisfying to set one's own course and to steer a craft with the latest propulsion technology than it is to huddle in a raft, gradually losing strength and waiting for rescue that may well not come.

Appendix

Krakoff
COMMUNICATIONS, INC.

Public Relations
&
Marketing Communications

University of Pittsburgh's University Library System (ULS)

Marketing Communications Strategy/Plan

Submitted: February 10, 2005

SITUATION ANALYSIS:

The mission of the University Library System (ULS) at the University of Pittsburgh is to provide and promote access to information resources necessary for the achievement of the University' s leadership objectives in teaching, learning, research, creativity and community service, and to collaborate in the development of effective information, teaching and learning systems.

To further the attainment of these goals, the ULS continues to be on the forefront of acquisition and library technology implementation. In fact, what sets the ULS apart from other university library systems are the depth, focus and comprehensiveness of the programs, services and special collections. During the Marketing Retreat, the comment was made that "We are innovative users not necessarily innovative creators of the technology. We are implementing what others are developing and talking about doing."

This mindset of advancement through user-friendly applications needs to be communicated to all pertinent parties. The ULS is faced with what most would consider a good problem to have—an identity disconnect coupled with an information conveyance void as a result of a multitude of programs and resources to aid specific populations within the University. As a result, a unified marketing strategy must be established to:
1. Brand these programs individually but under an umbrella, dominant ULS logo/brand.
2. Specify the end user/audience for each of these programs.
3. Determine a method or combination of methods through which to best deliver the information about each program to the appropriate end user.

Strengths of the ULS:

- Pound-for-pound, one of the best in the United States
- Seamless access and delivery of resources
- Quality of staff
- Depth of subject-specific material, wealth of collections
- Variety in forms of information:
    - Print collections
    - Electronic collections
    - Microfilm
    - Other archives

Overall Problems/Challenges:

- Target audience members unaware of the library's central role within the University, not thought of in high esteem
- General confusion/unaware as to the complete offerings of the ULS
- General confusion/unaware as to how to most-efficiently access the offerings

The challenge is to reassemble the fragmented programs/benefits of the ULS by creating a unified, comprehensive initiative to market specific programs and resources to appropriate end users.

OBJECTIVES:

1. Increase awareness/usage of resources and services while promoting and leveraging investments
2. Increase support/budget which will help to increase donations
3. Enhance professional perception and knowledge about capabilities and resources, both internally and externally

TARGET AUDIENCES:

Target audiences can be grouped into internal and external categories and then further categorized for targeting purposes as follows:

INTERNAL

1. ULS Staff
   - Librarians/Staff

2. University of Pittsburgh Decision Makers
   - Chancellor/Provost
   - Deans/Director
   - Inst. Advancement

3. Faculty
   - Admin./Department Chairs
   - Professors

4. Undergraduate and Graduate Students
   - Grad Assistants/T.A.s
   - Student Groups
   - Graduate Professional Associations
   - Distance Education Students

EXTERNAL

1. Current/Potential Donors
   - Alumni
   - Retirees
   - Foundations
   - Friends of Library Groups
   - Corporations (Local, National, International)

2. Current/Potential Users
   - Peer Institutions/Graduate Students
   - Researchers
   - General Community/Business
   - Not for Profits
   - Retirees
   - Local/National and International Companies
   - Other librarians

3. Decision Makers
   - Board of Visitors
   - Board of Trustees

4. Groups/Associations
   - Peer Institutions
   - Professional, Academic and Library Associations

Before we can identify specific strategies and tactics, we need to determine the desired results we wish to achieve from each group. Let's take a look at our "best case scenarios" for each of our target groups:

INTERNAL

1.ULS Staff
Desired Result: All staff members comprehensively informed about all new programs, collections, reference mechanisms and associated technologies to better help students/researchers at any level. By understanding the "big picture," they will have a more-positive outlook regarding their job.

2. University of Pittsburgh Decision Makers
Desired Result: Continually aware of the strides the ULS is making. Should be kept aware of prominent collections acquired, technological innovations and ULS rankings, and statistics as compared to other library systems nationally. This will help to increase funding and general awareness of the quality of the ULS.

3. Faculty
Desired Result: Readily incorporate library education and information into assignment plans and project sheets. General awareness of library capabilities and collections to accurately convey information to/answer questions from students—especially during their time of need i.e., finals, midterms, etc. This will increase usage of ULS services and resources.

4. Undergraduate and Graduate Students
Desired Result: Comprehensive understanding of library functionality and available collections/reference mechanisms. Comfort with research as a result of breadth of materials and user-friendly delivery mechanisms.

EXTERNAL

1. Current/Potential Donors
Desired Result: Donations (both in amount of donors and amount of individual donations) increase.

2. Current/Potential Users
Desired Result: Feel as though the ULS is an integral part of our region/nation/world supporting the educational and pragmatic efforts of businesses and individuals throughout without hassle, roadblocks or confusion.

3. Decision Makers
Desired Result: Equipped with the most up-to-date information about the ULS so recommendations can be made to senior University staff to impact funding/programs in the best interests of the students and the community.

4. Groups/Associations
Desired Result: Feel comfortable using the ULS as a resource and, more importantly, as a model for unparalleled ease-of-use programs and comprehensive acquisition plans.

STRATEGIES:

A mix of direct marketing, email communications, internal advertising and public relations efforts specific to each target group could be utilized to achieve all of the objectives stated above. From a graphics standpoint, a standard ULS look/logo (keeping within the identity rules of the University) will be established so every communications (printed or electronic) will have a consistent look.

The variation will be in the look of the programs that piece serves to publicize. For example, a HelpHub piece will look different than a ULS Special Collections piece but they will be instantly recognized as pieces associated with ULS through usage of the standard ULS umbrella logo and graphics standards such as placement of logo, general design of piece, etc. In addition, we recommend that targeted information be distributed to the various groups on a more frequent basis, mixing the delivery vehicle so that all audiences maintain a high awareness of the ULS and its services.

Below is an outline of how the ULS can accomplish the stated objectives while also achieving the desired results from each target group.

1. Increase awareness/usage of resources and services while promoting and leveraging investments

The purpose of this campaign will be to reach all target audiences in as many ways as possible while conveying the message of "What Can the ULS Do for Me." These communication mechanisms, including printed newsletters, enewsletters, printed postcards in mailboxes or email alerts will be benefit-specific for the target. They will also contain focused, organized and concise messages so they are (1) read and (2) processed.

2. Increase support/budget, which will help to increase donations

Through increased communication with current and potential donors about the ULS programs their funds are supporting, their dollars would be given more meaning so they feel connected to a specific collection or technological innovation. A bi-annual piece should be sent to all donors and prospects to educate them about where their funds are going, and, more importantly, why the projects their funds are supporting are integral to making the ULS and the University of Pittsburgh a researcher's destination. In addition, if they are kept informed about stages of implementation of programs they are helping to fund, they will start to personally identify with the project and feel a need to increase, continue or begin donations in order to "finish what they started."

Also, new sources for funding will be identified, emails and addresses will be collected, and regular, electronic communications will be developed.

3. Enhance professional perception and knowledge about capabilities and resources, both internally and externally

To accomplish this objective, we recommend playing up the prominence and prestige of the ULS among other comparable institutions including acquisitions rankings, technological advancements, ground breaking ease-of-use efforts, etc. This will help with internal comprehensive understanding and instill a sense of pride. An annual report for University "management" and administrators will be developed and disseminated. Externally, this piece will serve as intrigue and may increase traffic from curious locals or frustrated researchers or companies.

TACTICS

A. Printed Pieces

It is in these pieces where the graphics standard and the unified look (regardless of the message or target) will become apparent.

1. Postcards/Mailers:

A series of informational post cards can be developed and printed with message-specific copy to each target group. These post-cards can be used as a stand-alone piece or can be inserted into a target-specific pocket folder packet.

Ideas for postcard content:

- User testimonials for each group (a large business, a student, an outside researcher, a grad student, a faculty member, etc.)
- Quick resource/services guide about the ULS (this can include who to go to for what, quick research how-tos, etc.)
- A program and promotional post card can be developed to introduce the concept of a 'Research Challenge." Although this concept is best for undergraduate students, graduate students could participate as well. The idea is that classes or individuals could compete to find some piece of information in a special collection that is not often searched or a collection that has been newly acquired. The winner is the one who finds it first and a prize can be given. If these become monthly or annually this could prove to be an interesting PR piece as well.
- A 'Delivery" focused piece perhaps a spoof on all the food del ivery flyers undergrads and grads get that details the many convenient ways research materials can be delivered to them (email, etc.)

2. Folder:

For cost effectiveness, we recommend printing an 8.5 x 11 multi-purpose pocket folder introducing the new graphic standard for the ULS. The folder will feature general information on it about the ULS and be useful for ALL audiences. Target-specific information for each audience will then be inserted into the pocket and sent. Information that could be enclosed:

- Cover letter
- Appropriate postcard (testimonials, how-to info., etc.)
- Info for deans to use in promotions
- Updates on specific programs that donors have helped fund to keep them 'in-the-loop" and feel part of the project
- Annual or periodic report to inform staff/faculty of new info
- List of all collections, services and contact person for each or how-to access section for each

3. Direct Mail: Discipline-Based packets:

A two-color or four-color-process discipline-based packet can be developed for all faculty members and delivered during the summer months or at the start of each term to help with lesson planning. A similar packet can be distributed to TAs. This piece will contain information about what specifically the ULS can do for you or your students in Sociology, Math, etc. Also should include a section on what the ULS can do for students in terms of papers, theses, projects, comparative research, etc. and a similar info sheet for faculty.

4. Newsletters/Email Blasts

Internal and external newsletters should be printed 4 x a year and mailed to all target groups. The newsletter will contain a basic ULS update: new happenings, projects completed, projects in the works, new acquisitions, etc.

An e-newsletter will be emailed 4-6 times a year to complement the printed version and to keep people informed and aware of ULS activities. This can be tailored to all of the different target groups and will contain targeted information, unlike the hard copy newsletter. The effectiveness of implementing this enewsletter is based on the emails you have captured for all of your target audiences who are outside of the University system.

In addition, email blasts will be sent out to different groups on an as-needed basis if there seems to be confusion about a new policy, process or general information about something needs to be disseminated quickly. The enewsletter and email blasts could be used to introduce the opt-in regular ULS information option.

B. Educational Sessions & Special Events

There should be a library orientation for all new faculty, students and transfers. In addition, we recommend working with faculty to implement project-specific, mini-orientations and then incorporating these sessions into the syllabus for the class. This could be carried into educational outreach to the other target audience members. For example, host a wine and cheese event for donors during which you showcase a technology or collection their funds helped to facilitate.

Also, events could be planned for high-ranking officials/administrators at University of Pittsburgh and other institutions, business leaders, non-profit leaders, etc.

C. Publicity

Since all three objectives involve a better and broader communications effort, publicity will be a large component of the plan.

A comprehensive media list needs to be developed to include daily and weekly newspapers, magazines, radio, television and Web. The list will be used to distribute press releases on a variety of topics. This list will also include internal media exclusive to the University of Pittsburgh.

There will be two components to the media plan: volume and quality. One press release per month will be distributed announcing something new at ULS, a new hire, a promotion, etc. to maintain regular appearances in the media.

In addition, newsworthy feature stories should be pitched to key reporters/editors. For example pitches could be based around:

- each new collection or technological advancement
- superior public funding stats and acquisition rates
- Introduction of Ask a librarian to the regional libraries

Stories can also be ghost written and placed in numerous publications. One such example is the importance of past, present and future in a researcher's and library's success. A story focusing on the importance of current and historical collections to comprehensive research would provide a perfect opportunity to showcase the old and new collections at ULS. In addition, it would provide for a nice segue from how these historically relevant resources continue to be used to the ever-changing methods of accessing them.

Also, some of the testimonials in the printed pieces may be success stories that can be shared with the media.

In addition, articles should be secured in the University Times and/or the Pitt News that would focus on one aspect, collection or program in each issue. Maybe a regular column can be established in one or both regarding 'how to" pieces on reference/research challenges.

D.Web/Electronic—
The Web site could be redesigned to find out "up front" the interest of the visitor, and quickly getting them to the information that is most important for them. In addition, a 'facelift" for the Web could be performed during which the new umbrella ULS brand from the printed pieces could be incorporated on the Web. We recommend making the Web a place for further information. The idea is to print short, inexpensive pieces to obtain interest, then sending them to the Web for more details and specific information. For example, a person receives a postcard detailing delivery methods for all types of research but maybe the recipient wants to know a bit more. On the bottom of the post card it would say, For more information, go to this site. Once the recipient goes to the site, there will not only be more information about the postcard topic but there will also be an option to select to receive further library info and updates through email.

Finally, an area of the home page could be changed to announce the next library training session or new program being introduced.

EVALUATION

In order to rack the success of this program we recommend that surveys be distributed to each end-user group at the beginning or completion of the academic year to assess their level of knowledge/comfort with specific programs and to gage their feelings about ULS. Then, these results should be compared to survey results of previous years to see if measurable improvements have been made. In addition, informal evaluation sheets could be made available at all librarian stations and ULS entry/exit desks. A suggestion box could also be located prominently in high-traffic areas to gage what the target groups think could be improved upon. Finally, as comments are made in passing to staff from visitors of ULS, these should be documented (both positive and negative) and shared at staff meetings.

NEXT STEPS:

Establish clear parameters for objectives, budget to be allocated to this effort, then a final plan with schedules, responsibilities and line-item budgets can be developed, and the plan will be implemented.

Reference List

Abell, D., and J. Hammond. 1979. *Strategic Market Planning: Problems and Analytical Approaches.* Englewood Cliffs, NJ: Prentice-Hall.

Association of College and Research Libraries. 2004. *Standards for Libraries in Higher Education.* Chicago: Association of College and Research Libraries. Available at: http://www.ala.org/ala/acrl/acrlstandards/standardslibraries.htm. Accessed May 5, 2006.

Association of Research Libraries. 2005. *ARL Statistics.* Available at: http://www.arl.org/stats/arlstat/.

Bates, D. n.d. *Balancing the Books: Case Studies in Innovation: Blackwell's Technical Services in Action.* Oxford: Blackwell's Book Services.

Bechtel, M. 1995. *The Management Compass: Steering the Corporation Using Hoshin Planning.* New York: American Management Association.

Begay, W., D. Lee, J. Martin, and M. Ray. 2004. "Quantifying Qualitative Data: Using LibQUAL+™ Comments for Library-Wide Planning Activities at the University of Arizona." *Journal of Library Administration* 40 (3/4): 111–19.

Benaud, C. 1998. *Outsourcing Library Operations: An Overview of Issues and Outcomes.* Englewood, CO: Libraries Unlimited.

Bender, L. 1997. "Team Organization—Learning Organization." *Information Outlook* 1 (9): 19–22.

Bertot, J., and C. McClure. 2003. "Outcomes Assessment in the Networked Environment: Research Questions, Issues, Considerations, and Moving Forward." *Library Trends* 51 (4): 590–613.

Birdsall, D. 1997. "Strategic Planning in Academic Libraries." In *Restructuring Academic Libraries: Organizational Development in the Wake of Technological Change,* ed. C. Schwartz, 253–61. Chicago: Association of College and Research Libraries.

Blixrud, J. n.d. *Rethinking Public Services in the ULS.* Unpublished report, Washington, DC: Association of Research Libraries.

Boundless Connections [Booklet]. n.d. Pittsburgh, PA: University of Pittsburgh, University Library System.

Bradigan, P., and C. Powell. 2004. "The Reference and Information Services Team." *Reference and User Services Quarterly* 44 (2): 143–48.

Breivik, P. 1993. "Investing Wisely in Information Technology: Asking the Right Questions." *Educational Record* 74 (3): 47–52.

Bryson, J. 2004. *Strategic Planning for Public and Nonprofit Organizations: A Guide to Strengthening and Sustaining Organizational Achievement.* San Francisco: Wiley.

Butler, T., and J. Waldroop. 1999. "Job Sculpting: The Art of Retaining Your Best People." *Harvard Business Review* 77 (5): 144–52.

Cameron, K., and R. Quinn. 1999. *Diagnosing and Changing Organizational Culture: Based on the Competing Values Framework.* Reading, MA: Addison-Wesley.

Campbell, J. 2006. "Changing a Cultural Icon: The Academic Library as a Virtual Destination." *EDUCAUSE Review* 41 (1): 16–31.

Carnevale, D. 2003. *Organizational Development in the Public Sector.* Boulder, CO: Westview Press.

Chester, J. 2006. "The End of the Internet?" *The Nation* (February 1). Available at: http://www.thenation.com/doc/20060213/chester.

Cohen, A. 2000. "A Commentary on Galbraith and Hirshhorn." In *Breaking the Code of Change,* ed. M. Beer and N. Nohria, 177–91. Boston: Harvard Business School.

Collison, M. 1991. "Applications Down at Private Campuses, Up at Public Colleges." *Chronicle of Higher Education* 37 (25): A1–A28.

Cook, C., and F. Heath. 2001. "Users' Perceptions of Library Service Quality: A LibQUAL+ Qualitative Study." *Library Trends* 49 (4): 548–84.

Cresswell, J. 1998. *Qualitative Inquiry and Research Design: Choosing among Five Traditions.* Thousand Oaks, CA: Sage.

De Rosa, C., J. Cantrell, D. Cellantani, J. Hawk, L. Jenkins, and A. Wilson. 2005. *Perceptions of Libraries and Information Resources: A Report to the OCLC Membership.* Dublin: Ohio Computer Library Center.

Dempsey, B. 2005. "Power Users: Designing Buildings and Services from the End User's Viewpoint Transforms Access for Everyone." *Library Journal* 130 (20): 72–75.

Diaz, J., and C. Pintozzi. 1999. "Helping Teams Work: Lessons Learned from the University of Arizona Library Reorganization." *Library Administration and Management* 13 (1): 27–36.

Diaz, R., and S. Phipps. 1998. "Evolution of the Roles of Staff and Team Development in a Changing Organization: The University of Arizona Experience." In *Finding Common Ground: Creating the Library of the Future without Diminishing the Library of the Past,* ed. C. La Guardia and B. Mitchell, 408–23. New York: Neal-Schuman.

Dugan, R., and P. Hernon. 2002. "Outcomes Assessment: Not Synonymous with Inputs and Outputs: *Journal of Academic Librarianship* 28 (6): 376–80.

Druskat, V., and S. Wolff. 2004. "Building the Emotional Intelligence of Groups." In *Harvard Business Review on Teams that Succeed,* 27–51. Boston: Harvard Business School.

Faerman, S. 1993. "Organizational Change and Leadership Styles." *Journal of Academic Librarianship* 19 (3/4): 55–79.

French, W., and C. Bell. 1999. *Organization Development: Behavioral Science Interventions for Organization Development.* Upper Saddle River, NJ: Prentice Hall.

Galbraith, J. 1997. *Organization Design.* Reading, MA: Addison-Wesley.

———. 2000. *Designing the Global Corporation.* San Francisco: Jossey-Bass.

————. 2005. *Designing the Customer-Centric Organization: A Guide to Strategy, Structure, and Process.* San Francisco: Jossey-Bass.

Garvin, D., and M. Roberto. 2004. "What You Don't Know about Making Decisions." In *Harvard Business Review on Teams that Succeed,* 99–121. Boston: Harvard Business School.

Giesecke, J. 1994. "Reorganizations: An Interview with Staff from the University of Arizona." *Library Administration and Management* 8 (4): 196–99.

Giesecke, J., and B. McNeil. 2004. "Transition to the Learning Organization." *Library Trends* 53 (1): 54–67.

Goldstein, P. 2006. *The Future of Higher Education: A View from CHEMA.* Washington, DC: Council of Higher Education Management Associations.

Gratch-Lindauer, B. 2002. "Comparing the Regional Accreditation Standards: Outcomes Assessment and Other Trends. *Journal of Academic Librarianship* 28 (1/2): 14–25.

Gulati, J., and J. Oldroyd. 2005. "The Quest for Customer Focus." *Harvard Business Review* 83 (4): 92–101.

Gumbus, A., and B. Lyons. 2004. "How Unilever HPC-NA Sold Its Employees on the Balanced Scorecard." *Strategic Finance* 85 (10): 42–46.

Hackman, J. 2002. *Leading Teams: Setting the Stage for Great Performances.* Boston: Harvard Business School.

Hawkins, L. 2006. "Lost in Transmission—Behind GM's Slide: Bosses Misjudged New Urban Tastes." *Wall Street Journal* (March 8).

Hernon, P., and R. Dugan. 2002. *An Action Plan for Outcomes Assessment in Your Library.* Chicago: American Library Association.

Higgins, J. 1982. *Human Relations Concepts and Skills.* New York: Random House.

Hiller, S., and J. Self. 2004. "From Measurement to Management: Using Data Wisely for Planning and Decision-Making. *Library Trends* 53 (1): 129–55.

Holbrook, C., R. Houbeck, T. Richards, and J. Wilhelme. 1984. "The Merging of Serials Units: A Case Study." *Journal of Academic Librarianship* 10 (1): 29–32.

Holloway, K. 2003. "Developing Core and Mastery-Level Competencies for Librarians." *Library Administration and Management* 17 (2): 94–98.

————. 2004. "The Significance of Organizational Development in Academic Research Libraries." *Library Trends* 53 (1): 5–16.

Hymowitz, C. 2006. "Two More CEO Ousters Underscore the Need for Better Strategizing." *Wall Street Journal* (September 11).

Kaplan, R., and D. Norton. 1992. "The Balanced Scorecard: Measures that Drive Performance." *Harvard Business Review* 70 (1): 172–80.

————. 2001. *The Strategy-Focused Organization: How Balanced Scorecard Companies Thrive in the New Business Environment.* Boston: Harvard Business School.

————. 2006. "How to Implement a New Strategy without Disrupting Your Organization." *Harvard Business Review* 84 (3): 100–109.

Katzenbach, J., and D. Smith. 2001. *The Discipline of Teams.* New York: Wiley.

————. 2004. "The Discipline of Teams." In *Harvard Business Review on Teams that Succeed,* 1–25. Boston: Harvard Business School.

Kent, C. 1997. "Rethinking Public Services at Harvard College Library: A Case of Coordinated Decentralization." In *Restructuring Academic Libraries: Organizational Development in the Wake of Technological Change,* ed. C. Schwartz, 180–92. Chicago: Association of College and Research Libraries.

Knapp, A. 2004. "We Asked Them What They Thought, Now What Do We Do? The Use of LibQUAL+™ Data to Redesign Public Services at the University of Pittsburgh." *Journal of Library Administration* 40 (3/4): 157–71.

Knapp, A., J. Miller, and K. Thomes. n.d. *Rethinking Public Services Final Report*. Available at: http://www.library.pitt.edu:8000/planning/reference/. Accessed February 1, 2005.

Kohberger, P. n.d.a. "Reengineering Technical Services Processes." PowerPoint presentation, University Library System, University of Pittsburgh.

———. n.d.b. "Technical Services Reengineering Narrative Timeline." Unpublished report, University Library System, University of Pittsburgh.

Kohberger, P., D. Hayashikawa, D. Lucas, and D. Silverman. 1996a, November 14 [rev. December 1996]. "Technical Services Reorganization Plan." Unpublished report, University Library System, University of Pittsburgh.

———. 1996b, November 14 [rev. January 1997]. "Technical Services Reorganization Plan." Unpublished report, University Library System, University of Pittsburgh.

Kollen, C., N. Simons, and J. Tellman. 1997. "Librarians in Split Positions with Both Technical and Public Services Responsibilities." In *Advances in Library Administration and Organization*, ed. D. Williams and E. Garten, 201–25. Greenwich, CT: JAI Press.

Kotler, P., and S. Levy. 1969. "Broadening the Concept of Marketing." *Journal of Marketing* 33 (1): 10–15.

Kurz, K., and J. Scannell. 2005. "Repositioning Price." *University Business* 8 (1): 23, 25.

Lakos, A., and S. Phipps. 2004. "Creating a Culture of Assessment: A Catalyst for Organizational Change." *Portal* 4 (3): 345–61.

Landesman, M. 2004. "Libraries Investing in the Future First—Some Practical Suggestions." *ARL Bimonthly Report* 234:1–7.

Larson, C. 1998. "Customers First: Using Process Improvement to Improve Service Quality and Efficiency." *Reference Services Review* 26 (1): 51–60.

Lee, S., B. Juergens, and R. Werking. 1996. "Commentaries on Choosing Our Futures." *College & Research Libraries* 57 (3): 226–33.

Leonard, P. 1985. "The Rest of the Organizational Development Equation." *Journal of Academic Librarianship* 11 (1): 34.

Lientz, B., and K. Rea. 2004. *Breakthrough IT Change Management: How to Get Enduring Change Results*. Oxford: Elsevier Butterworth-Heinemann.

Lipow, A., ed. 1993. *Rethinking Reference in Academic Libraries*. Berkeley, CA: Library Solutions Press.

Lubans, J. 1996. "'I Ain't No Cowboy, I Just Found This Hat': Confessions of an Administrator in an Organization of Self-Managed Teams." *Library Administration and Management* 10 (1): 28–40.

Lynch, C. 2003. *Reflections Toward the Development of a Post DL Research Agenda*. Chatham, MA: NSF Post Digital Libraries Futures Workshop. Quoted in A. Wilson, ed. 2003. *The OCLC Environmental Scan: Pattern Recognition: A Report to the OCLC Membership*. Dublin: Ohio Computer Library Center, 78.

Marcum, D. 2005. "The Future of Cataloging." Paper presented at the American Library Association Midwinter meeting in an EBSCO Information Services' Executive Seminar for research library directors, Birmingham, AL.

Marcum, J. 2003. "Visions: The Academic Library in 2012." *D-Lib Magazine*, 9 (5). Available at: http://www.dlib.org/dlib/may03/marcum/05marcum.html.

Miller, J., K. Thomes, and A. Knapp. n.d. "Rethinking Public Services in the ULS." PowerPoint presentation, University Library System, University of Pittsburgh.

Miller, R. 2002. "Shaping Digital Library Content." *Journal of Academic Librarianship* 28 (3): 97–103.

Miller, R., and B. Ferketish. n.d. "Living the Vision at the University of Pittsburgh Libraries." PowerPoint presentation, University Library System, University of Pittsburgh.

Nair, M. 2004. *Essentials of Balanced Scorecard.* Hoboken, NJ: Wiley.

National Science Foundation. 2005. *Federal Science and Engineering Support to Universities, Colleges, and Nonprofit Institutions: FY 2002.* Available at: http://www.nsf.gov/statistics/nsf05309/. Accessed May 4, 2006.

Northwest Association of Schools and Colleges and Universities. 2003. *Evaluation Committee Report.* Seattle: University of Washington, Commission on Colleges. Available at: http://www.washington.edu/about/accreditation/EvaluationCommReport.pdf. Accessed May 25, 2006.

OhioLINK. 2006a. "Connecting People, Libraries, & Information for Ohio's Future—2006 and Beyond; Continuing the Task: The OhioLINK Program Vision, Priorities, and Strategic Activities." Available at: http://www.ohiolink.edu/ostaff/lac/pdf/031606-newvision2006_3–06draft.pdf. Accessed May 29, 2006.

———. 2006b. "OhioLINK 2006 Regional Briefing." PowerPoint presentation, OhioLINK, Columbus, OH.

Oltmanns, G. (2004). "Organization and Staff Renewal Using Assessment." *Library Trends* 53 (1): 156–71.

Oltmanns, G., and J. Self. 2002. "Assessment and Flexibility: Implementing the Balanced Scorecard, Reassigning Staff." PowerPoint paper presented at University of Arizona Living the Future 4 conference, Tucson, AZ. Available at: http://dizzy.library.arizona.edu/conferences/ltf4/pres/uvl_files/frame.htm.

Owens, I. 1999. "The Impact of Change from Hierarchy to Teams in Two Academic Libraries: Intended Results vs. Actual Results Using Total Quality Management." *College & Research Libraries* 60 (6): 571–84.

Pfeiffer, J., and J. Jones. 1971. *1972 Annual Handbook for Group Facilitators.* La Jolla, CA: University Associates.

Phipps, S. 1993. "Transforming Libraries into Learning Organizations—The Challenge for Leadership." In *Catalysts for Change: Managing Libraries in the 1990s,* ed. G. Von Dran and J. Cargill, 19–37. New York: Haworth.

———. 1999. "Performance Measurement as a Methodology for Assessing Team and Individual Performance: The University of Arizona Experience." In *Proceedings of the 3rd Northumbria International Conference on Performance Measurement in Libraries and Information Services,* ed. P. Wressel, 113–17. Newcastle upon Tyne, UK: Information North for the School of Information Studies, Univ. of Northumbria at New Castle.

———. 2004. "The System Design Approach to Organizational Development: The University of Arizona Model." *Library Trends* 53 (1): 68–111.

Polzer, J., and R. Luecke. 2004. *Harvard Business Essentials: Creating Teams with an Edge: The Complete Skill Set to Build Powerful and Influential Teams.* Boston: Harvard Business School.

Pulley, J., A. June, S. Hebel, J. Brainard, et al. 2003. "Special Report: Financial Outlook 2004." *Chronicle of Higher Education* 50 (17): A1–A17.

Quinn, J. 1993. "The Tax Payers versus Higher Education." *Newsweek* 122 (20): 51.

Renaud, R. 1997. "Learning to Compete: Competition, Outsourcing, and Academic Libraries." *Journal of Academic Librarianship* 23 (2): 85–90.

Robbins, H., and M. Finley. 2000. *The New Why Teams Don't Work: What Goes Wrong and How to Make It Right.* San Francisco: Berrett and Koehler.

Rogers, R., J. Hayden, and B. Ferketish. 1985. *Organizational Change that Works*. With R. Matzen. Pittsburgh, PA: Development Dimensions International.

Russell, C. 1998. "Using Performance Measurement to Evaluate Teams and Organizational Effectiveness." *Library Administration and Management* 12 (3): 159–65.

Russell, K., and D. Stephens. 2004. "Introduction to Special Issue on Organizational Development and Leadership." *Library Trends* 53 (1): 1–4.

Schaffer, R., and H. Thomson. 1992. "Successful Change Program Begins with Results." *Harvard Business Review* 70 (1): 80–89.

Schatz, A. 2006. "Tech Firms Defend China Web Policies." *Wall Street Journal* (February 16).

Schneider, K. 2006. "The User Is Not Broken." Free Range Librarian. Available at: http://freerangelibrarian.com/2006/06/the_user_is_not_broken_a_meme.php. Accessed September 15, 2006.

Schwartz, C. 1997. *Restructuring Academic Libraries: Organizational Development in the Wake of Technological Change*. Chicago: Association of College and Research Libraries.

Senge, P. 1994. *The Fifth Discipline: The Art and Practice of the Learning Organization*. New York: Doubleday/Currency.

———. 2001. "Leading Learning Organizations." In *Contemporary Issues in Leadership*, ed. R. Rosenbach and R. Taylor, 125–39. Boulder, CO: Westview Press.

Shanghai Jiao Tong University. 2005. "Academic Rankings of World Universities." Available at: http://ed.sjtu.edu.cn/rank/2005/ARWU2005TOP500list.htm.

Shoaf, E. 2004. "New Leadership for Libraries: Who Has the Right Stuff?" *College & Research Libraries News* 65 (7): 363–65, 375.

Sigband, N., and J. Biles. 2004. "While Enrollments Climb Rapidly, Available Seats Decline Dramatically." *Phi Kappa Phi Forum* 84 (4): 37–38.

Stephens, D., and K. Russell. 2004. "Organizational Development, Leadership, Change, and the Future of Libraries." *Library Trends* 53 (1): 238–57.

Stoffle, C. 1995. "The Upside of Downsizing." In *The Upside of Downsizing: Using Library Instruction to Cope*, ed. C. La Guardia, S. Bentley, and J. Martorana, 1–13. New York: Neal-Schuman.

Stoffle, C., B. Allen, J. Fore, and E. Mobley. 2000. "Predicting the Future: What Does Academic Librarianship Hold in Store?" *College & Research Libraries News* 61 (10): 894–901.

Stoffle, C., B. Allen, D. Morden, and K. Maloney. 2003. "Continuing to Build the Future: Academic Libraries and Their Challenges." *Portal* 3 (3): 363–80.

Stoffle, C., S. Phipps, M. Ray, and C. Russell. 1998. "Team-Based Management in the Research Environment." *InfoManage* 5 (11): 1–10.

Stoffle, C., R. Renaud, and J. Veldorf. 1996. "Choosing our Futures." *College & Research Libraries* 57 (3): 213–25.

Stringer, R. 2002. *Leadership and Organizational Climate: The Cloud Chamber Effect*. Upper Saddle River, NJ: Prentice-Hall.

University of Arizona Libraries. 1999. "Current Situation Analysis: 1998/1999." Available at: http://www.library.arizona.edu/library/teams/slrp/csa/98–99/csa_98–99.html. Accessed January 11, 2005.

———. 2000. "Current/Future Situation Analysis: 1999/2000." Available at: http://www.library.arizona.edu/library/teams/slrp/csa/99–00_home.htm. Accessed January 11, 2005.

————. 2002, January. "Current Situation Analysis." Available at: http://www.library. arizona.edu/library/teams/slrp/csa/01–02/CSA2002.htm. Accessed January 11, 2005.

————. 2003a, January. "Strategic Long Range Planning Team: 2002/2003 Current Situation Analysis." Available at: http://www.library.arizona.edu/library/teams/slrp/ csa/02–03/CSA0203.htm. Accessed January 11, 2005.

————. 2003b, November 18. "Strategic Long Range Planning Team: 2003/2004 Current Situation Analysis." Available at: http://www.library.arizona.edu/library/teams/slrp/ csa/03–04/CSA0304.html. Accessed January 11, 2005.

————. 2003c, November 18. "Strategic Long Range Planning Team: 2003/2004 Current Situation Analysis; Summary." Available at: http://www.library.arizona.edu/library/ teams/slrp/csa/03–04/CSA0304Summary.html. Accessed January 11, 2005.

————. 2003d. *University of Arizona Libraries Annual Report 2002.* Tucson: University of Arizona.

————. 2004. *University of Arizona Libraries Annual Report 2003.* Tucson: University of Arizona.

————. 2005a. "Social Science Team: 2004/2005 Current Situation Analysis." Available at: http://www.library.arizona.edu/library/teams/sst/csa0405.htm. Accessed January 11, 2005.

————. 2005b. *University of Arizona Libraries Annual Report 2004.* Tucson: University of Arizona.

University Library System, University of Pittsburgh. 1996a. "Task Force on Building a Balanced Collection." Available at: http://www.library.pitt.edu:8000/spsc/bctf/. Accessed May 25, 2004.

————. 1996b. "Task Force on Creating a Positive Workforce." Available at: http://www. library.pitt.edu:8000/spsc/pwtf/. Accessed May 25, 2004.

————. 1996c. "Task Force on Creating an Agenda for diversity." Available at: http:// www.library.pitt.edu:8000/spsc/dtf/. Accessed May 25, 2004.

————. 1996d. "Task Force on Delivering Quality Service." Available at: http://www.library.pitt.edu:8000/spsc/qstf/. Accessed May 25, 2004.

————. 1996e. "Task Force on Educating Users." Available at: http://www.library.pitt. edu:8000/eutf/. Accessed May 25, 2004.

————. 1996f. "Task Force on Information Technology." Available at: http://www.library. pitt.edu:8000/spsc/ittf/. Accessed May 25, 2004.

————. 1996g. "Task Force on Targeting Opportunities for Specialized Collections." Available at: http://www.library.pitt.edu:8000/spsc/sctf/. Accessed May 25, 2004.

————. 1996h. "ULS Diversity Committee. Cultivating Diversity: Rediscovering Ourselves, Our Services, and Our Clients." Unpublished report, University Library System, University of Pittsburgh.

————. 1997a. "ULS Strategic Plan Implementation." Available at: http://www.library. pitt.edu:8000/planning/document2.html. Accessed May 26, 2004.

————. 1997b. "University Library System (ULS) Strategic Plan." Available at: http:// www.library.pitt.edu:8000/spsc/document1.html. Accessed May 25, 2004.

University of Pittsburgh, Office of Institutional Research. 2005. *University Fact Book.* Available at: http://www.ir.pitt.edu/factbook.

Von Dran, G., and J. Cargill. 1993. *Catalysts for Change: Managing Libraries in the 1990s.* New York: Haworth.

Wachter, M. 2002. *8 Lies of Teamwork.* Avon Lake, OH: CorporateImpact.

Weinberg, W. 2006. Email to OhioLINK User Services Committee Listserv. February 15, 2006. Athens, OH: Ohio University Libraries.

Wood, E. 1988. *Strategic Marketing for Libraries: A Handbook.* With V. Young. Westport, CT: Greenwood.

Younger, J. 1996. "Recommendations on Technical Services." Unpublished report to R. Miller, Dean of Libraries, University Library System, University of Pittsburgh.

Index

About the Authors

ELIZABETH J. WOOD, holding an AMLS and BA in German from the University of Michigan and an MBA from Murray State University in Kentucky, has both library and business training. Author of the first in the Greenwood Library Management Series *Strategic Marketing for Libraries* (1988) as well as a chapter in James Rettig's *Distinguished Classics of Reference Publishing* (1992), Ms. Wood was keynote speaker at the 1986 LOEX Conference, has written several articles, and has presented many workshops about academic library marketing and strategic planning.

A veteran of more than 30 years of academic library service—first as a student employee, later as the business subject specialist and reference/instruction librarian, and some 12 years as head of the Information Services Department at University Libraries (Bowling Green State University). She has served under many deans and has participated in more organizational development processes than she cares to remember.

DR. RUSH G. MILLER earned a BA, MA, and PhD in Medieval History along with the MLS. His library administrative career spans 32 years, including 12 years in his current position as Hillman University Librarian and Director of the University Library System at the University of Pittsburgh. Prior to Pittsburgh, he was Dean of Libraries and Learning Resources at Bowling Green State University, and Director of Libraries at Sam Houston State University and Delta State University. He has authored numerous articles and presentations dealing with subjects including management, digital libraries, organizational development, fund raising, diversity, and staff development. He currently serves on the board of the *Journal of Academic Librarianship*. At Pitt, Dr. Miller is known as an innovative leader and has launched a number of wide-ranging initiatives on campus and internationally. He has served on the Boards of the Association of Research Libraries, the Pennsylvania Academic Library Consortium, the

Philadelphia Area Library Network (which represents more than 600 libraries, information centers, museums, archives, and other similar organizations in neighboring states), and other professional organizations.

DR. AMY KNAPP, Assistant University Librarian at the University of Pittsburgh's University Library Systems, holds an MA in English Literature, an MLS degree, and a PhD in Library Science, all from the University of Pittsburgh. For several years before accepting her current position, she paid her dues and learned the realities of academic library work as Assistant Head of Database Searching and Coordinator of Library Instruction.

Dr. Knapp has taught classes in Information Retrieval and U.S. Government Resources in the Graduate School of Information Sciences at the University of Pittsburgh for 10 years. Her dissertation research focused on how faculty members access U.S. Federal Government documents in an electronic age. A long-time advocate of a user focus in academic libraries, she has published in the areas of faculty and student use of electronic resources and applications of LibQUAL+™ data to academic library planning and operations.